AFTER THE HONEYMOON

How Conflict Can Improve Your Relationship

Daniel B. Wile

WILEY

John Wiley & Sons, Inc.
New York • Chichester • Brisbane • Toronto • Singapore

Library of Congress Cataloging-in-Publication Data:

Wile, Daniel B.
    After the honeymoon : how conflict can improve your relationship /
Daniel B. Wile.
       p.   cm.
     ISBN 0-471-85346-1.   ISBN 0-471-85347-X (pbk.)
     1. Marriage.   2. Interpersonal conflict.   3. Communication in
marriage.   I. Title.
HQ734.W74   1988
646.7'8—dc19   87-35057
                                                                   CIP

Printed in the United States of America

10 9 8 7 6 5 4 3

To Joanne,
my principal source of conflict and resolution

Preface

My name is Dan Wile, I'm the author of this book, and I want to turn your partner into a better person. And I'm going to try to do this without your partner having to do anything and without you having to do anything except read this book.

This may seem like a lot to promise. And I know that we've all been told that we shouldn't want to change our partners and that we should take responsibility for changing ourselves.

But don't we all really wish that we *could* change our partners?

So here's my recommendation. Read the first six or seven chapters and then look at your partner. If I'm right, your partner won't appear quite so unloving, neglectful, demanding, insensitive, withholding, controlling, selfish, self-righteous, or afraid of intimacy.

Read another six or seven chapters, and look at your partner again. By this time he or she ought to have begun developing signs of nobility. And that's because you'll begin to see that:

> What appears as your partner's defensiveness and excessive arguing may actually be the result of his or her inability to argue adequately and to present his or her case in a way that you'd appreciate and understand.
>
> What appears as your partner's angry tantrums or unrealistic fantasies may actually be potentially useful clues to important hidden issues in the relationship.
>
> And what appears as your partner's uncompromising attitude and unwillingness to meet you halfway may actually be the result of his or her *over*compromising attitude and giving in too much.

For example, in preparing for a vacation, your partner may have left all the work (all the arranging and packing) to you. But that may be because he or she has already *over*compromised. In an effort to be agreeable and accommodating, your partner may not have sufficiently stood up for the kind of vacation he or she really wanted.

Your partner probably won't do anything differently while you read this book—in fact, he or she could be asleep on the couch the whole time—but somehow that person, your partner, will have changed. That's because *you* will have changed, or rather, your *view* of your partner will have changed. In your eyes your partner will have turned into a better person.

Reading this book, you may better appreciate the odds your partner is working against in his or her efforts to establish a halfway decent relationship. The source of our problems is habits of thought that cause us to think of ourselves and our partners in condemning ways: as too sensitive or too insensitive, as too selfish or too self-sacrificing, as too dependent or too afraid of intimacy.

I said I wanted to turn your partner into a better person. But I also want to turn your partner's partner into a better person. And that's you.

After reading the first six or seven chapters, look at yourself. If I'm right, you, too, won't appear quite so unloving, neglectful, demanding, insensitive, withholding, controlling, selfish, self-righteous, or afraid of intimacy. And after six or seven more chapters, look at yourself again. You, too, ought to begin looking more noble.

Now, it may appear that I'm saying you should try to view your partner and yourself more positively. What I'm actually saying, however, is that once you understand the situation from this new vantage point, you'll *automatically* view your partner and yourself more positively.

And it may appear as if I'm saying that you shouldn't criticize your partner. What I expect to happen, however, is that once you understand the situation, you will feel more justified in criticizing your partner.

True, you'll feel more sympathetic toward your partner for what you now see he or she has to go through. But you'll also feel more sympathetic toward yourself for what you now see you have to go through.

So when you finish this book, and if you've really gotten its message, it'll be even money whether you'll go over to the couch and wake your partner:

To express your appreciation.

Or to give him or her a piece of your mind (but in a more pointed, more effective, and more satisfying way).

The reason this book causes us to view our partners and ourselves sympathetically is that it counteracts our usual tendencies, which are to view our partners and ourselves *accusingly*. And that's what this book is about—it's about the accusing ideas, beliefs, rules, judgments, or habits of thought that we don't know we have but that interfere with our ability to think and talk effectively about problems.

These accusing habits of thought include:

1. The *character-flaws* habit of thought—the belief that relationship problems arise from our character defects; for example, our self-ishness or dependency.
2. The *you-must-have-wanted-it-that-way* habit of thought—the belief that we really want our problems. We are getting too much out of them to want to give them up.
3. The *back-to-childhood* habit of thought—the belief that couple problems are the result of unfinished business (emotional baggage) from childhood that we're dragging into the present.
4. The *bad-habits* habit of thought—the belief that problems are simply the result of bad habits and bad behavior.
5. The *unrealistic-expectations* habit of thought—the belief that problems are the result of our failure to accept reality, give up unreasonable expectations, and make compromises.

You may be surprised that I'm describing these as *accusing* habits of thought. We use them all the time, and we think of them not as accusing but just as *true*. Neighbors talking over the fence use them. Barbers and hairdressers chatting with their customers use them. Characters on television sitcoms use them. Psychotherapists use them. I use them, although these days I try not to.

And these habits of thought *are* true, or, rather, they are partly true. They are *misleading* partial truths. They have enough of the truth to be convincing (there is no doubt, for example, that problems *do* go back to childhood), but they skew our view of things. Once we use the back-to-childhood habit of thought and, for example, trace a man's outbursts at his wife to his being spoiled as a child, all that we now see when we look at him is a spoiled little boy who has tantrums if he doesn't immediately get his way. It becomes difficult to consider the possibility that he might have good reason for being upset.

This book is about the five accusing habits of thought that *block* our thinking and make it difficult to work out our problems. And it's about the following seven *non*accusing ways of thinking that *un*block our thinking and *help* us work out our problems:

1. The *universal-issues* way of thinking—the belief that partners in an unsatisfying relationship are experiencing clear and intense forms of *common* couple problems. This realization allows the person to feel less weird, neurotic, or freakish and to feel a greater sense of his or her common humanity.

2. The *ordinary-feelings* way of thinking—the belief that underlying our seemingly strange, provocative, and childish behavior are ordinary, understandable, garden-variety adult feelings.

3. The *point-not-gotten-across* way of thinking—the belief that our seemingly strange, provocative, off-the-wall behavior is a result of the failure to get something important across to the other.

4. The *hidden-appropriateness* way of thinking—the belief that our seemingly strange, provocative, off-the-wall behavior makes sense once you get to the bottom of it. In an unrecognized way, it *is* appropriate to the immediate situation, even though it may appear exaggerated.

5. The *hidden-clue* way of thinking—the belief that our strange, provocative, off-the-wall behavior not only makes sense, but can also be useful. It can serve as a clue to important underlying feelings or hidden issues.

6. The *special-sensitivities* way of thinking (which is a direct antidote to the back-to-childhood habit of thought)—the belief that although we have special sensitivities growing out of our childhoods, these are special sensitivities to things that are actually happening at the present. Our reactions are now seen not as completely inappropriate holdovers from the past but as reactions to something that is actually going on. For example, a wife's childhood-based special sensitivity to being ignored—she felt rejected by her mother—can enable her to detect the subtle ways in which she is *actually* being ignored by her husband *now*.

7. The *solutions-become-problems* way of thinking—the belief that problems result from the attempts to solve them. For example,

forcing yourself to have sex in an effort to overcome a temporary loss of interest in sex (that is, turning sex from a pleasure into a duty) may lead to a longer-lasting and now serious loss of interest in sex. Realizing that attempts to solve problems often intensify the problem puts the person in a better position to deal with this difficulty.

Although these five habits of thought and seven ways of thinking will be discussed most directly in Chapters 9 and 10, examples of them are given throughout the book.

Imagine the difference it would make if we were to use these *non-accusing* ways of thinking rather than the *accusing* habits of thought that we typically use. This is what I mean when I say that reading this book will enable you to look at your partner and at yourself in a new way. The nonaccusing forms of thinking point to a whole new way of having a relationship:

The goal is to be able to have a relationship about your relationship; that is, to develop a shared nonjudgmental vantage point for looking at your relationship.

The ideas in this book apply to heterosexual couples, to gay and lesbian couples and, to some extent, to people in nonromantic relationships; for example, business colleagues, roommates, friends, relatives, and tennis partners. That's because the issue of accusing versus nonaccusing thinking is critical in all relationships.

And where did I get these ideas? I got some from conventional wisdom; that is, from principles that you and I have always been taught. I got others from *non*conventional wisdom; that is, from principles that fly in the face of what you and I have always been taught. This book is in part an elaboration of ideas that I got from Bernard Apfelbaum, a psychologist in Berkeley, California, who developed a way of thinking about people and their problems that he calls *ego analysis*. This book also comes from my twenty years as a psychotherapist, my eleven years as a couples therapist, and my twenty years as a husband.

Some who have read this book see me as overly pessimistic; some as overly optimistic. Those who see me as overly pessimistic point to my saying that solving our relationship problems may require having conversations that are very difficult to have. And I *do* say this. In fact, in the hope that we will have improved our ability to have such conversations in the future, I even considered titling the book: *A Couple's Manual for the Twenty-Third Century (And What to Do in the Meantime)*.

Those who see me as overly *optimistic* consider me as having a goody-goody view of human nature. These readers are critical of what they see as my failure to appreciate that many partners *are*, in fact, manipulative, controlling, withholding, narcissistic, dependent, uncooperative, dishonest, exploitive, resistant, sadistic, passive-aggressive, small-minded, self-destructive, or evil.

From these critics' point of view, I am too *slow* to accuse.

From my point of view, they are too *ready* to accuse. Accusatory thinking is an obstacle to genuine understanding. People call their partners "manipulative" or "controlling," for example, and get into a fight, or, in order to avoid the fight, they talk in an overly bland way. In neither case do they get a chance to talk about any of the issues.

I hope to win you over to my point of view.

Whatever the situation in your relationship, there's a way of thinking about it—and a conversation you can have with your partner—that can make a difference. It's just difficult to figure out what this conversation is. This book is an attempt to help you figure it out.

DANIEL B. WILE

Oakland, California
April 1988

Acknowledgments

Carolyn Pape Cowan, Philip A. Cowan, Betty J. Wenz, Eleanor Bulova, Daniel Berman, Robert Epstein, Norman Livson, Ronald Spinka, and Carol Swanson thoroughly read the manuscript and made valuable suggestions. Howard P. Wile, Margery B. Wile, Patricia Blanche, Philip Blanche, and Peg Kemper made important comments on specific sections of the book.

Joanne R. Wile, Bernard Apfelbaum, Nan Narboe, Carol Carr, Alan Rinzler, Diana Weinstock, and Dean Delis read several drafts of the book and, in addition to their invaluable detailed comments, made useful suggestions about the book's overall style, tone, and organization.

Grateful acknowledgment is made to Alfred A. Knopf, Inc. for permission to reprint passages from *Heartburn* by Nora Ephron. Copyright © 1983 by Nora Ephron.

D.B.W.

Contents

1

USING THE RELATIONSHIP TO SOLVE YOUR PROBLEMS

A husband became irrationally jealous and accused his wife of seeing other men. Feeling jealous was his way of sensing the subtle *disconnections* between himself and his wife. He imagined her *connecting* to someone else; that is, he became jealous.

If this husband and wife *knew* that his jealousy was a way of experiencing subtle disconnections between them, they might be able to use his feeling as an instrument for detecting these disconnections. They'd be able to turn this problem (his irrational jealousy) into a clue.

In Chapters 1 and 2, I discuss how to make your problems work for you and, in particular, how to turn your problems into clues.

In Chapters 3 and 4, I challenge several common beliefs about relationships. I suggest, despite the fact that you might have been told the opposite, that:

> You *can* expect your relationship to solve your problems.
> You *can* use your relationship to fill gaps in your personality.
> You *don't* have to learn to love yourself before you are able to love someone else.
> You *don't* have to stop being dependent to make your relationship work.

1

Blending the Problem into the Relationship

What we all want to do with our problems, of course, is solve them. In fact, we expect to solve them, and we feel like failures if we don't.

But maybe we should realize that certain problems are unsolvable. And that goes double for relationship problems. While each relationship has its own special set of satisfactions, each relationship appears also to have it own special set of unsolvable problems.

> You and your partner are pretty unusual—and pretty lucky—if you
> can't immediately think of two or three or a dozen problems that
> keep coming up and that you don't know how you are ever going
> to solve.

Imagine another thirty years of struggling with the same problems you've been suffering from since the beginning of the relationship. It's enough to make a person want to separate or divorce. And that's what a lot of people do. A lot of other people resign themselves to what they feel is a kind of second-class relationship. And a lot of other people just try not to think about it.

But there is a *fourth* thing you can do: you can *blend* your problems into the relationship so that they no longer threaten the relationship and, in fact, may even contribute to it.

A CHALLENGE FROM A DISGRUNTLED READER

Mr. Skeptic: Now wait a minute, Wile. Not so fast. I, for one, don't *want* to blend my problems into my relationship. I want to *eliminate* them.

3

And what does "blending your problems into the relationship" even mean? Doesn't it make more sense to try to ignore your problems, work around them, devote yourself to solving them, or, at least, try not to mind them?

Wile: Well yes, those are all good things to try. And such efforts often work.

Mr. Skeptic: Well, I'm glad you'll admit it.

Wile: But such efforts often *don't* work. Think of the last time you tried to ignore something that upset you about Mrs. Skeptic—the fact that she doesn't talk much to you, for example, or doesn't want to have sex often enough, or wants to stay home when you want to go out, or doesn't help out in the yard.

Since bringing it up would just start an argument, you keep your mouth shut. If you're lucky, your feeling of resentment passes. That's because:

You satisfy your need to talk by calling a friend.

She surprises you and wants to have sex after all.

You get her at least to sweep the walk, so you no longer mind so much the fact that you do most of the yard work.

Or you discover that you're content to stay at home.

You've prevented an argument that would have ruined the evening and the evening ends up not too bad.

Mr. Skeptic: That's what I mean. If you don't go around all the time having to express every little resentment, things will take care of themselves.

Wile: Yeah, but only if you're *lucky*. If you're *unlucky*, your feeling of resentment *won't* pass. Instead, it'll grow:

Calling the friend just makes you *more* aware of how you miss being able to talk to your wife.

Your wife says something that suggests she might be interested in sex after all. But it's a false alarm. By the time you get to bed, she's asleep. You feel set up.

She agrees to sweep the walk but puts off doing even that.

Sitting home watching television another evening turns out to be even more boring than you had thought.

Mr. Skeptic: Well sure, such things happen sometimes.

Wile: And when they *do* then you're in *real* trouble because, if you're like a lot of people, you make the complaint you would have made two hours before, but now with ten times the force. And the resulting fight is ten times worse than if you had stated your complaint in the first place.

Mr. Skeptic: But suppose I *don't* make the complaint? Suppose I keep my mouth shut?

Wile: Well, that's what you've been doing all along, of course—keeping your mouth shut and stifling yourself—except now you've got a lot more to stifle. And stifling takes its toll. Soon you might not even *feel* like talking or having sex or going out. Another fraction of an inch of thickness has been added to the wall between you and your wife.

Mr. Skeptic: This whole discussion is depressing me. Okay, just for sake of argument, let's say I agree with you. What do you suggest we do?

Wile: Well, if ignoring the problem doesn't work, let's do what I said earlier and try to blend the problem *into* the relationship. This would mean:

1. Holding an ongoing conversation about the problem rather than doing what you have been doing, which is trying to avoid talking about it and then having sporadic angry exchanges about it.
2. *Expecting* the problem to recur, and in fact *planning* for its recurrence, rather than simply hoping that it won't recur.
3. Turning the problem to whatever positive use you can, rather than simply trying to put up with it.

Mr. Skeptic: I don't see how *expecting* the problem is going to help. In fact, the whole thing sounds pretty idealistic to me. Can people really do any of these things?

Wile: Well, it's not easy. But, as I shall try to show, there's a way.

HOLDING AN ONGOING CONVERSATION ABOUT THE PROBLEM

Blending a problem into your relationship requires that you have an effective ongoing way of talking about the problem. Of course, you're right, Mr. Skeptic, that partners have good reason *not* to talk about their problems. Their attempts to do so typically turn into arguments that make matters worse. Let's take an example.

Paul and Alice are a couple in their late twenties who have been married for five years. Paul is a mechanic for a rent-a-car agency and Alice is a kindergarten teacher. Paul is upset at the way Alice acts at parties. Driving home one night, he tries to talk with her about it.

PAUL: You acted like an idiot. You talked loud. You laughed like a fool. Everyone was looking at you.

ALICE (feeling accused and fighting back): That's nonsense. I didn't talk louder than anyone else. In fact, *you're* the one who looked like an idiot. You hardly spoke to anyone the whole evening. Everyone was wondering what was wrong with you.

PAUL (defending himself): I talked to plenty of people. And if I was quiet at times, it was only because I was embarrassed by the way *you* acted.

ALICE: *I'll* say you were quiet. You sat in the corner reading a book.

PAUL: Well I was tired of listening for the umpteenth time to how you were raised on a farm. I'd like to go to *one* party in which you didn't have to tell everyone the story of your life.

The argument rages for twenty minutes and then neither speaks to the other for two days. Paul vows to himself never to go to another party with Alice again.

Then the whole thing blows over. The good will that they generally feel toward one another returns. Paul forgets his vow, and they again begin going to parties. Everything is okay the first several times they go out with others. And then the whole thing happens again. They go to a picnic where they hardly know anybody and:

> Alice feels self-conscious.
> She talks loudly and laughs nervously.
> Paul gets quiet.
> They have an argument on the way home.
> Paul vows never again to go to another party with Alice.
> It's two days before they start talking.
> But then they do start talking.
> And then they do start going to parties.
> And three months later the whole thing happens again.

It's easy to imagine Alice and Paul going on like this for the next thirty years. So let's try to imagine how they might be able to talk about it in a way that would work out. First, Alice and Paul would need to do something that they never do: *talk* about the problem when they *aren't* fighting. They never do it because they're afraid that this would just restart the fight.

Mr. Skeptic: And they're right. It probably would.

Wile: Well yeah. So Alice and Paul need a way of talking that *doesn't* immediately turn into an argument. But that's not easy—which I guess is *your* point, Mr. Skeptic. There are several traps that Alice and Paul can quickly fall into. For example, suppose before the next party, Alice *were* to try to talk with Paul about the issue. She'd probably say something like this:

ALICE: I'm tired of your always picking fights with me when we come home from parties.

But this wouldn't work out well because Paul would probably answer back:

PAUL: Well I'm tired of the way you always *act* at parties.

And they'd be off. The conversation wouldn't even have begun and already it would have become an argument. So let's begin again and see if we can at least get the conversation started. Instead of Alice beginning with an accusation ("I'm tired of your always picking fights with me"), let's have her do what a psychotherapist would recommend she do: express her *feelings*, and in this case, her fears:

ALICE: I'm *worried* about our getting into a fight after the party this Saturday.

And instead of Alice just launching into the discussion, let's have her start by explaining to Paul what she's trying to do:

ALICE: I've been thinking about the arguments we get into when we go to parties, and I'm worried about the Collins' party this Saturday. I think I'd feel better if we could at least talk a little about it.

Paul's intrigued. He's never heard Alice talk this way before. And that's not surprising: hardly *anyone* ever talks this way. That's my point, of course: partners don't talk the way they need to in order to have things work out between them.

Paul's intrigued, but he isn't very hopeful. He can't believe that they could actually talk about the problem without getting into an argument. The only way to solve a problem, he believes, is to try not to have it. So he says:

PAUL: Thinking it will happen will just make it happen. You shouldn't go to the party with such a negative attitude.

Feeling criticized, Alice criticizes back:

ALICE: I don't have a negative attitude. I'm just facing reality, which obviously you're afraid to do.

Again the conversation would have become an argument before hardly getting started. So let's back up again and try to imagine what Paul could have said that might have worked out better. Instead of criticizing Alice for having a negative attitude, he could have said what he was feeling:

PAUL: I'm worried that talking about the party will just lead to an argument.

Even if Paul had said this, there would *still* be a chance for misunderstanding. Alice might take Paul's comment as meaning that he absolutely refuses to talk. If so, she might say in exasperation:

ALICE: You never want to talk about anything.

Paul would criticize back:

PAUL: You always have to talk everything into the ground.

And again they'd be into an argument. So what could Alice say that would work out better? She could say what she's feeling. Paul had just said, "I'm worried that talking about the party will just lead to an argument." Alice could say:

ALICE: Yeah, me too. It's just so important that we work something out about parties, I think it's worth the risk.

When your partner acknowledges the validity of your concerns about what he or she wants to do, you're more likely to want to go along with it. Alice's willingness to acknowledge that talking about the party is chancy causes Paul to feel like saying:

PAUL: Well sure, let's give it a try.

Having explained what she wants to do and having gotten Paul's agreement, Alice now launches into the discussion. And the fact that it's a discussion and not an argument makes a big difference. Alice admits something that she'd never otherwise admit:

ALICE: You know, maybe you're right about how I am at parties. I get nervous when I'm around people I don't know. And I get loud and awkward when I get nervous.

Paul is grateful that Alice is acknowledging what he had been trying so hard to get her to acknowledge. He softens. He admits something *he'd* never otherwise admit:

PAUL: You know. You're not the only one who gets nervous around strangers. I do too, except that when I get nervous, I get quiet and self-conscious.

And suddenly the reason for their problem is clear. It's not just that Alice gets loud and awkward when she gets nervous. And it's not just that Paul gets shy and self-conscious when he gets nervous. It's that Alice's way of getting nervous conflicts with Paul's way. Paul becomes *more easily embarrassed* and Alice starts doing things *that are more embarrassing*.

It's not just Alice's problem. It's not just Paul's problem. It's a joint problem. And for a moment at least that's how they see it.

Alice and Paul have made a good start in talking about their problem. But how can talking really help? It can help because inadequate or ineffective talking is a major part of the difficulty.

A relationship problem is really two problems:

1. *There is the problem itself.* In the case of Alice and Paul, it's the interaction between the different ways that they get nervous at parties.
2. *There is the problem of how partners talk (or don't talk) about the problem.* The way Alice and Paul talk about the problem—keeping quiet about it and then getting into arguments over it—is the bigger part of the problem. That's what is largely responsible for the difficulties that arise between them.

Solving the problem of how Alice and Paul talk about the problem could go a long way toward detoxifying it and blending it into the relationship. Alice and Paul would be talking together about how their problem at parties drives them apart. They would no longer be cut off from one another. They would no longer be privately preoccupied, each with his or her own particular troubled thoughts about the matter.

The goal is for Alice and Paul to be able to talk about the problem, not just this once, but in an ongoing way. Just as people on a midwestern farm need to keep in constant contact about the possibility of tornadoes —checking with one another about the weather and about whether the storm cellar has sufficient provisions—so couples need to keep in contact about their relationship problems. Each couple has its own set of private tornadoes to keep watch on.

PLANNING FOR THE PROBLEM

The first step in blending a problem into the relationship sets the stage for the second. Once partners have established an ongoing way of talking about the problem, they can then make joint plans about it.

The following is an example of Alice and Paul making joint plans. It's an idealized version. It leaves out all the blowups, false starts, dead ends, and conversation breakdowns that typically occur. Later chapters will show how blowups and breakdowns can themselves be blended into the relationship. For the moment, however, let's just look at what emerges at the end of the process.

Alice and Paul sit down together to decide how they want to handle their recurring problem about parties. They decide that they don't have to worry about *every* party. It's only parties at which they don't know many people that give them trouble. But that's exactly what's facing them this coming weekend at the Collins's party.

What are they going to do about the Collins's party? What they *had* been doing at parties is to try to adopt a "positive attitude." As Paul said, "If you go expecting problems, that's exactly what you'll find."

A positive attitude sounds like a good idea, but it may have serious drawbacks. If you're not expecting problems, you may be unprepared to deal with them. There's a certain advantage, accordingly, in adopting a "negative" attitude. There's the power of negative thinking just as there's the power of positive thinking. If you expect something to go wrong, you'll be prepared if it does.

So Alice and Paul go to the Collins's party. And they adopt a "negative" attitude:

> They jointly predict that Alice is going to get loud and that Paul is going to get embarrassed.

Alice's anticipating that she might get loud, Paul's anticipating that he might get self-conscious, and both anticipating that Paul might get embarrassed by Alice's loudness and that Alice might get embarrassed by Paul's withdrawal, give them a joint platform from which to view their behavior. It provides them a way to get outside of and be less affected by the problem.

After predicting that they might have their usual problem, Alice and Paul make plans to deal with it. They agree to:

> Check with one another during the party to see whether what they fear is happening. Compared to previous parties at which they had ended up enemies, they would now be allies.
>
> Leave the party early if they begin to feel too uncomfortable. Compared to previous parties at which they felt trapped, they now have escape hatches.
>
> Help one another out. Alice, who doesn't realize when she begins to get loud and awkward, asks Paul to point out when she does. Paul, who can get stuck in a funk at a party, asks Alice to notice when he is and help pull him out of it. Compared to previous parties at which they were left to deal with their problems alone, they would now be appealing to one another as resources.

There are many things that partners can do once they begin to blend the problem into their relationship. After the party, Alice and Paul know that they'll be able to:

> Commiserate with one another if, as may be the case, just what they feared might happen *did* happen.
>
> Celebrate the fact, if this is the case, that what they feared might happen did *not* happen.

I recommend that partners deal with couple problems in the same way that people deal with the flu. People are careful to avoid conditions that might lead to the flu, but they also keep on hand a supply of aspirin, and they are alert to the first signs of symptoms. When a child in the family gets a fever, everyone snaps into action.

So Alice and Paul go to the Collins's party, and here is what happens:

> Alice is loud only for a short period and Paul, to his surprise, hardly minds it when she is.
>
> Paul does get self-conscious, and Alice, as planned, comes to talk with him about it. The chance to tell Alice that he wants to go home, and Alice's willingness to do so, makes a big difference. Paul no longer feels trapped. He no longer feels alone. He no

longer feels self-conscious. And, surprisingly, he no longer wants to go home.

In fact, Alice and Paul are among the last to leave. And instead of arguing on the way home as they usually do, they chat about the party.

Jointly predicting a problem makes it (1) less likely to occur and (2) less distressing and easier to deal with if it does.

CHOOSING A PARTNER
IS CHOOSING A SET OF PROBLEMS

Mr. Skeptic: Well, okay, so Alice and Paul—what was the word you used?—*blended* their problem into the relationship. But it sure took a lot of effort. I can't help thinking that they're just poorly matched and that they'd each be better off married to someone else.

Wile: Well, that may be. On the other hand, problems would arise no matter *who* they married. There are always points in any relationship where sensitivities of one partner grate against the sensitivities of the other. True, if Paul had married either of his previous two girl friends, he wouldn't have had the particular problem at parties that he had with Alice. Neither of these girl friends got loud and awkward when nervous. And neither objected when Paul got quiet at parties.

> But if Paul had married Susan, he and Susan would have gotten into a fight before they even arrived at the party. That's because Paul, who is rarely ready for parties on time, would have kept Susan waiting. Susan would feel taken for granted, which is something she is sensitive about. And Paul would take her complaint about his always being late as domination, which is something *he* is sensitive about.
>
> And if Paul had married Gail, he and Gail wouldn't have gotten to the party at all. That's because they would be too upset about an argument earlier that day about Paul's not helping with the housework. Gail experiences his not helping as abandonment, which is something she is sensitive about, and Paul experiences Gail's insistence that he help as domination, which, as I just said, is something *he* is sensitive about.

Each potential relationship has its own particular set of inescapable recurring problems. If Alice had married either of her previous two boy friends, she wouldn't have had the particular problem at parties that she had with Paul.

> If she had married Steve, she'd have had the *opposite* problem. Steve gets louder at parties than she does. He'd get drunk, she'd get angry at his drunkenness, she wouldn't speak to him, and then they'd get into a fight.
> And if she had married Lou, she and Lou would enjoy the party but would have trouble when they got home and Lou wanted sex. That's because Alice and Lou respond in opposite ways to minor disagreements, such as the one that, let us imagine, they had had earlier that day. Lou responds by wanting sex. Sex is his way of feeling closer. Alice responds by *not* wanting sex. Sex is something she wants only when she *already* feels close.

No one ever begins a relationship in the following way—it would be too unromantic—but there is value, when choosing a long-term partner, in realizing that you will inevitably be choosing a particular set of unresolvable problems that you'll be grappling with for the next ten, twenty, or fifty years.

I recommend that we *start* thinking this way. It's as if you bought a car you really loved but that you knew had a temperamental carburetor. So you become an expert in adjusting carburetors. And whenever you go driving, you take along a set of tools and a manual. In a couple relationship, partners need to become joint experts, and they need to have a joint set of tools and, perhaps, *this* manual.

> Each relationship has its own set of unsolvable problems that can best be dealt with by developing a shared nonjudgmental vantage point from which to view these problems.

As time goes on, the couple problem may become less of a problem and more something partners may even be able to laugh at. A few months later, Paul said:

PAUL: Of course I'd never really want us to do this but wouldn't it be something if we brought a videocamera to these parties. We could start a videotape collection of me being withdrawn and you being loud.

People who can share a joke like this have gone a long way toward blending the problem into the relationship.

Building a Relationship On a Problem

"*B*lending your problems into your relationship" isn't just learning to live with them. It's also turning them to advantage. Problems have two particularly powerful advantages. They can be used as:

1. Pathways to intimacy.
2. Clues to important issues in the relationship.

These are significant benefits. It's possible in some cases to turn your problems—the things that most distress you—into the things that most help you. Partners who are able to do this are using their problems to help build their relationship.

Mr. Skeptic: I know what you're trying to do. You think it's clever to take what everyone knows is clearly a bad thing and try to prove that it's really a very *good* thing. But there's no way around it. Problems are bad things and should be eliminated.

Wile: Well, I'm just trying to find better ways to eliminate them. I want to use problems that we *know* we have to deal with problems that we *don't* know we have. And I want to use problems to increase intimacy.

USING PROBLEMS AS PATHWAYS TO INTIMACY

Intimacy is what everyone seeks in relationships. Everyone seeks it except those who have given up hope of ever getting it or who never knew it was possible to get in the first place. There is a great misunderstanding about intimacy, however. Many people think that intimacy comes from spending a lot of time together, enjoying the same things, and having the same interests. But intimacy comes from something entirely different.

> Intimacy comes from telling your partner the main things on your mind and hearing the main things on your partner's mind.

Intimacy is the contact partners make with one another *about* their wishes, concerns, and problems, and, in particular, about their wishes, concerns, and problems about the relationship.

Everyone knows that problems can lead to a *loss* of intimacy. The honeymoon ends when problems begin. Intimacy can be regained, however, by the way people solve their problems. Here's an example.

Mary and Dennis are a married couple in their early thirties. Dennis is a construction foreman and Mary is a quality control inspector on an automobile assembly line. Mary feels resentful that Dennis doesn't help more around the house. She blurts out:

MARY: We've got a great division of labor here. You mess the house and I clean it.

DENNIS (defending himself): What are you talking about? I do a *lot* around here. And speaking about messes, take a look at your desk some time.

And they get into a fight. So far, that is not new. In fact, that is what everybody does. One partner is sarcastic, the other is defensive, and they get into a fight.

But then Mary and Dennis do something that *is* new. After they have the fight, they *use the fight*. They use it as an introduction to a conversation and as a pathway to intimacy. The next day, when both have cooled off, Dennis comes up to Mary and talks about the fight. He says that he didn't realize it at the time, but he felt disappointed. He had been making an effort to do more around the house and Mary didn't seem to notice. And he was also disappointed in himself because, now that he thinks about it, he hasn't really been doing as much around the house as he had vowed to do.

Suddenly Mary and Dennis are having a conversation rather than an argument. Since Mary isn't being accused, she doesn't need to defend herself. And when people don't need to defend themselves, they are able to acknowledge things:

MARY: Well you *have* been helping more, and I appreciate it, so I don't know why I'm still upset about it.

And when people don't feel the need to defend themselves, they are able to discover things:

MARY: I guess I'm upset because the fact that you *are* helping makes me realize that we don't work well together. You have your own way of doing things and I have mine. We're really very different people. And we lead such separate lives. I've got my friends and you've got yours. I've got my job and you've got yours. I take care of the house, even if you are helping more, and you take care of the yard and the car, and I hardly help you at all in *those* jobs. Sure, we do our jobs okay, but we go our separate ways and don't connect very well. And I'm upset about that.

Dennis says that he has been feeling the same way and that his trying to help with the housework was an effort to connect a little better.

And now Mary and Dennis aren't just talking about the problem of who does housework. They are using this problem to discover another more general problem: their worry that they don't connect as much as they'd like to.

If Mary and Dennis have the view of intimacy that a lot of people have—that is, if they believe that intimacy is spending a lot of time together, enjoying the same things, and having the same interests—they're likely to have the nightmare view that:

They're just incompatible.
Getting married might have been a mistake.
And that's all there is to it.

The conversation is likely to bog down at this point—they don't feel there's anything more to say. And each partner is likely to go away feeling discouraged.

If they were to have the view of intimacy that I'm talking about, however, they'd know that:

Talking about not being intimate can, itself, be an intimate act.

That's because talking about feeling unconnected can be connecting. For a moment at least, Mary and Dennis would be in it together. Confiding about concerns such as feeling too separate is perhaps the fullest way in which people can join.

> A relationship is a busy place. It's like an airport with lots of things going on—scheduled and unscheduled feelings arriving and departing.

If a relationship is an airport, then intimacy—the main thing everyone's seeking—is the traffic controller. It's the contact that partners feel, whether spoken or unspoken, as they go about doing everything else. Intimacy is created by the way partners talk about what's happening in their lives and, in particular, what's happening between them. It's a consequence of their ability to be mutual confidants.

Conflicting work schedules may limit partners' time together to five minutes a day. Business travel may limit their contact to a phone call a day. But a phone call or a five-minute talk may be enough. Partners who, in such a phone call or talk, are able to get across how they feel will experience greater intimacy than partners who, although spending a lot of time together, are unable to do so. And among the major things that partners need to get across, and in a way that doesn't just lead to arguments, are feelings, worries, and dissatisfactions about the relationship.

Without such talks, long periods of time together may be difficult. A wife may think that she'd love to spend more time with her husband. When he retires, however, and spends much of the day at home, she discovers she doesn't like it. He is underfoot, and he interferes with her schedule. This husband and wife don't have a functioning relationship traffic controller. Neither has a way of letting the other in on what he or she is thinking and feeling. And neither has a way of talking about problems. The wife can't tell her husband about her difficulty having him home. If she *were* able to talk to him about it, and in a way that wouldn't just lead to a fight, she might feel better about having him home.

> Depending on how partners talk or don't talk about them, problems can lead to an increase or to a decrease in intimacy.

USING PROBLEMS AS CLUES

Couples can use their problems in another way: as relationship barometers for detecting moment-to-moment fluctuations in the relationship atmosphere. Partners have certain unwanted feelings that keep coming up. Many have repeated periods in which they are preoccupied with imperfections in their partners, such as:

An unattractive physical feature.
A nervous habit.
A slouch.
Untidiness.
Overtidiness.
Dressing sloppily.
Not having interesting enough things to say.

Many have repeated periods in which they are preoccupied with resentment about their partners':

Not being affectionate enough.
Not wanting to talk enough.
Not initiating things to do together enough.
Not wanting to have sex enough.
Not helping with the housework enough.
Watching sports on TV too much.
Being too involved with the kids,
Or not involved enough.
Not being careful enough with money.

Some have repeated periods in which they are preoccupied with:

Jealous thoughts about their partners' past romantic relationships.
Worries about suspected current ones.
Envious thoughts about their partners' greater professional achievement or closer relationship with their children.

Recurring feelings such as these may reflect general ongoing problems that need to be dealt with on their own terms. But they may have hidden potential uses.

A recurring relationship problem is like a trick knee. No one would ever want to have one. But it does have a side benefit. You'll know when it's going to rain.

In a similar way, a recurrent relationship problem can be used to measure the current relationship climate.

The following is an interchange in which Mary and Dennis do just that. I think you'll find striking how foreign and unfamiliar this interchange seems. It's hard to imagine ourselves or anyone we know talking this way. The fact that it is so foreign shows how infrequently we ever think to use our problems as relationship barometers.

Mary finds herself stewing again about having to do all the housework. She complains about Dennis's not helping and they get into a fight. Later, however, she uses her feeling as a clue. She comes to Dennis and tells him:

MARY: I know that housework is a big problem between us, and I'm not sure how we are ever going to solve it. But I seem to be feeling *particularly* upset about it at the moment. And I think it means what it usually means when I'm feeling particularly upset about housework: that I'm feeling really distant from you.

And she adds:

MARY: I've been feeling that we've each been off in our own worlds the last couple of days.

Dennis *has* been off in his own world. He's been having private resentful feelings about the fact that Mary doesn't want to have sex as often as he does.

At this point, Dennis could express his anger. He could accuse Mary of being sexually cold, and they could get into a fight. That's what usually happens. But in this idealized example, he doesn't. Instead, he uses his feeling as a clue:

DENNIS: Well, you're right, I *have* been off in my own world. I've been having my usual angry thoughts about your not wanting to have sex as much as I do. And I think it means what it often means: that I'm feeling neglected.

And he adds:

DENNIS: But I don't know why I would feel neglected. Nothing special has happened that should make me feel that way.

And then Mary, again making an ideal response, says:

MARY: Well, maybe that's the problem—the fact that nothing special *has* happened. I haven't been talking much to you. I've been preoccupied by problems at work. And I don't know why I *haven't* been telling you about them because I think I'd feel better if I did.

Between them Mary and Dennis have thus figured out what has happened:

Mary got preoccupied by problems at work and stopped talking to Dennis.

As a result, Dennis felt neglected. And he did what he usually does when he feels neglected: he felt like having sex.

But Mary didn't feel like having sex, which made Dennis feel even more neglected. He became resentful and stopped talking to her.

As a result, Mary felt cut off from Dennis. And she did what she usually does when she feels cut off from Dennis: she became preoccupied with resentment about his not helping more around the house.

By using their distressing feelings as clues, Mary and Dennis were able to figure all this out.

Mary and Dennis might even be thought of as *fortunate* that they have these problems about housework and sex. Mary's feeling resentful that Dennis wasn't helping enough with the housework allowed them to figure out that she felt cut off. Dennis's feeling resentful about Mary's not wanting to have sex allowed them to figure out that he felt neglected. If they hadn't had their respective concerns about housework and sex, or something like them, they mightn't have been able to make these important discoveries.

And these discoveries led to changes. Talking about feeling distant made Mary feel less distant. And talking about feeling neglected made Dennis feel less neglected.

The fact that Mary's resentment about housework and Dennis's resentment about sex can be used as clues doesn't mean that these issues aren't of major concern in their own right:

Mary's resentment about having to do most of the housework can mean that she feels distant, *and* it can mean exactly what it looks like: that she hates having to do all the housework and that she wishes Dennis would do more.

Dennis's resentment about Mary's not wanting sex as much as he does can mean that he feels neglected, *and* it can mean exactly what it looks like: that he wants sex more frequently.

DEFANGING YOUR INTERNAL PROSECUTOR

Why is this ideal conversation that I've described for Mary and Dennis so foreign to us? Why is it so hard to imagine anyone talking this way? And, in general, why don't we all develop relationship traffic controllers and use our problems as clues? Something gets in the way. And we need to know what this something is if we're to move it out of the way. This "something" is the internal prosecutor.

Using your problems as clues requires having a calm, unhurried, unself-critical attitude about your problems. It requires having the presence of mind to say to yourself, "Oh, how interesting. Here I am again resenting having to do all the housework. Or, here I am again resenting there not being enough sex. I wonder what it means? I wonder why I'm having these feelings now?"

Of course, people hardly ever think like that. Instead, they start accusing:

MARY (to herself): What's wrong with me that I resent doing most of the housework? I know I talk a lot about a fifty-fifty relationship, but, really, I'm the one who wants the house "just so." *I'm domineering. I'm controlling. I'm a nag.* Why do I always have to have everything my way? Dennis does lots of things for us. In his own way he does as much as I do. And what's wrong with me that I'm not more interested in sex? *I'm cold. I'm inhibited.*

DENNIS (to himself): What's wrong with me that I'm so preoccupied with sex? *I'm immature. I'm selfish. I use women as objects.* And what's wrong with me that I don't do more of the housework? *I'm lazy. I'm selfish. I'm spoiled.*

They blame themselves. Their internal prosecutors have taken over. Or they blame their partners:

MARY (to herself): No, it's not me. It's *Dennis.* Something's wrong with him that he won't do more of the housework. *He's lazy. He's selfish.*

He's spoiled. He's used to having everybody do everything for him. He thinks only of himself. And something's wrong with him that he's so preoccupied with sex. *He's immature. He treats women as sex objects.*

DENNIS (to himself): No, it's not me. It's *Mary.* Something's wrong with her that she's so preoccupied with cleaning the house. *She's a perfectionist. She's unable to relax and enjoy life.* And something's wrong with her that she has to have me do it with her. *She's trying to control me. She's a nag.* And something's wrong with her that she isn't more interested in sex. *She's cold. She's repressed. She's inhibited. She wants to frustrate me.*

Such blaming blocks effective thinking and talking about the issue. What Mary and Dennis need, and what we *all* need, are ways to defang our internal prosecutors and to see beyond our blaming.

> The more we are able to defang our internal prosecutors and see beyond our blaming, the more we will be able to blend our problems into our relationships and to build our relationships upon them.

BUILDING YOUR RELATIONSHIP
ON YOUR NEGATIVE FEELINGS

People hope to build their relationships on their positive feelings and their good times. I recommend that they also build them on their negative feelings and their bad times. The ability of partners to talk about their recurring negative feelings, and to use them as clues, can provide a solid foundation for a relationship.

The following conversations are examples of building the relationship on your problems. They are discussions that are hard to have and that we suffer from not being able to have. I'm presenting these conversations because knowing about them may make it more possible to begin to have them.

Ralph and Betty are a couple in their mid-forties. They have been married for five years. Each had been married before. Ralph is a postal carrier and Betty is a waitress. Here is the exchange they had while at a party.

RALPH: I saw you flirting with Malcolm just now. In broad daylight, with everyone watching. Why do you have to humiliate me like that?

BETTY: That's ridiculous. I don't even like Malcolm. You're driving me crazy with your jealousy. And I don't appreciate your criticizing me for things I'm not doing.

RALPH: Well *I* don't appreciate your doing what *you're* doing—wagging your little fanny in front of every pair of pants that has a zipper in front.

BETTY: I'll wag my little fanny in front of anything I want to. I certainly wouldn't bother wagging it in front of you. You wouldn't even notice. You're so busy being jealous.

RALPH: That does it. We're going home.

BETTY: That's fine with me. You've completely ruined the party for me.

The following is the conversation that Ralph and Betty needed to have but didn't. In this idealized conversation they engage their relationship traffic controller and use the problem of Ralph's jealousy as a clue.

RALPH: You were flirting with Malcolm just now, and I'm upset about it. I thought you told me that you don't like him.

BETTY: I don't.

RALPH: Well, you'd never guess it. You were hanging on to his every word. And you were laughing at all his stupid jokes.

BETTY: Is that how it looked? How embarrassing. I was trying to be polite. I didn't want it to show that I don't like him. I guess I overdid it.

RALPH: Well that's really something. Here I am getting crazy jealous over Malcolm, and you're just trying to hide the fact that you don't like him.

In the conversation that Betty and Ralph *did* have, they never got the chance to discover this misunderstanding. And they never got the chance, as they are about to do, to use Ralph's feeling as a clue.

RALPH: But it's more than just Malcolm. I've been having my usual jealous thoughts about your first husband. I've been thinking that you wished you were still married to him.

BETTY: Well, if you're thinking that again, maybe it means what it usually means when you're thinking that—that we haven't been connecting well recently. I don't know if this is it, but I have been all involved arranging Sarah's (their three-year-old daughter's) birthday party.

RALPH: That could be it. You've been real busy arranging the party, and I've been feeling left out.

BETTY: I thought I was doing you a *favor*. I thought you wouldn't want to be bothered with the party.

RALPH: Ordinarily I *wouldn't*. But this time I miss not being included.

BETTY: Well, if you *want* to be included, I could sure use the help. The party's gotten way out of hand.

Betty and Ralph would thus have used Ralph's jealousy as a clue to the fact that they haven't been connecting well recently and as a pathway to intimacy; that is, as a means of *reconnecting*. In this sense they'd be building their relationship on Ralph's problem of jealousy.

Here's an example with another married couple, Jane and Tony. Jane is a loan manager at a bank and Tony is a planning director for the city. Again, let's start with the conversation these partners *did* have. It's the kind of ordinary, slightly disagreeable conversation that partners often have and that almost everyone will recognize:

JANE: Do you love me?

TONY: You know I do.

JANE: Yes, but it's nice to hear you say it.

TONY: I'm not very good with words. I express it in other ways.

JANE: *What* other ways?

TONY: Lots of ways. I tell you how good you look. I bring you flowers.

JANE: It's not the same.

TONY: Well, I don't know what to do, then.

JANE: You could tell me that you love me.

TONY: OK, "I love you."

JANE: Well, all right, but next time say it as if you mean it.

Jane and Tony are caught in a discussion neither of them wants. Jane doesn't like being the beseeching, love-sick wife. Tony doesn't like being the withdrawn, depriving husband. How could they have avoided this disagreeable exchange? And, now that they are in it, how can they get out of it?

The answer is to recognize Jane's "Do you love me?" *as a clue* rather than as just a question that Tony should answer. Feeling unloved is Jane's relationship barometer. It's her way of registering any of a number of possible disruptions or disturbances in the relationship. It's a *rough* measure, however. It indicates that something's wrong, but it doesn't say exactly what.

What Jane and Tony need, accordingly, is a conversation in which:

1. Instead of simply getting Tony to say he loves Jane, they jointly recognize that she feels unloved.
2. They jointly find out what her feeling of being unloved is about.

Here's a conversation in which they do this. It's an ideal conversation because it omits all the false starts and breakdowns that generally occur.

JANE: I just caught myself about to ask my usual "do you love me?" question.

In one sentence, Jane rescues them from their typical impasse. Instead of simply asking, "Do you love me?", Jane reports her *wish* to ask it.

If Jane were to say, "Do you love me?" Tony would feel criticized for not having spontaneously thought to say it. He'd get defensive. He'd say in a beleaguered tone of voice, "You know I do."

In saying that she caught herself *about* to ask "my usual 'do you love me?' question," Jane is clearly criticizing herself, not Tony. Since Tony doesn't have to defend himself, he feels like helping her out:

TONY: Well, if you want me to tell you I love you, I guess you must be feeling *unloved*.

Instead of sparring with one another, Jane and Tony are now on the same side. In fact, each acts as the other's second. Jane protects Tony from her question about whether he loves her. Tony then helps her discover and state that she feels "unloved." The collaborative tone is set.

JANE: Well, I *have* been feeling unloved, and I don't even know why. . . . Well, actually, it's not so much that I feel unloved. It's more that I feel unsatisfied.
TONY: About what?
JANE: I don't know. It just *seems* that lately we haven't had much to say to one another.

In the discussion that they *did* have, Jane and Tony argued about his reluctance to say "I love you." But it wasn't about love at all. It was about feeling unsatisfied and about not having much to say to one another.

Tony answers Jane's comment that they haven't seemed to have had much to say to one another lately:

TONY: Well, I guess I *have* been engrossed in my own thoughts. And you've seemed kind of quiet too.

JANE: What's been so engrossing?

TONY: I've been stewing about how my boss has been treating me. I didn't tell you because I didn't want to sound like a broken record.

JANE: Well, I'd like to hear about it, broken record or not. And after you tell me about what's happening with your boss, then I'll like to tell you what's happening with my supervisor, because that's what *I've* been stewing about. And *I* haven't been telling you because *I* didn't want to sound like a broken record.

Everything now becomes clear. Jane and Tony kept their worries to themselves and, in so doing, shut one another out because neither wanted to be tiresome to the other. Jane's response to this mutual shutting out was to feel unsatisfied and unloved. In the discussion that they did have, they argued over whether Tony should say "I love you." In the conversation that they could have had, they used Jane's feeling of being unloved as a clue that they were shutting one another out. And discussing how they had been shutting one another out was a way of letting one another in.

Mr. Skeptic: That's all well and good, but didn't you just say that this was an idealized conversation that's almost impossible to have? How is such a conversation going to help Jane and Tony if they can't have it?

Wile: Just knowing that there *is* such a thing can help. Realizing that their problem is primarily how they *talk about* the problem may make it less likely that Jane and Tony will be stuck with dismal doomsday views such as:

Jane is just too needy.
Tony is just inadequate.
And they should just throw in the towel.

Realizing how such conversations ideally can occur may enable partners to make tentative starts toward having them. And any movement in this direction, however hesitant and stammering, can make a big difference.

3

Using The Relationship To Cure Your Problems

*P*eople hope that love will transfigure their lives. All that's needed, they believe, is to meet the right person and everything will change. Discontents and insecurities will drop away. Life will take on a richer meaning. Everything will be better.

And people are afraid that love *won't* transfigure their lives. They are worried that it's true, as everyone is always telling them, that:

> You can't expect your relationship to solve your personal problems. In fact, you'd better solve your problems first or you'll screw up the relationship.
>
> You can't expect a partner to make up for what you lack in yourself.
>
> You've got to learn to love yourself before you'll be able to love anyone else.
>
> You've got to learn to become independent before you'll be capable of a mature relationship.

I have a different view. I believe:

> You *can* expect your relationship to solve your personal problems.
>
> You *can* expect your partner to make up for what you lack.
>
> Finding someone who loves you is a good way to learn to love yourself.
>
> Forming a couple relationship is a good way to learn to become independent and, at the same time, to become more skillfully *dependent*.

Mr. Skeptic: I think you just enjoy disagreeing with what *everyone* else says.

Wile: Well, actually, it's not that much fun. I'd rather *agree* with everyone. In fact, I'd like to *convince* you that filling lacks in your personality, learning to love yourself, and becoming independent are what relationships can accomplish rather than what people must achieve prior to beginning them.

A RELATIONSHIP IS A GOOD PLACE TO SOLVE YOUR PROBLEMS

The romantics are right, but not in the way they think. Romantics think that love solves all problems. As soon as the right person comes along, they say, your troubles will be over.

> There are lots of women out there who thought that the right person had come along but who are now divorced, alone, and supporting a couple of children.
>
> There are lots of men out there who thought that the right person had come along but who are now divorced, alone, separated from their children, and sweating under child support payments.

But the romantics are partly right. Relationships *can* in some ways solve the problems that come up in everyday life.

> A man submits to abuse by his boss because he feels he has no right to complain or because he fears that his boss might fire him. And his boss *might*.
>
> A woman feels justified in complaining about a male co-worker's smoking (since it is now more socially acceptable to do so) but not about his other disagreeable habits, such as loud talking and noisy gum-chewing. She feels it's petty of her to be bothered by such things.

In general, people hesitate to complain directly to friends, bosses, or co-workers when they feel irritated by them. By the same token, they stifle many of their positive feelings. They feel it would be boastful and self-centered to make too much of their successes or to gloat over their rivals' defeats. A great many of the everyday feelings that people have are defined by them, and by society, as inappropriate or small-minded.

So people arrive at the end of a day, a week, or a year choked with feelings to which they feel unentitled or which, for other reasons, they are unable to express. This is a major cause of the tiredness that people can feel at the end of the day. And this a major reason why people try to get away on weekends and why they need vacations.

A major positive value of a couple relationship is the opportunity to express some of these held-back feelings.

> In the privacy of the couple relationship, people can sometimes let themselves engage in a little boasting, gloating, and griping; that is, "self-centeredness" and "small-mindedness."

Here, the usual standards about what is appropriate to say and to feel may be relaxed.

The chance to talk to their partners about what happened during the day is, for many people, the premier event of the evening. Some couples run through the events of the day immediately upon meeting. Others are silent at first and then spill out these events in the course of the evening, the next day, or the next month.

Such mutual confiding is a way of dealing with problems from the day by getting out into the open what has been rattling around in your head and by feeling that someone is on your side.

Mutual confiding is so important that partners who don't engage in it can, by this fact alone, be considered deprived.

A RELATIONSHIP IS A GOOD WAY TO MAKE UP FOR PERSONAL LIMITATIONS

We are told not to expect relationships to fill gaps in our personalities. But that's exactly what we can expect.

Harry, who has been modest and reserved throughout his life, is charmed by Cathy, who is expressive and expansive. He's intrigued by someone who doesn't mind drawing a little attention to herself. She makes up for what he lacks. And a little of it begins to rub off on him. He becomes more expressive himself.

Depending on the qualities you lack and the qualities that your partner has, you can learn from your partner:

How to have fun; how to be serious.
How to take a vacation; how to hold a job.
How to be angry; how to be unperturbed.
How to be organized; how to be spontaneous.
How to follow rules; how to bend them.

Forming a relationship is like entering a new culture. And if it's broadening to travel to another culture then it's broadening to form a new relationship.

Entering the new culture of a relationship produces problems, however. The goal is to obtain the benefits of this new culture and, at the same time, to be able to deal with its problems. Here is an example.

Sid and Barbara have been seeing one another for six months. Sid is the head librarian at a local junior college and Barbara is an aerobics instructor. Both are in their mid-twenties. Sid is enchanted by Barbara's spiritedness and adventurousness. She is always thinking of interesting things to do, whereas Sid gets caught in ruts.

The first months of their relationship are the most exciting in Sid's life. Barbara gets them to do all kinds of things that Sid would never think of—canoeing, scuba diving, flying kites, riding roller coasters. And now he's beginning to initiate such activities himself. Being with Barbara is teaching him how to be this other type of person.

Barbara is charmed by Sid's style. He's always saying everything in graceful and engaging ways, whereas Barbara always feels awkward and self-conscious. Barbara loves being with someone who has such elegance and poise. And now, she's beginning to be more poised herself. Being with Sid is teaching her how to be this other type of person.

What Barbara and Sid most like about one another, however, can, in a moment, turn sour. Sid can worry that he's not spirited and adventurous enough for Barbara. It's an issue that he's sensitive about. All his life, Sid has worried about being unspontaneous. And Barbara can worry that she's not charming and smooth enough for Sid. It's an issue that *she's* sensitive about. All her life, she has been worried about being awkward.

Barbara and Sid are driving back from a backpacking trip. Sid's quiet. He didn't enjoy the trip as much as he did the other excursions Barbara had planned. They kept getting lost, there were lots of bugs, it rained, and their tent leaked. Furthermore, Sid wasn't used to such primitive bathroom methods. So, he's cold, tired, itchy, wet, and constipated.

A hot shower, a good night's sleep, a flush toilet, and Sid could be as good as new. But there's an added problem. Sid thinks he *should* have enjoyed the trip. His internal prosecutor tells him:

SID (to himself): I can't believe it. You let a few insects and a little constipation get you down. You're a spoilsport. You never enjoy anything. Look at Barbara. She went on the same trip and nothing's bothering her. She's chatting away merrily.

Sid feels too ashamed about not enjoying the trip to say anything about it to Barbara. And that's too bad because if he *were* to tell her, she might admit that she didn't enjoy the trip either. Sid would be relieved, and they'd be able to share a new common goal: looking forward to getting home.

But Sid *doesn't* tell her. In fact, he doesn't say anything. And Sid's quietness worries Barbara. She sees it as confirming her worst fear, that she's too inelegant for Sid. Her internal prosecutor tells her:

BARBARA (to herself): Look at how quiet Sid is. You're probably driving him crazy with your nervous chatter.

In order to cheer Sid up, Barbara suggests that they stop at a winery. Barbara's suggestion, which is meant to help, puts Sid deeper in the dumps. He already feels he's a killjoy for not enjoying backpacking. And now he has to show that he's an even worse killjoy for not wanting to stop at the winery.

So he does what people often do in such situations. He shifts from blaming himself to blaming his partner. "It's not that I never want to do anything," he tells himself, "it's that Barbara always has to do everything." So he asks Barbara:

SID: Can't you even sit still for a second?

Barbara feels hurt and insulted. She forgets that she doesn't really want to stop at the winery either and that she suggested it only because she thought it would cheer up *Sid.*

BARBARA: It's not that I can't sit still. It's just that you never want to do anything.

This is hard for Sid to take, partly because it's exactly what he's been accusing himself of. So he blurts out:

SID: Well, I'd want to do more if you weren't driving me crazy with your mindless chatter. . . .

Which is a crushing blow to Barbara, since she's already worried about being inelegant.
Barbara sulks.
Sid sulks.
Neither speaks for the next forty miles. The day has turned into a disaster.

Mr. Skeptic: I think Barbara and Sid are just too *different*. And I think it shows that it may be a *mistake* to try to make up for a personal lack by finding a partner who has the missing quality.

Wile: But the problem isn't Sid and Barbara's differences. It's how these partners talk (or don't talk) about these differences. There were several things that Barbara and Sid needed to say that they didn't get to say. Driving home from the backpacking trip, Sid needed to say:

SID: I didn't enjoy the trip and I feel bad about it. I'm worried that I'm a killjoy.

Since Sid was unable to say this and instead fell silent, Barbara was then in the position in which *she* needed to say:

BARBARA: I'm worried that you're quiet because you're put off by my chattering.

Since Barbara was unable to say this and, instead, suggested they stop at the winery, Sid was then in the position in which *he* needed to say:

SID: I'm worried that this will disappoint you, but I feel like going home. In fact, this whole weekend makes me think that I can't keep up with you. You're still bouncing and I'm dragging.

Since Sid was unable to say this and, instead, said, "Can't you even sit still for a second?" Barbara was then in the position in which *she* needed to say:

BARBARA: That's hard to hear because I was already worried that my awkwardness and chattering might be getting to you.

Since Barbara was unable to say this and, instead, said, "You never want to do anything," Sid was then in the position in which *he* needed to say:

SID: That's hard to hear because I was already worried about being a killjoy.

Since Sid was unable to say this and, instead, said "Well, I'd want to do more if you weren't driving me crazy with your mindless chatter," Barbara was then in the position in which *she* needed to say:

BARBARA: Well, that's exactly what I'm worried about—that I chatter too much and that I'm not fun to be with. That's why I suggested the winery—to try to make it more fun to be with me.

Barbara and Sid wouldn't have had to think of *all* these things. Any one of them might have stopped the argument. (In a way, it doesn't take much to reestablish a collaborative spirit.) The problem is that at such moments, people are generally unable to think of *any* of these things.

Choosing a partner who has qualities that you lack is a good way to try to complete your personality. But such qualities can turn into sources of conflict. At such times, it's even more important than usual to find a way to talk about what's happening that doesn't just end in fights and hurt feelings.

A RELATIONSHIP IS A GOOD PLACE TO LEARN TO LOVE YOURSELF

We are advised not even to attempt a relationship until we have first learned to love ourselves. Of course, no one ever follows this advice. Learning to love yourself is a difficult task. Not many of us are very good at it. If we were to wait until we learned to love ourselves, few of us would start a relationship before the age of 93.

Fortunately, we don't have to wait. Learning to love yourself is what relationships can help accomplish rather than what you must do prior to beginning them. People can become more self-appreciative, more self-confident, and more self-respecting as a result of their relationships.

Why is it so frequently said, then, that you have to learn to love yourself before you will be able to love anyone else? It's because people who don't love themselves can often be:

Sensitive to slights. Since they doubt their lovability, they take slights as meaning that they are unlovable.

Prone to jealousy. They can easily believe that their partners would rather be with someone else.

And these can lead to serious problems in a relationship. Sensitivity to slights and proneness to jealousy are not in themselves the major difficulties, however. Everyone is sensitive or prone to something. The major difficulties are the partners' self-criticism about the fact that they have this sensitivity or proneness and their consequent inability to think and talk about it effectively.

Barry is a shy, 23-year-old computer programmer who is attracted to Patsy, a vivacious 21-year-old secretary who lives in his apartment building. Encouraged by her friendliness, he asks her out. They begin seeing a lot of one another and become involved.

Barry is a prime example of a person who could easily be seen as "needing to love himself before he will be able to love anyone else." His sensitivity to slights and proneness to jealousy threaten his relationship with Patsy. The real problem, however, is his *inability to think and talk about* his sensitivity to slights, proneness to jealousy, and inability to love himself.

When Patsy first said she loved him, Barry couldn't believe it. And then he began to believe it. He was ecstatic.

But it was easy for him to begin not to believe it again. They went to a party and Barry couldn't help thinking that Patsy wished she were with one of the other men. And driving home, when Patsy didn't snuggle up to him as she usually did, he became further upset. And the next day, when he called her at work and she didn't seem glad to hear from him, he became even more upset.

That did it. He left his own work, rushed over to Patsy's office, and yelled at her for being so cold to him and for throwing herself at other men.

And that did it for Patsy. She said he was being ridiculous, that she didn't know what he was talking about, that she didn't want him coming to her office and creating a scene, and that he had to learn to stop being so insecure.

Barry is a person whose difficulty loving himself makes it hard for him to believe that Patsy, or anyone else, could love him. He easily panics when Patsy behaves in ways that are less than fully loving. He thinks this shows that Patsy doesn't really care for him, which is what he has been fearing all along.

Barry's reactions aren't completely off the wall, however. He is right that something funny happened at the party. It's just that it wasn't what he thought.

Patsy wasn't thinking that she wanted to be with another man. She had gotten a haircut that day that she thought made her look awful. She was thinking that *no man* would want to be with *her*. That's why she acted in the hesitant and stiff manner that made Barry think that she would rather be with another man.

Barry is also right that something funny happened on the way home. Patsy *didn't* snuggle up to him. But again, it wasn't for the reason that Barry thought. Patsy didn't think he'd want to be snuggled up to by someone who looked so terrible.

Barry is also right that something funny happened when he called the next day. This time, however, it *is* for the reason he thought, or at least very close to it. Patsy was beginning to react to the coldness that Barry had begun to show toward her. Barry's fear that Patsy had begun to care less for him caused him to act in a way that *caused* her to begin to care less for him.

Barry's problem wasn't simply that he didn't love himself. His problem was his inability to think and talk about his sensitivity to slights and proneness to jealousy and the difficulty he had loving himself. He kept these worries to himself. And when he did finally say something, it was to blurt out accusations.

Let's imagine how it would look if Barry *were* skillful in thinking and talking about these worries. On the drive home from the party, he might have said something like:

BARRY: I'm feeling really insecure tonight. I kept thinking you wished you were with someone else. And I really miss your not snuggling up to me as you usually do. And this is really hard to talk about—and I almost didn't—because I'm *ashamed* of how insecure I can get.

Just saying this could be a big relief. And it could give Patsy an opportunity to say:

PATSY: Well, I'm glad you're telling me because I've been thinking that *you* must be wishing that *you* were with someone else—someone whose hair didn't look so awful.

Patsy, as it turns out, has her own version of Barry's problem. A bad haircut is all it takes to make her feel unattractive. And she, too, feels too self-conscious about having such worries to talk easily about them.

Learning to love yourself can be a difficult task, and most of us can use all the help we can get. Finding someone who *does* love us is often a good first step.

Relationships are a resource. But they are a resource with a hazard. It's easy to keep your fears of rejection to yourself, as Barry did, and then spew them out in a way that *causes* your partner to reject you.

4

Becoming Skillfully Dependent

I' ve described three ways in which relationships can cure: by providing a live-in confidant, by filling gaps in your personality, and by helping you love yourself.

But there is a fourth: helping you become independent *and* dependent.

Some people say that you should become independent *before* beginning a relationship. "Dependence dooms relationships," they say. "You've got to stop trying to turn your partner into a parent. You've got to stop being so dependent." I have a different view. I believe that:

Learning to become independent is what relationships can help accomplish rather than what must be done prior to beginning them.
At the same time, relationships are good places to accomplish the opposite task: learning to become successfully *dependent*. Dependency isn't a deficiency that needs to be overcome but a skill that needs to be developed. Dependence is too important a task to be left to children.

In other words, relationships are good places to develop skill in being both dependent *and* independent.

A COUPLE RELATIONSHIP PROVIDES
A SPECIAL OPPORTUNITY FOR DEPENDENCY

I'm going to talk about dependency in an unusual way: as something you can be good or poor at. Since children are well known for being dependent, you might think that they'd be good at it. But they're not. Children have only crude ways for getting people to comfort them (for example, by crying) or to pay attention to them (for example, by yelling "Look at me"). Adults have more subtle, flexible, and effective means of satisfying their needs for dependency. Adults are also freer to choose where to seek such satisfaction and, if disappointed, freer to look for it elsewhere.

The shift from childhood to adulthood is traditionally thought to require giving up childhood dependency. I suggest, however, that a couple relationship provides a special opportunity for dependency. In a couple relationship, you have a person—your partner—who is able to respond to your needs at a time in your life (adulthood rather than childhood) when you are better able to pinpoint what you really want.

Adults aren't necessarily less dependent than they were as children. What has happened is that they have developed better ways of being dependent. We don't notice that adults are dependent because of the relatively smooth, subtle, and skillful ways in which they typically fulfill their dependency needs. We *do* notice that children are dependent because of the relatively awkward, obvious, and unskillful ways in which they typically seek to do so.

RESCUING A RUINED IDEA

"Dependency" is a ruined idea. There's no way to refer to "being dependent" that's not a put-down. When people wanted to find a way to talk about dependency in a nonaccusing way they had to invent a new term: "support system." While it's bad to be dependent, it's okay to need a support system.

It's hard to think of "dependent" in any way other than just as something you shouldn't be. If a five-year-old wants to deliver a devastating blow to his three-year-old brother, he says "You're just a baby. You can't do anything by yourself." No other remark will have quite the same effect. Independence is seen as good and dependency is seen as bad. And growing up means shifting from dependency to independence. And that's all there's suppose to be to it.

Mr. Skeptic: Wait a minute, Wile. All this stuff you're saying is a just a lot of word games. I don't even think that *you* believe it. Dependent *is* bad and independent *is* good. And growing up *does* mean giving up childish dependency. What other possible way is there to think about it?

Wile: Well, let's *try* to think about it in another way. And let's start by looking at exactly how we use the term, dependent. And we use it to describe people who do annoying and disagreeable things such as:

Make whiny complaints about your neglecting them.

Put on long, pleading, beseeching, hurt looks.

Feel easily slighted or neglected.

Hang around waiting for you to pay attention to them rather than doing things on their own.

Have tantrums about your avoiding or rejecting them.

Follow you around when you take them to parties rather than circulating by themselves.

Wait for you to initiate activities and complain if you don't.

Such behavior is generally ineffective in getting you to *want* to take care of them, even though you might try to force yourself to do so.

In other words, we use the word "dependent" to describe people who are *unsuccessful* at getting us to want to take care of them. They turn us off. That's the irony. They're *poor* at being dependent.

People who are *good* at being dependent don't even look dependent. They just look like warm, engaging, appreciative, responsive, and loving people whom you feel like giving things to and doing things for. They are people who are successful in getting you to want to comfort them and take care of them. They make it fun to do so. They are people you'd want as friends. They are people you'd want to marry.

"How dependent is the person?" is the wrong question. I suggest that everyone is very dependent. The question is "how skillful is the person at being dependent?"

And the answer for most of us is *"not very,"* even if we *are* more skillful than we were as children.

That's because it's difficult to ask for things—and it's even more difficult to complain about not getting them—without, at times, your request being experienced as a pressure and the whole thing turning into an issue.

So some people don't even *try* to ask for things; they don't want it to turn into an issue. And they don't want to be seen as "dependent."

And some people try to ask for things anyway, even though it turns into an issue.

And some people deal with the problem by ritualizing the kinds of things they give to and do for one another. For example, a wife may automatically bring her husband a can of beer when they sit down to watch television in the evenings, and she may get him a quart of Rocky Road whenever she goes to town, and she may always have the house prepared and refreshments ready for his regular Wednesday night poker games. He doesn't even have to ask. And he does things for *her*, and *she* doesn't even have to ask. He keeps her car filled with gas, he accompanies her on her weekly visits to her parents (which she really appreciates), and he takes care of the kids on Sundays so that she can have some time to herself.

This kind of ritualistic giving runs the risk of going stale and no longer satisfying the needs—both for getting and for giving—that it was designed to meet.

TALKING SKILLFULLY ABOUT BEING UNSKILLFULLY DEPENDENT

So, since most of us are unskillful at being dependent, we need a way to deal with the effects of our lack of skill.

Dora is unskillful at being dependent. She stays at home taking care of her ten-year-old daughter and eight-year-old son, while her husband Ned works as an attorney.

Dora appears to have little of a life of her own, although she seemed quite independent before her marriage. She spent two years in Ecuador as a Peace Corps volunteer and traveled throughout Europe by herself. When Dora and Ned go to parties, she clings to him. On weekends, when Ned has work to do, Dora hangs around waiting for him to finish. She doesn't seem able to entertain herself. And every once in a while she lashes out at him for not spending enough time with her and for being married to his work.

And then Ned lashes back:

NED: You don't give me an inch of breathing room. You hover over me. You never let up for a minute. I'd like to come home *one* time without you ambushing me at the door. I'd like to go to *one* party where you didn't wear out the sleeves of my jacket hanging onto them.

Dora's the kind of person you'd want to tell to stop being so dependent and to go out and develop a life of her own. And that's what Dora privately tells herself.

Mr. Skeptic: And that's what Dora *should* tell herself. You call her unskillful at being dependent, but she seems pretty skillful to me. She's living off other people. She's insatiable. She's a bottomless pit. Look at all she's getting from Ned.

Wile: I don't see her as getting very much. In fact, she's getting very little. It's hard to enjoy the attention of a person you feel sees you as a pest. And that's how Ned sees her—as a pest. Her hanging onto him just makes him want to get away. And her sporadic lashing out at him for not spending enough time with her makes him feel like spending even *less* time with her. So Dora's unskillful at being dependent. Ned is put off by her rather than wanting to take care of her.

What Dora needs, and what many of the rest of us need, is a way to deal skillfully with the effects of being unskillfully dependent. To show what this looks like, I'm going to turn Dora into another person, Dora-2, who is *skillful* in dealing with the effects of being unskillfully dependent. Ned and Dora-2 go to a party and she clings to him. But then she says:

DORA-2: I hate the way this party's going. I'm hanging onto you in a way I don't like—and I'll bet you don't care much for it either—and I'm not even getting that much from it.

Ned is shocked. He's used to Dora-1. And Dora-1 would never say anything like this.

Instead of just acting on her feelings, Dora-2 is standing back and reporting them.
Instead of blaming Ned, she's sympathizing with him for what she imagines must be her impact on him.

And Dora-2 has more to say:

DORA-2: This isn't how I want to be—clinging to you in this needy way. I don't even know why I do it. Somehow I don't get reassured enough. I keep sticking around hoping there'll be more, because I don't get enough.

There's a danger here. Ned could easily feel that Dora-2 is blaming him for not reassuring her enough and for not giving her enough. They could get into a fight.

But Dora-2 makes clear that she's *not* blaming him:

DORA-2: And I don't get enough because I'm hanging onto you in a way that would drive anyone away.

Ned appreciates Dora-2's willingness to look at her clinginess from *his* point of view. And it makes him feel a little more like looking at the situation from *her* point of view. Instead of feeling resentful, as he usually does, he feels sympathetic. Dora-2 is talking skillfully about having been *un*skillfully dependent.

Mr. Skeptic: Wait a minute. I've been sitting here patiently giving you the benefit of the doubt, but now you've gone too far. I've known plenty of people like Dora, and none of them could *possibly* talk in this way—I don't care if you call her Dora-2 or even *Dora-3*.

Wile: Well that doesn't surprise me because hardly anyone talks in such a nondefensive and fully aware way. *I* don't talk this way, and I wrote this book. Dora-2 is a figment of my imagination. But a person who *could* talk this way is my idea of someone who is really good at recovering from being unskillfully dependent. Dora-2 is knowing and saying what she wants. And she is doing so in a way that really gets it across. And since she isn't criticizing Ned, he's able to hear it.

> Being able to talk with Ned in this way can accomplish in ten minutes what can't be accomplished in ten years of following him around at parties. It can provide the sense of intimacy and connectedness that Dora is seeking.
> And if partners could talk this way, they'd be more likely to *feel* like doing things for one another and like taking care of one another.

USING YOUR RELATIONSHIP TO BECOME INDEPENDENT

I've been talking about relationships as a way to become more effectively *dependent*. Now I want to talk about them as a way to become more effectively *independent*.

And, ironically, partners can become independent as a result of feeling more securely dependent.

> The more people feel they can *depend* on their partners, the more emboldened they may feel to do things on their own.

The experience of feeling emotionally backed and of having a built-in confidant—someone reliable with whom to debrief the day—can enable people to approach the world more boldly and self-confidently.

I shall use the example of Dora and Ned to show how a relationship can undermine a partner's striving for independence and how, alternatively, it can facilitate it.

Dora has had a depressing day at home. She doesn't want to bring Ned down, however, so when he returns from work, she conceals her feeling from him and, instead, talks *gaily* about neighborhood gossip. Dora's hollow cheerfulness gets to Ned. He tries to be patient, but finally blurts out:

NED: Why are you telling me all this boring stuff? Staying home is rotting your mind. You should go out and meet people, or maybe take some courses, or maybe even get a job.

Getting a job isn't a bad idea, and Ned could be seen as offering a useful suggestion and encouraging her independence. Instead of feeling encouraged, however, Dora feels put down. She's upset at Ned's seeing her as tiresome and uninteresting. Her confidence, already low, slips further. Instead of enjoying the possibility of getting a job, she doubts that anyone would want to hire her.

The relationship has had an undermining effect. It has hindered Dora's move toward greater independence. It's one of those unfortunate situations in which each partner's attempt to make things better made things worse. Dora's attempt to avoid bringing Ned down brought him down. Ned's effort to listen respectfully led to his disrespectful outburst.

Let's take it again from the top and this time show how the relationship might have had an empowering effect. This time when Ned comes home, Dora *doesn't* try to be cheerful. Instead, she tells him:

DORA: I've been feeling depressed today. In fact, I've been feeling depressed a lot recently.

Ned had noticed that she had been feeling down and is glad to have a chance to discuss it:

NED: Yeah, I've been worried about you. You seem to be feeling the way I felt when I was laid up that year and couldn't work. It really got me down. It sounds as if something has really gotten *you* down.

Dora feels understood. Her eyes fill with tears:

DORA: You know what? Being at home all day isn't such a great idea. Maybe I should think about getting a job.

Let's look at what has happened:

First, Dora has been successfully dependent. She has talked in a way that gets Ned to sympathize with her.

Second, being successfully dependent—feeling that Ned is on her side—enables Dora to feel more *independent*. As before, the idea of a job comes up. But now Dora feels inspired to look for one. The relationship has empowered her. It has made her more *independent*.

Once we stop labeling dependence as childish, we'll be able to see that dependence and independence are twin needs of adults. And these twin needs are *inter*dependent:

Dependence—feeling secure in a relationship—can allow a person to become more independent; that is, to deal more resourcefully with the world.

And being able to deal more resourcefully with the world includes being able to deal more resourcefully with the world of people; that is, knowing more what you want from others (including your partner) and being able to ask for things more comfortably, less accusingly, and in a way that is more likely to get others to want to provide it. Thus, becoming more independent can lead to becoming more skillfully *dependent*.

"Independence" is often viewed as *having no needs*. But, as I suggest here, it can also be viewed as competence and resourcefulness in *fulfilling* your needs.

II

MAKING TALKING LESS DANGEROUS

*N*o matter what we discuss—intimacy, dealing with problems, learning to love ourselves, filling gaps in our personalities, becoming skillfully dependent, or becoming independent—it all comes back to one thing: talking.

So in Chapter 5, I talk about talking. I show that the heart of a relationship is saying what you need to say and feeling that it has gotten across.

But talking is dangerous. It destroys as many relationships as it saves. In Chapters 6 and 7, I show why it is dangerous and how to make it less so.

5

Having the Conversation That's Been Missing

*T*he heart of a couple relationship has been described as:

Sharing common interests.
Companionship.
Raising children.
Doing things together.
Trust.
Loyalty.
Commitment.
Sex.
Love.

I disagree. The heart of a couple relationship is saying what you need to say and feeling that it has gotten across. And that's what makes sharing common interests, companionship, doing things together, having sex, and raising children together enjoyable and worthwhile things to do. And that's what can establish trust, loyalty, commitment, and love.

Sally, who has been a traditional wife for the ten years of her marriage to Stuart, nervously asks him if it's all right if she goes out for dinner one night a week with two of her women friends. Here's what Stuart needs to be able to say:

STUART: Sure, once a week is fine, if that's all it means. But since things have been so rocky between us recently, I'm worried that this is the first step in our drifting apart.

If Stuart were to say this, then the issue of Sally's going out with friends would be put in proper perspective. Stuart's not against it; he's just worried that he and Sally are drifting apart.

But Stuart is *unable* to tell her this, in part because he doesn't know that he feels this and in part because he isn't used to thinking and talking in such terms. He knows that there's something about Sally's going out with friends that he doesn't like, but he doesn't know what.

STUART: Why can't you just talk to your friends on the phone?
SALLY: But the whole point is to change my routine and get out a little on my own.
STUART: I just don't think it's a good idea. It's dangerous to be out at night.
SALLY: Don't be silly. I won't be alone. There will be three of us women.

It looks like there's going to be no way to talk Sally out of it. So Stuart just puts his foot down:

STUART: Well, you're married to me and you should stay at home in the evenings and make dinner.

In one lunkish sentence, Stuart has regressed thirty years in the history of man–woman relationships. Any modern person hearing him would immediately side with Sally, although wondering why Sally is so meek: Why is she asking him? Why isn't she telling him?

But what can be said about Stuart—a husband living in this day and age—who insists that his wife devote herself en'irely to his needs? The problem is his inability to tell Sally what he needs to tell her. He experiences her request for a night out as a threat and, in a way, as an attack. And he does what people who feel threatened and attacked—and who can't tell their partners about it—often do. He simply attacks back. He tells her to stay home.

People say and do lunkish things when they have important feelings that they are unable to express. (A "Peanuts" character was too shy to tell a girl he was sweet on her. "I didn't know what else to do," he told a friend, "so I hit her".) Until Stuart is able to tell Sally that he is worried about their drifting apart, he may be stuck making doltish claims about a husband's natural rights.

And having made these doltish claims, Stuart tries to defend them. The more he says, however, the worse he sounds, even to himself. People can sound pretty ridiculous when they try to defend indefensible positions. Even so, Sally is unable to stand up to him. Sally tries to answer and gets twisted in her words. Later, she thinks of the responses she wishes she had made.

STUART: You've *always* made my dinners.
WHAT SALLY *WISHES* SHE HAD SAID: Yeah, so maybe it's time you made mine.
STUART: You know I'm all thumbs in the kitchen.
WHAT SALLY *WISHES* SHE HAD SAID: Well, you can use your thumbs to fry an egg.
STUART: I think it's your friend Sue that put you up to this.
WHAT SALLY *WISHES* SHE HAD SAID: Yes, she's a very *wise* friend.
STUART: I work hard all day supporting you and it's only right that you do your part.
WHAT SALLY *WISHES* SHE HAD SAID: Well, now that you mention it, that's another thing I'd like to talk to you about. I'd like to go back to work and have us *both* do the housework.

Sally clearly is not making her point. She has pertinent comebacks, but thinks of them only hours later. Many people might suggest that Stuart needs consciousness raising and that Sally needs assertiveness training.

Easily missed, however, is the fact that Stuart is making his point no better than is Sally. He has the last word, and most of the words in between, but he isn't saying what he really needs to say. He's not telling her that he's afraid that her going out with friends is a further step in their drifting apart.

Hardly anyone looking at this interchange between Stuart and Sally would ever guess that the problem is Stuart's failure to say what he needs to say. That's because it's so easy to attribute the problem to Stuart's character defects (and also to Sally's). Sally's friends tell her:

He thinks only of himself.
He wants to keep you under his thumb.
He wants a mother, not a wife.
He's a male chauvinist.
Get rid of him. You're worth ten of him.
Why do you let him treat you this way? You must enjoy suffering.

And it's not just Sally's friends who talk this way. If Sally were to consult a psychotherapist who has an extreme version of the kind of thinking that I object to, he or she might say (or at least think):

Stuart's making outrageous claims of narcissistic entitlement.

He's seeking omnipotent control.

He's functioning at an early childhood stage in which he's symbioti-
cally attached to his mother.

You're adopting the cultural role of the submissive wife and are repeating the sadomasochistic relationship you had with your father.

You're afraid to leave him because early childhood losses have made
you fearful of separation.

Being dominated must serve a function for you. You must be getting
something out of playing the victim with Stuart.

Stuart is seen by nearly everyone (and secretly by himself) as a spoiled,
selfish, and manipulating bully. Nothing more is thought necessary to say.
Once a problem is attributed to a person's character defects, it's difficult
to consider the alternative possibility that the problem might be a result of
his or her inability to get a point across.

But if Stuart and Sally *were* to consider such a possibility—that is, if
they were to consult a psychotherapist who believed in the kinds of thinking
I'm trying to promote—these partners would now recognize that:

If Stuart's spoiled, he's also deprived. He's deprived of a basic need
that people have: to be able to talk about what is foremost on
their minds.

If he's selfish, he's also unable to ask for what he really needs. He
needs to know how Sally feels about him.

If he's manipulative, he also lacks any real control. He's unable to
talk to Sally about what is really bothering him.

And if he's bullying, he's also oppressed and up against the wall. He
can't think of anything to do that doesn't just make matters worse.

Looked at in this way, Stuart seems much less the evil, exploitive, malicious,
"bad" partner. He appears more like a poor guy struggling ineffectually
against difficult odds.

Mr. Skeptic: You bleeding-heart do-gooders are all alike. All this
mumbo-jumbo about Stuart being a poor-guy-struggling-against-difficult-
odds just muddies the water. He's a bully, and he shouldn't be allowed
to get away with it. You want to forgive everybody. I'm just glad you're
not on the Supreme Court.

Wile: Now wait a minute. I'm not talking about forgiving Stuart or letting him get away with anything. Just because we *understand* Stuart's behavior, this doesn't mean that we have to like it, or that Sally has to stop resenting it, or that she has to put up with it.

But if Sally and Stuart *were* to think about Stuart's behavior in this new way, they'd have the possibility of talking usefully about it. Imagine what might happen, for example, if Stuart were to tell Sally that he's worried about their drifting apart. Imagine further that he were to tell her that he's *ashamed* of having these worries; he feels that a real man wouldn't be so frightened about such things.

Problems often seem more manageable when discussed, particularly when discussed with the person they concern. Having aired his worries, Stuart might now feel more comfortable with the idea of Sally going out.

Even if he didn't, Sally and Stuart would at least be able to talk directly about these important feelings. In fact, talking about such feelings is what Sally has been seeking all along. That's why she wants to go out with friends. She wants to spend time with people with whom she *can* talk about personal things.

> Thus, as paradoxical as this might seem, confiding in Sally about his reservations about her going out could make it less necessary both for Sally to go out and for Stuart to keep her home.

There are thus two problems. The first problem is a failure to have needed conversations. Difficulties occur when partners are unable to say what they need to say. The second problem is that people don't know that this is the problem. It's so easy for partners to attribute their difficulties to character defects that they fail to see that the problem is missing conversations.

WHAT PEOPLE NEED
AND WHAT THEY THINK THEY NEED

Partners need to have certain types of conversations, and they need to have them all the time:

> They need to be able to talk about their gripes and worries (particularly those about the relationship).
> They need to be able to talk about their wishes and fantasies (partic-

ularly those about the relationship) and about how these wishes
and fantasies are being disappointed.

They need to be able to talk about their hesitation in bringing up
dissatisfactions that they fear might hurt or anger the other.

And they need to be able to talk about how they occasionally blurt
them out anyway.

They need to have conversations and not just arguments about all
these things.

They need a chance jointly to lament the fact that relationships are
so hard.

And they need a chance jointly to realize that their relationship is not
as abnormal and different from everyone else's as it sometimes
seems to be.

And that they themselves are not as screwed up as they sometimes
feel they are.

Partners need all these things, and they generally get none of them.
And they don't even know that they are deprived of them. It's hard for
people to notice that they're deprived of something that they didn't know
they needed.

Partners have an entirely different idea of what they need:

They think they need to have "common interests," by which they
mean spending a lot of time together and having things to say
to one another.

They think they need to have "common goals," by which they mean,
among other things, agreement on the number of children they
are going to have, who's going to take care of these children,
who's going to take care of the house, who's going to work, and
where they're going to live.

They think they need to be able to "get along," by which they mean
not have too many arguments.

They think they need to be "compatible," by which they mean not
have too many arguments.

They think they need to be able to "communicate," by which they
mean not have too many arguments and not have too many
silences.

They think they need to be "sexually compatible," by which they
mean to want sex as often as their partner does, not lose too
much interest in having sex, and be able to have orgasms.

These are the grounds on which people judge whether or not their relationships are satisfying and whether or not they have a right to feel deprived.

In other words, while partners may sense that something is lacking in their relationships, they feel unjustified in feeling deprived unless they can point to established reasons such as "incompatibility" or "lack of common interests." They don't realize that, more than anything else, they are deprived of conversations.

SEEKING OUT THE MISSING CONVERSATION

If partners *were* to realize that they are deprived of conversations, they could say to themselves:

What is the conversation that would take care of this problem we are having (or, at least, would tell us *why* we're having it)?

Once you begin looking for the conversations you're missing, you'll discover that they're not difficult to find. Here are some examples:

(1) A man who had been divorced for several years called his eight-year-old daughter, who lived with his ex-wife, and asked if she wanted to go for ice cream. His ex-wife had a busy schedule—she worked full time and was in the process of planning her second marriage. The man's taking his daughter for ice cream interfered with his ex-wife's evening and violated their agreement that all visits with his daughter be prearranged. The man was puzzled himself about why he did it. He generally prided himself on sticking to arrangements and making things easy for his ex-wife.

Asking his eight-year-old daughter for ice cream was what this man was left doing because he was unable to tell his ex-wife, "I know that this is ridiculous—I was the one, after all, who wanted the divorce—but I think I always had a secret belief that we would somehow get back together. Your getting remarried makes me finally realize we'll never be a family again and that I'm going to lose everyday contact with Sarah. And I'm feeling really bad about it."

Since this man was unable to express these feelings—he didn't even fully know that he had them—he had no choice but to act on them. Taking his daughter for ice cream was a desperate and totally ineffectual effort to maintain everyday, casual, spur-of-the-moment contact with her.

(2) In their book, *Therapy for Couples*, Billie Ables and Jeffrey Brandsma

tell of a wife who annoyed her husband by opening his mail. Opening his mail, the authors suggest, was what she was left to do because she couldn't say what she needed to say, which was something like: "I haven't told you this before, but I don't feel as close to you as I thought I would. We have such separate lives. I feel left out of your life more than I want to be."

Opening her husband's mail was a desperate although totally inadequate and even counterproductive effort to include herself more in her husband's life.

People underestimate the power of words. It is said that:

Actions speak louder than words.
One picture is worth a thousand words.
Sitting here talking about the problem all day isn't going to solve it.

But it depends on what the words are. The right words can be worth a thousand pictures. And the right words can lead to actions and solve problems, as the following example shows.

(3) A woman was hesitant to tell a man, whom she had just started dating, that a pair of slippers he had bought her in Mexico were too tight. He seemed so pleased with his gift to her—they *were* a splendid pair of slippers—that she had difficulty telling him that she couldn't wear them. When she finally did tell him, she found out that he really didn't mind. And here's the surprise. When she went home to try on the slippers again, they now fit.

I know this sounds like a fairy tale—*Cinderella* without the stepmother—but it's not hard to figure out how it happened. When the woman put on the slippers after just receiving them, she was *afraid* that they might not fit. She took the slight pressure on her toes as indicating that they were "too tight." After *telling* her boyfriend that the slippers didn't fit, however, and, in so doing, dealing with her fears, she now experienced the pressure on her toes in an entirely new way—as indicating that the slippers were "snug"; that is, as slippers should be. The pressure was off *having* to like them.

Expressing what you need to express doesn't always have such dramatic effects—it doesn't always make your slippers fit—but it does often help matters, as the following example shows.

(4) A husband resented the fact that his wife invited her sister to dinner without first checking with him. All he needed to do was to complain about it—and to feel that his wife understood how he felt—to then feel perfectly

comfortable and even happy to have her sister come. In fact, having made the complaint, he was then particularly gracious toward the sister during dinner.

Let's suppose, however, that his wife had refused to listen to his complaint and had said instead: "I'll invite my sister anytime and anywhere I damn please." The husband would never have gotten the chance to do what he needed to do (to make the complaint and to feel that his wife understood) to enable him to change his attitude about his wife's sister's coming to dinner. And when she came, he might have been rude the whole evening.

So it's important to be able to express your complaints. And, as the following example shows, it's important to be able to express your worries.

(5) Bernard Apfelbaum, my mentor in ego analysis, describes how people behave when, during sex, they find themselves unaroused. They withdraw into their heads and try to conjure up erotic scenes. An alternative is for them to tell their partners how they feel, saying something like: "For some reason I don't feel very turned on and I'm worried about disappointing you." People hesitate to say such things for good reason, Apfelbaum says, because doing so might completely destroy the mood for sex.

But it might also *create* the mood for sex, he continues. A common effect of telling your partner that you're not aroused is then to begin to *become* aroused. By confiding in your partner, you are breaking out of the shut-down, cut-off, struggling-in-isolation effort that's turning you off.

Everyone knows how expressing a fear, worry, or grudge can, at times, diminish or even eliminate the fear, worry, or grudge. I'm simply suggesting that this idea be raised to a major principle:

> Whenever you find yourself feeling less satisfied with, less in love with, less turned on by, more walled off from, more disgruntled with, or more bored with your partner, look for feelings, wishes, worries, or complaints that you are not telling him/her and that he/she is not telling you—and see if you can talk to your partner about them.

People start acting in crazy, confused, offensive, and desperate ways when they are unable to say important things that they need to say.

6

Avoiding Conversational Booby Traps

Mr. Skeptic: Okay Wile, you keep making this big point about talking. But if talking is as wonderful as you say it is—if it's the way to become intimate—why haven't we all figured this out long ago. If it's so great, why do we do so little of it?

Wile: Because talking is also dangerous. Here's what can happen:

1. Your partner tells you about a problem he or she has and you offer advice or try to give reassurance. Instead of feeling grateful, however, your partner gets angry. You get into a fight, and both of you wish that he or she hadn't told you about the problem in the first place.

2. Your partner tells you about his or her day. Instead of being interested, as you think you should be, you feel *bored*. You pretend you aren't bored, however, because you don't want to hurt your partner's feelings. So you sit there bored. And it doesn't even do any good because your partner senses that you are bored and feels hurt and angry.

As I shall try to show, the best way to deal with these traps is to *expect* to stumble into them and to become skillful at climbing out of them.

THE UNWANTED-ADVICE TRAP

Trap Number One: Offering advice or trying to give reassurance when your partner wants to tell you how he or she feels.

Annie and Joel are a couple in their late twenties. Joel is an engineer for the water company and Annie, who works full time as a file clerk for a Savings and Loan, is trying to get a college degree by going to school at night. Annie comes home one evening and says:

ANNIE: It's all too much for me. I've got a ten-page paper due in class Monday evening and I haven't even started it yet.

JOEL (rushing in with reassurance): Don't worry, you'll get it done. You always do. You've never failed to hand in a paper in your whole life.

ANNIE: Yeah, but this time's different. And, anyway, it's not just that. Two people at work are on vacation and my boss has given me their work to do. I don't see how she expects me to do everyone else's work and still finish mine.

JOEL: You shouldn't put up with it. You've got to tell her that you can only do so much.

ANNIE: Yeah, but she'll just tell me that I should work harder. You can't reason with her.

JOEL: Well, then maybe you should talk about it to *her* boss.

ANNIE: Yeah, but I'd only get into trouble if I went over her head.

JOEL: Well, then maybe you should get another job.

ANNIE: Yeah, but it's not that easy to get another job.

Annie doesn't know why they are discussing quitting her job; that isn't what she wanted to talk about, although she isn't exactly sure what it is she *did* want to talk about. She knows that Joel's comments aren't helping, but she can't figure out why. She worries that she is being ungrateful for not appreciating Joel's suggestions.

And Joel feels that she is being ungrateful for not appreciating his suggestions. Every time he suggests something, she comes up with a reason why it won't work. She's keeps saying "yes, but."

Of course, we could turn the whole thing around and ask not why Annie refuses to accept any of Joel's suggestions but, rather, why he has to make them. Joel has been talking to Annie less than two minutes and has already made three suggestions including that she quit her job.

Joel may be acting this way because he's impatient with Annie. He may be the kind of person who feels that it's a waste of time to worry about your problems; what you should do instead is try to solve them or, at least, learn to live with them. He may feel that it would be a mistake for him to be too understanding and too sympathetic because that might just encourage Annie in her tendency to complain and feel sorry for herself.

Although Joel has a touch of this belief, his major reason for giving Annie the advice he does is that he thinks Annie expects him to solve her problem. And he does what people often do when they feel responsible for solving another person's problem. He offers advice, and then when the other person fails to take it, he blames the other person:

JOEL: I don't think you really *want* to solve your problems. You get too much enjoyment out of complaining about them.

This is the kind of conversation that makes people not want to have conversations. The next time Annie feels troubled by problems at work or school, she keeps them to herself. She wants to avoid repeating this tense and unsatisfying conversation. And Joel wants to avoid it too.

As I said, Joel thinks that Annie wants him to solve her problems. But that *isn't* what she wants. What she wants is for Joel to appreciate how she feels. She would love it if he were to say something like: "Poor baby. Everything's coming down on you all at once."

What Joel says, unfortunately, makes her feel that he *doesn't* appreciate how she feels:

By reminding her that she *always* finishes her papers for school, Joel is telling her, in effect, that she has no reason to be upset and that she *shouldn't* be upset.

By advising her to confront her boss and, if that fails, to quit, Joel is telling her, in effect, that her problem has direct and straightforward solutions if she would only apply them and, again, that she has no reason to be upset.

Joel is trying to reassure Annie that she has no reason to be upset while Annie is wanting him to appreciate that she does. It's an unfortunate misunderstanding. Joel feels burdened with responsibility to do something for Annie that she doesn't even want him to do. It would be a great relief for him, accordingly, if he were to realize:

That Annie *doesn't* expect him to solve her problem.

That she doesn't even *want* him to try to solve it.

That she simply wants him to appreciate how she feels.

That his doing so would mean a lot to her, since a major part of her problem is feeling all alone in her feelings.

And thus, in a sense, Joel, acknowledging how she feels, *would* be solving her problems (by enabling her to feel that she *isn't* all alone in her feelings).

I'm not saying that Joel is wrong to try to give advice and reassurance. At *other* times, Annie might have been reassured by Joel's reminder that she always gets her papers written. And she *might* have appreciated and, in fact, felt supported by Joel's advice to confront her boss or, even, to quit her job. On *this* occasion, however, Annie experiences his quickness to reassure and his readiness to offer solutions as efforts to talk her out of her feelings.

Joel needs an important piece of knowledge. He needs to know that there are two *very different* things that Annie might want from him when she comes to him with a problem:

1. She might want him to help solve the problem and, perhaps, to reassure her that it isn't such a big problem; that is, she might want him to talk her out of her feelings.
2. *Or* she might want him to listen to how she feels about the problem and, perhaps, to appreciate how *big* and unsolvable the problem really is or, at least, how big and unsolvable it *seems* to her at the moment.

If Joel had known that there were these *two* different things that Annie might be wanting, he might have been able to say at the end of their disagreeable interchange:

JOEL: Hey, I just thought of something. Here I've been rushing in with all this advice and all these solutions. And maybe that's not at all what you're wanting from me.

Annie would be relieved if Joel were to say this. She had felt all day that no one had understood how she felt. In hearing these words from Joel, she would finally feel that someone had.

And there is something further that Joel needs to know. He needs to know that choosing the "wrong" response—giving Annie advice when she wants to be listened to—is a *common* error.

The ideal attitude, in fact, is for Annie and Joel to realize that giving reassurance and advice when your partner really wants to be listened to is not only a common error but an inevitable one, and that both of them are repeatedly going to make it.

The more Joel sees that the error he's making is common and unavoidable, the less of a failure he will feel for making it and the more matter-of-factly he will be able to discuss it.

And the error *is* common and unavoidable. As a couples therapist, I make my living, in part, by showing people how they give reassurance and advice when their partners really want them to listen to how they feel. So you'd think I would know a lot about it. And I do. But that doesn't stop me from repeatedly making the same error with my wife Joanne.

If Joanne and I differ from other couples, it's not that we avoid giving each other unwanted advice and reassurance. It's that we feel less upset and more matter-of-fact about it when we do.

I might say, "This conversation isn't going right, so maybe you're not wanting all this advice I'm giving." Or Joanne might say, "I don't know why but I'm not appreciating your advice. Maybe I just want you to understand how I feel."

As long as I see giving unwanted advice and reassurance as an error that anyone can make—and that *everyone does* make—and not as indicating that there is something wrong with me, it is easy for me to switch gears and start listening. So that's the goal: to become good at noticing when you are giving unwanted advice (or when your partner is) and to have a matter-of-fact way of talking about it when you do.

THE BOREDOM TRAP

Trap Number Two: Your partner gets *bored* when you say what's on your mind or talk about your day.

As I have said, telling your partner what's on your mind and hearing what's on your partner's mind is what produces intimacy; it's how you can feel close to someone. But what do you do if hearing what's on your partner's mind *bores* you or if saying what's on *your* mind bores your partner.

Brenda and Jack are a couple in their late forties. Jack is a pharmacist and Brenda works in an ad agency. They have been married for twenty-three years. Brenda comes into the living room where Jack is reading the paper and tells him about her day.

She describes the ad that she designed that morning. She says that she drew it with a fine-line pen to get a special shading effect, that she filled it in with reds and yellows, that she used script to provide elegance, and that she put the written copy *within* the art work rather than beneath it as is usually done.

Jack is bored by the details of ad design. He pretends he isn't bored, however, because he doesn't want to hurt Brenda's feelings or reveal himself as a husband who isn't interested in what his wife says. He worries that he's a self-centered person who cares only about himself.

Noticing that Jack is beginning to get bored, Brenda switches to a topic that she hopes might interest him. She tells him about the surprise lunch-hour potluck that people in her office threw to celebrate her promotion next month to vice president. (Her promotion means leaving the people she had been working with for fifteen years and moving to the tenth floor executive offices.) She describes the dishes that everyone brought to the potluck. Carmen, her office mate, brought a lobster marinade that took two days to prepare. Peter, her secretary, baked a cake. Kris, her buddy down the hall, brought fresh strawberries.

Jack is getting even more bored, but he now feels *justified*. "Why should anyone care," he thinks, "what someone else has for lunch?"

Brenda senses Jack's increasing boredom and worries that it's because she's a boring person. She tries to talk in a more animated way in a renewed effort to engage his interest. She tells him about something funny that happened at the potluck:

BRENDA: You're not going to believe this, but *three* people all made the same dish. You should have seen Edna's face when she walked in with her chicken casserole and saw that both Sandra and Johnnie had brought in the same dish.

Brenda laughs while telling the story, hoping that Jack, too, would see it as funny and laugh.

He doesn't.

"I guess you had to be there," Brenda says.

It's an unfortunate situation. The harder Brenda tries not to be boring, the more awkward and less interesting she becomes and the more bored Jack becomes.

BRENDA (feeling hurt and frustrated): You're not listening to me. You haven't heard anything I've said.

JACK (defending himself, and trying to prove that he *has* been listening): Yes I have. You told me about your new ad. And then you told
me about the party they gave you. And then about the three people
who brought in chicken casseroles.

BRENDA: Yeah, but you weren't *really* listening. You weren't *interested*.

JACK: Well, it's just that we have different interests. I don't know much
about ads. And I don't know most of the people in your office. And
I never was one for office gossip.

BRENDA: It isn't just gossip. You just aren't interested in people.

Between them, Brenda and Jack have come up with three ideas of
why Jack is bored:

1. They just have different interests. (This is what they have just said.)
2. Jack is self-centered. (This is a hidden fear.)
3. Brenda is boring. (This is another hidden fear.)

If Brenda and Jack are to get out of this spot, they will need to develop
different ideas. And that's difficult to do because the ideas that Brenda
and Jack already have—that Brenda is boring, that Jack is selfish, and
that they are incompatible—are *nightmare* ideas. These nightmare ideas
completely fill their minds and make it difficult for them to consider the
possibility, for example, that Jack's boredom is the result of:

1. Brenda's not saying how she feels.
2. Jack's failure to make a sufficiently active response.
3. Brenda's awkward attempts to reengage Jack's interest.
4. And Jack's failure to recognize how much Brenda is getting out
   of talking to him.

Let's go over these one at a time—

**Idea number one: Brenda and Jack need to know that Brenda
is being boring, but that's because she's leaving out the most
important parts. She is leaving out how she *feels* about the
events she is describing.**

Jack says that he isn't interested in ads. He *would* be interested,
however, if Brenda were to tell him:

BRENDA: I was really *pleased* with the ad. It made me feel good all day. It's the best thing I've ever done, and it makes me think that maybe it's possible to be an artist and an ad woman at the same time.

Jack may not care about Brenda's job, but he does care about how *Brenda* cares about it. If Brenda *had* told Jack the major point, which is that she felt really pleased with the ad, he might have wanted to hear more about it; that is, he might then have been interested in the details. Without hearing the major point, however, he would have understandably little interest in the details.

Details can be dull when you don't know why your partner is telling them. In discussing the surprise potluck, Brenda again omitted the most important parts, which were that:

> She was deeply touched. No one in the office had ever been given a party like that before. It was clear that people at work really cared for her and that they were sorry that she was leaving. And she felt momentarily sad, thinking how she was going to miss them.

Jack would *not* be bored hearing that. And once Brenda's feeling about the potluck became clear, the reason for her describing what everyone brought to it would also become clear. She was touched by how everyone tried so hard to make it special. Nancy spent two days preparing a dish. Kris went clear across town to get fresh strawberries. And Peter even tried to bake a cake.

Why did Brenda leave out the most important parts—her *feelings*? She did so because she was afraid that expressing them would be like tooting her own horn. She felt that telling Jack that she did a super job on the ad would be too boastful. So, instead, she told him *how* she composed it. She hoped he might guess from her description of it how good the ad really was. And she was self-conscious about how flattered and honored she felt about the party. She gave details that, by themselves, were not interesting because she was shy about relating feelings that ironically *would* have been interesting.

Brenda's effort not to be too boastful made her boring.

Most of us are boring when we the describe events without stating our feelings about them. We become less boring as we become increasingly aware of our feelings and increasingly skillful at expressing them.

> **Idea number two: Brenda and Jack need to know that Jack's boredom is as much the result of what *he* is doing as it is the result of what she is doing. It's a consequence of Jack's inability to make a sufficiently active response to what Brenda is saying and, in general, his sense of helplessness to do anything other than to sit there and listen.**

Brenda's being boring is only half the story. The other half is that Jack was unable to engage Brenda in what she was saying. He sat there helplessly, listening to Brenda, trying to be the dutiful husband. Brenda had, at times, complained that Jack didn't listen to her. At those times, Jack defended himself; he said he *did* listen. Privately, however, he worried that she might be right. He had the nightmare view of himself as a selfish person who had no feeling for his wife and who didn't care about anyone but himself.

So when Brenda came into the living room to talk to him, Jack felt that anything less than his full and uninterrupted attention would be further evidence that he was unwilling to listen to her. He felt that he didn't have the option to tell her that:

She was describing the ad in too much detail for him.

And that, anyway, he wanted to read the paper and would prefer to talk *after* dinner.

So Jack was bored, not just because Brenda was relating details without telling him how she felt, but also because his commitment to listen patiently and uncomplainingly prevented him from doing what *anyone* would need to do in that situation to remain engaged.

People get bored because they don't have a good way to talk about being bored.

It's *hard* to tell your partner that you're bored by what he or she is saying. You think that you *shouldn't* be bored or, if you are, that you should at least have the decency to keep quiet about it.

Of course, not everyone feels the need to keep quiet. Jack's friend

Mack wouldn't sit still for two seconds if Tammy, his wife, described the dishes people brought to a potluck that she had gone to. He'd say:

"You're boring."
Or, "I don't want to hear that crap."
Or, "I don't see why you keep going to those stupid parties."
Or, "Hey, that reminds me of a funny story I heard today . . ."
Or, "What's for dinner?"

Of course, Mack never has to say such things anymore because Tammy had long ago given up trying to talk to him about her day. She just feels bullied by him.

Mack's way of dealing with feeling bored is to blurt out "You're boring." Jack's way is to keep his mouth shut. Each approach has serious disadvantages. So let's try a third approach. Let's have Jack try to *talk* about his dilemma:

JACK: Please don't take this wrong, but I'm having trouble listening to the details of how you put together that ad.

Jack's being able to say this, of course, would immediately relieve his boredom. He'd be making an active response.

If Jack is to be able to say this, of course, he'll have to be at least partly free of his nightmare view that he's just a "selfish person."

And if Brenda is to be able to tolerate hearing what Jack says, she'll have to be at least partly free of her nightmare view that she's just a "boring person." She might then be able to talk about it:

BRENDA: Well, I *do* take it a little wrong. I worry that I've been boring you.

And having said this, she might then be able to say:

BRENDA: Now that you mention it, though, I *did* get caught up in a lot of details.

Brenda would be using Jack's report that he felt bored as a clue to discovering that she had gotten caught up in details. And she might be able to go still further:

BRENDA: I wanted to show you what a fantastic job I did on that ad. I guess I didn't just come out and say I did a great job because I didn't want to toot my own horn.

Once Jack understands why Brenda was telling him about the ad, he might then become *interested* in the details.

JACK: How was it different from the other ads you've done recently?
BRENDA: I was *trying* to tell you. I came at it in an entirely different way.
I used colors that pop right out at you. I used script to provide elegance. And I put the copy right in the middle of the picture where no one would expect to find it.
JACK: Did you bring home a copy for me to see?

In order not to be bored, people may need a straightforward way of talking about being bored. And in order not to be boring, people may need a straightforward way of talking about being boring.

Idea number three: Brenda and Jack need to know that being boring is a consequence, in part, of trying *not* to be boring.

When Jack began to show signs of boredom, Brenda tried to talk in a wittier, more expansive, and more animated way in an effort to reengage his interest. Although some people are skillful at bringing their partners back from the precipice of boredom, most, like Brenda, just push them over it. At such times:

Their poise crumbles.
Their cleverness disappears.
Their charm abandons them.
They become nervous, awkward, hesitant, and self-conscious.

In other words, Brenda was being boring because she was trying not to be boring. Let's imagine what it would look like if, instead, Brenda were to talk to Jack about being boring. Let's say she goes to Jack later in the evening and says:

BRENDA: You know when we were talking earlier tonight, I was afraid I was boring you. So I did what I usually do—I tried *even harder* to be interesting. I keep forgetting that I become awkward and nervous and *even less* interesting when I do that.

Jack is unlikely to be bored hearing this. In fact, he is likely to feel *relieved*. Since Brenda would be saying that she was *being* boring, he wouldn't have to attribute his boredom to his own self-centeredness.

So let's collect all these ideas about why Brenda was boring. She was boring:

Because she left out the important feelings that might have made the details interesting.

Because she was worried about being too boastful.

Because she was worried about being too boring; that is, her efforts not to be boring made her more boring.

And, most important, because she was unable to recognize and to talk to Jack about any of this.

Mr. Skeptic: Not so fast. All that sounds nice, but what do you think you've really proved? Okay sure, maybe you've explained why *Brenda* is boring. But what about people who are *always* boring? What about people who are, well, *just boring*?

Wile: Those are people who *always* leave out the important feelings, who *always* worry about being too boastful, who *always* worry about being too boring, or who *always* are unable to recognize and talk to their partners about any of this.

> **Idea number four: Brenda and Jack need to know that Jack becomes bored, in part, because he feels left out and unimportant. He doesn't realize how crucial a role he has. He doesn't recognize what it means to Brenda to be able to tell him about her day.**

Jack felt that he didn't have a role. He thought that it didn't even matter to Brenda that she was talking to him. He thought that she was chattering away about the ad and about the party because she had nothing better to do; she could have been talking to anybody. He felt ignored and unimportant. And all this made him feel bored. He didn't realize that:

Brenda had been looking forward all day to talking to him. And it had to be him; no one else would really do.

Telling him about her success with the ad would be the capping event in her celebration of it.

Much of her pleasure in the party that people at her work threw for her was the prospect of being able to tell him about it.

Telling him about her sadness at leaving the people she had been working with for fifteen years (and getting him to understand how she felt about it) was her way of trying to deal with this sadness.

Jack didn't realize any of these things, partly because Brenda didn't make it clear that she was feeling them. If he *had* realized it, or if Brenda had told him, he wouldn't have felt so left out and bored.

So these are some of the major booby traps that we can stumble into when we try to talk to our partners:

> Instead of doing what our partners want us to do, which is to listen to them and to appreciate how they feel, we offer solutions, which makes them feel that we *don't* appreciate how they feel.
>
> We become boring because we leave out the most important parts— our feelings—and as a result of our efforts not to be boring.
>
> We become bored because we don't know how to talk about being bored and because we don't realize how much our partners are getting out of talking to us.

When you think about how easy it is to fall into these booby traps, and how discouraged we get when we do, it's amazing that any of us still talk to our partners at all.

7

Using Communication Errors as Clues

*T*alking is dangerous. In an effort to make it less so, communication skills trainers have developed rules for good communication. Here are some of them:

1. Make "I statements" rather than "you statements" (e.g., say "I felt hurt and angry when you came home late last night" rather than "You're completely irresponsible; you don't think about anybody but yourself").
2. Don't say "always" or "never" (e.g., "You *never* lift a finger around here").
3. Don't interrupt your partner.
4. Paraphrase what your partner says so he or she will know that you have heard (e.g., "I hear you say that you feel. . . . Do I have it right?")
5. Don't "mindread"; that is, don't speculate about what your partner is feeling, thinking, or trying to do (e.g. "You're trying to make me feel guilty").
6. Stick to one topic.
7. Don't bring up resentments from the distant past.
8. Don't get sidetracked in an argument over irrelevant issues (e.g. "It happened in September." "No, it was October." "No, I distinctly remember it was September").
9. Don't label or name-call.
10. Don't store up complaints (e.g., "And another thing. . . . And also . . . And why did you have to. . . .?").

I shall discuss these rules and describe my modified versions of them.

In the following short conversation, Juanita and Jose violate all ten rules:

JUANITA (making a "you statement" and using the word "never"): You never talk to me anymore. The only time we. . . .

JOSE (interrupting and failing to paraphrase): What do you mean I never talk to you? Remember last weekend at the park? We talked the whole afternoon and. . . .

JUANITA ("mindreading"): You call that talking? You spent the afternoon complaining about my mother coming over. You were trying to punish me and make me feel guilty.

JOSE: I wasn't trying to make you feel guilty. I just don't think we have to invite your mother over so much.

JUANITA (changing the subject): Yeah, what about all the evenings we've spent with your *brother*.

JOSE (bringing up an old resentment): I didn't hear you complaining ten years ago when *your* sister came to dinner and left *three months* later.

JUANITA: She'd had a bad time. Her husband just left her. Besides, she only stayed *two* months.

JOSE (sidetracked over an irrelevant issue): It was *three* months.

JUANITA: It was *two*.

JOSE: It was *three*.

JUANITA (name-calling): It was *two* months. I remember for sure. And it was *ten years* ago. You've got to be *crazy* and *paranoid* to hold a grudge that long.

JOSE (dumping out stored-up complaints): I'll tell you who's crazy. It's someone who tells me to be ready to leave in time for a party and then keeps me waiting half an hour. It's someone who says she wants sex and then, when I'm raring to go, changes her mind. And it's someone who takes care of every stray dog off the street, but pays no attention to her husband. And it's. . . .

Let's look at Juanita and Jose's violations of these communication rules one at a time.

Communication rule 1: *Make "I statements," not "you statements."*

In starting the conversation by saying "You never talk to me anymore," Juanita thought she was just stating a fact. And, in a way, she was.

Jose *hadn't* been talking to her as much as he used to. But she was also accusing him. There is no way that anyone could hear the statement "You never talk to me anymore" without immediately feeling accused of doing something wrong. Juanita was accusing Jose without knowing it.

A number of years ago, a psychologist, Thomas Gordon, discovered a clever way of helping people recognize when they are accusing people without knowing it. He pointed out that statements that begin with a "you" or a "you are" tend to be accusations, and that a way to avoid making such accusations is to say, instead, "I" or "I feel."

There are exceptions, of course. Some statements that begin with a "you are" are *not* accusations; for example, "*You are* wonderful." And some statements that begin with an "I feel" *are* accusations; for example, "*I feel* you are a jerk." In general, however, Gordon's principle is useful.

> Gordon's observation has been turned into the following rule: make "I statements," not "you statements." Don't say "You aren't listening." Say "I feel frustrated because I feel I'm not getting my point across."

"You statements" are easy to argue with. The person is making a claim about what the other person is doing or feeling ("You aren't listening") that can easily be challenged. ("You're wrong," the other person can say. "I *am* listening"). "I statements" are difficult to argue with. The person is simply saying what he or she feels. ("I feel frustrated"). And it's difficult to argue with that.

If Juanita were to have made an "I statement," she wouldn't have said "*You* never talk to me anymore." She would have said something like:

JUANITA: I feel hurt and angry because I take your talking less to me these days as meaning that you're not as interested in me as you used to be.

There is little doubt that Juanita and Jose would have been better off if she had said this. Since her emphasis is more on what she is feeling rather than on what Jose is doing wrong, Jose is less likely to become defensive.

Juanita, however, might not *feel* like making an "I statement"; that is, she might not *feel* like saying "I feel hurt and angry." She might only feel like saying "You never talk to me anymore." In fact, the words "I feel hurt and angry" *might not even occur to her.*

As a couples therapist, I have done a lot of communication skills training, so I know the communication rules pretty well. In the heat of the battle with *my* wife, however, the "I statement" rule can go out the window. I don't even think about it.

Everyone makes "you statements," even communication skills trainers. Sometimes you just feel like accusing. Sometimes nothing else but a good "you statement" will do. So I've got my own revised version of the "I statement–you statement" rule. In my version, it's not what you do that is important. It's what you *know*.

The major problem with Juanita's saying "You never talk to me anymore" is that she *doesn't know* that she's being accusing. She thinks she is just expressing her feelings. And since she doesn't know she's being accusing, she has no choice but to take Jose's defensive and accusing response as indicating, "You can't talk to Jose. He gets upset for no reason at all."

The biggest problem with "you statements," in other words, is not that you become accusing. And it's not that your partner becomes defensive. It's that you end up feeling that there is no way to talk to your partner and that your partner ends up feeling that there is no way to talk to you.

So here is my revised "I statement-you statement" rule:

1. Make "you statements" if you feel like doing so, but *know* that you are doing so, so that you won't be surprised by the effect; namely, your partner getting defensive or angry.
2. Know *how* to make "I statements," so that you will be able to do so if you want to.

And there is a third part to this rule:

3. Recognize "you statements" as clues to hidden "I statements."

"You statements" (accusations) are not all bad. In fact, they can be useful. They are rough first approximations to "I statements." The "you statement," "*You are* completely selfish and irresponsible," can be thought of as a rough first approximation to the "I statement," "*I feel* taken for granted when you come home late as you did tonight."

"You statements" may not reveal very clearly what's askew, but they indicate that *something* is.

"You statements" indicate that there is something that needs to be talked about. "I statements" provide the means to do so.

The hope is to obtain full benefit from your "you statements" without suffering too much from their costs; that is:

To be able to make "you statements" without you and your partner getting too terribly upset about it.

To be able to use these "you statements" as stepping stones to "I statements" in which you really are able to talk about the matter.

Here is the conversation that Juanita and Jose's argument could have been a stepping stone to:

JUANITA: I said some pretty strong things earlier tonight. I didn't realize it at the time, but I was feeling really hurt and angry.

JOSE: It was clear enough that you were angry, but I couldn't have guessed that you felt *hurt*.

JUANITA: Well, "hurt" might not even be the right word. Maybe, it's worry. I'm worried because I haven't been feeling as close to you as I used to.

JOSE: Well, I've been worried about that, too. We used to talk a lot more. I miss the way you used to confide in me. And, for some reason, these days when I have things to say I keep them to myself.

As this short conversation shows, the use of "I statements" changes everything. Jose *himself* has brought up the very issue that Juanita had before so unsuccessfully tried to raise: he *admits* that he doesn't talk to her as much as he used to. And Juanita and Jose discover that they are missing the *same* thing: a sense of closeness. And since they are talking about what is on their minds—even if it's about how they don't feel close—they are to that extent reestablishing a sense of closeness.

Communication rule 2: *Don't say "always" or "never."*

Juanita's opening statement—"You never talk to me anymore"— has another element that communication skills trainers would question: her use of the word "never."

The problem with the word "never" is that it's an exaggeration. Juanita doesn't really mean that Jose *never* talks to her anymore. She simply means that he doesn't talk to her as much as he *used to* and as she would like him to. And the problem with such an exaggeration is that it gets the other person angry.

Another problem with the word "never" is that it makes Juanita's charge easier to try to refute. All Jose has to do is to point to an exception. And that is what he does. He says, "What do you mean I never talk to you? Remember last weekend at the park? We talked the whole afternoon."

> The terms "never" and "always" are too powerful. They provoke the other person unnecessarily. And they are too weak. They are too *easy* to refute.

Because of these hazards, communication skills trainers have established the rule: Don't say "always" and "never." But there is a problem with this rule, as there is with all communication rules. *Communication errors are clues to use rather than just mistakes to correct.*

> Rather than telling people *not* to violate communication rules, I would want them to *expect* to violate these rules and then to use their violations as clues.

When people say "always" or "never," they do so for a reason. It's a means of emphasis and an expression of frustration. Juanita's saying "never" is:

> An expression of how frustrated she feels about the matter.
> A consequence of having previously held back her complaint. Now that it is finally coming out, it is doing so in this exaggerated form.
> A way of being emphatic and making sure to get Jose's attention on the matter.

Juanita wouldn't have to say "never" if she had a more direct way of indicating all this. But since she *doesn't*, it's a good thing that she can at least say "never."

So when Juanita says "never," it isn't just a communication error. It's a stand-in for, and thus a clue to, what she's feeling. Instead of telling Juanita, "Don't say 'never,' " I would want to help her discover and express the feelings for which the word "never" is a stand-in. I would want to help her say that she feels really frustrated about the matter and that she is worried about not getting through to Jose about it.

So here is my revision of the "always-never" rule:

1. *Know* that "always" and "never" are likely to slip out of your mouth even if you work conscientiously to suppress them.
2. *Know* that—whenever you find yourself saying "always" or "never" —you've got a frustrated person on your hands and that the person is you.
3. *Know* that you are likely to end up feeling even *more* frustrated because your partner will almost inevitably respond to your "always" or "never" by pointing to an exception.
4. *Know* that the words "always" and "never" are stand-ins for important feelings and, as such, can be used as clues to discover what these feelings are.

Communication rule number 3: *Don't interrupt your partner.*

Juanita has barely gotten into what she wanted to say. "You never talk to me anymore," she says. "The only time we. . . ." And we'll never know how that sentence is going to end because Jose immediately interrupts: "What do you mean I never talk to you? Remember last weekend at the park? We talked the whole afternoon and. . . ." And we'll never know how Jose's sentence is going to end because Juanita immediately interrupts back: "You call that talking? You spent the afternoon complaining about my inviting my mother over."

Everyone knows about the disadvantages of interrupting:

It deprives your partner of the chance to have his or her say.
It makes your partner angry.
It makes your partner feel like not listening to *you*.
Since you aren't letting your partner finish, you may be jumping to false conclusions about what he or she was going to say.

So it's understandable that communication skills trainers would make the rule: Don't interrupt your partner. Few people, however, know about the *dis*advantages of not interrupting. The more you force yourself to sit there quietly while your partner makes what seem to you to be unfair charges:

The less you'll be able to listen to what he or she says.
The angrier you may be when you finally get your turn. By that time, you may be unable to do anything else but throw a tantrum.

The more dispirited you may be when you finally get your turn. By that time, you may not feel like saying anything at all.

The more you interrupt your partner, the more you may squelch him or her. The problem is that the *less* you interrupt your partner, the more you may squelch *yourself.*

So here is my revision of the "Don't interrupt your partner" rule:

1. Interrupt your partner if that's what you want to do, but know the danger; that is, that your partner may become an angry or dispirited person who can't listen.
2. Refrain from interrupting your partner if that's what you want to do, but know the danger: that is, that *you* may become an angry or dispirited person who can't listen.

And here is the third part to this rule:

3. Become an expert in the art of interrupting without interrupting; that is, in finding ways of expressing your objections that don't completely cut off your partner.

Here are some examples of interrupting without interrupting:

"I don't want to interrupt, but I want you to know that I *feel* like interrupting."

"I'll want my chance because you're saying a lot of unfair things. But go on."

"You're probably making a good point, but I'm too angry at how you're saying it to want to listen."

"I know that I shouldn't interrupt, and I won't, but I want you to know that I'm having a hard time listening to these inaccurate and unfair charges that I feel you're making and I can hardly wait to get my chance to have *my* say."

In each case, the speaker is making *enough* of an objection—*enough* of a statement about how he or she feels—so that he or she might now be able to hear the end of the partner's statement. At the same time, the objection is *sufficiently* short and *sufficiently* noninflammatory so that the person who had been talking may be able to continue without feeling cut off.

Communication rule number 4: *Paraphrase what your partner just said.*

In Jose's response, "What do you mean. . . . Remember last weekend. . . . We talked the whole afternoon," he is violating another communication rule. He is *reacting* to what Juanita just said rather than *paraphrasing* it.

When your partner is trying to tell you how he or she feels, communication skills trainers say, paraphrase what he or she says (put it in your own words) and then check to see whether you've got it right. For example, say: "I hear you saying that you feel. . . . Do I have it right?" Or, "Let's see if I understand what you're saying. You're saying. . . . Am I right?"

Mr. Skeptic: I can't understand how you psychologists think anyone can say such a thing with a straight face? It's so stiff and phony. You'd never catch me talking that way.

Wile: Well sure, it *can* sound stiff and phony sometimes. And that's too bad because communication skills trainers are onto something pretty important here. One of the big problems in communicating—the reason fights get started and become unresolvable—is that neither partner listens to, thinks about, or acknowledges what the other says. Instead of thinking about what Juanita says, Jose *argues* with her. He said, "What do you mean I never talk to you? Remember last week. . . ."

And here's where the paraphrasing rule can be useful. Paraphrasing —that is, saying, "I hear you saying . . . Is that right?"—would *force* Jose to pay attention to what Juanita just said. He can't immediately try to answer or refute it. He can't immediately go on to give his view. He has to think about what Juanita said. His whole attention is directed to trying to understand what Juanita said and to make clear to *her* that he understands it.

And all this seems like a good thing, even though, as you say, Mr. Skeptic, paraphrasing can seem contrived sometimes.

And there's a bigger problem. People feel like paraphrasing *least* just when they may need to do it most. Here are Juanita and Jose in the office of a communication skills trainer, who is trying to teach them to paraphrase.

TRAINER: Okay, let's start again, but this time, Jose, remember to paraphrase. Go ahead, Juanita.

JUANITA: Well, as I said, I'm worried that we will spend another weekend without really talking to one another. You'll invite your buddies over and spend the whole time watching football and I'll feel deserted and resentful.

JOSE: I can understand how you feel, but. . . .

TRAINER: No, Jose, telling Juanita you understand isn't the same as paraphrasing what she says. How does she *know* you understand? The only way she can tell for sure is if you put it in *your own* words.

JOSE: Okay. (Turns back to Juanita) I hear you saying that you're afraid that we won't talk and that I'll leave you out and get all involved with football and my friends, but. . . .

TRAINER: Check it out with her.

JOSE: Is that right?

JUANITA. Yes.

TRAINER: Good.

Jose's heart is clearly not in paraphrasing. He is showing only token compliance with the task. The reason, we can imagine, is that he is eager to get to the "but"; that is, to the place where he can begin stating his defense. And he wants to state his defense, we can also guess, because he feels unfairly accused. In other words, Jose feels too misunderstood by Juanita to want to try to understand her.

> So here is what often underlies the communication error of not paraphrasing: People don't feel like paraphrasing—they don't feel like acknowledging their partners' feelings—when they feel that their partners aren't acknowledging their feelings.

The paraphrasing rule is based on an important insight; namely, that people often stop listening to one another *without realizing it.* They don't fully see that they have temporarily slipped into an adversarial mode. The paraphrase rule is an effort to get partners to listen to one another when they hadn't realized that they weren't.

I suggest using the insight but eliminating the rule. Or, to put it another way, I suggest profiting from the rule and, at the same time, profiting from *violations* of the rule.

The following is an example of what Jose might say to himself if he were to use his violations of the paraphrasing rule as a clue:

JOSE: Since I've stopped paraphrasing what Juanita is saying, it must mean that I don't feel like listening to her. And if I don't feel like listening to her, it must be because I'm feeling unlistened to myself.

So here is my revised paraphrasing rule:

1. Appreciate how important listening to your partner is, how quickly problems arise when you don't, and how easy it is to think you are listening when you're not.
2. Know *how* to listen to your partner's feelings (how to paraphrase what he or she says) so that you will be *able* to do so when you want to.
3. Use your "violations" of the paraphrase (listening-to-your-partner) rule as a *clue* to the fact that at the moment you may be feeling unlistened to yourself.

If you appreciate all this, you will then see that your arguments with your partner are often not even about the *issues* that you and your partner *think* they are about. They are results of the fact that both you and your partner are feeling unlistened to.

Communication rule number 5: *Don't "mindread."*

Let's return to Juanita and Jose's original argument. Jose responds to Juanita's charge by saying, "What do you mean I never talk to you? Remember last weekend at the park? We talked the whole afternoon."

Juanita replies, "You call that talking? You spent the afternoon complaining about my inviting my mother over. You were trying to punish me and make me feel guilty."

In so saying, Juanita commits another communication rule error. She "mindreads."

"Mindreading" is telling people what you think they are thinking, feeling, or trying to do rather than *asking* them or waiting until they tell *you*.

"Mindreading" can be clearly provocative. Statements such as:

"You were trying to punish me."
"You were trying to make me feel guilty."
"You don't like any of my friends."

"You *feel* threatened by my successes."
"You're jealous of me."
"Unconsciously you hate me."
"You're afraid of commitment."

can bring reasonable conversation to a halt. People don't like others making such guesses about their feelings and intentions. And they particularly don't like it if these guesses are wrong, which they often are.

The "mindreading" statement, "Why are you so angry at me?" can lead into the following familiar argument:

Wife (mindreading): Why are you so angry at me?
Husband (raising his voice): I'm not angry.
Wife (raising hers): Listen to your voice. You sound pretty angry to me.
Husband: Well, I'm angry now. But I wasn't angry before. What got me angry was your *saying* I was angry.

Such interchanges are frustrating to *both* partners. It's understandable, therefore, that communication skills trainers would offer the rule: don't "mindread."

There is a problem with this rule, however. Although "mindreading" may be seen as *jumping* to conclusions (usually thought of as a bad thing), it may also be seen as simply *drawing* conclusions. In this latter meaning of the term, even psychotherapists "mindread." Some psychotherapists tell their clients, for example: "You're angry at your father," "You're depressed," or "You're jealous of your siblings."

And even when "mindreading" *is* jumping to conclusions—that is, when it *is* a clear communication error—it isn't *just* an error; it's a clue.

When a person says, "You don't like any of my friends," what he or she might really mean is "I'm *worried* that you don't like any of my friends. And it's important to me that you *do* like them."

And that's what a certain type of "mindreading" error often is. It's an expression of the person's *own* feeling—often a feeling of worry or fear—put in the form of an assertion about the *other* person's feeling. It's a worry or fear stated as a fact. Thus:

"You're jealous of me" might mean "I'm *worried* that you might be jealous of me."

>"Unconsciously you hate me" might mean "I'm *afraid* that you might
> hate me. You've been quiet lately and I'm worried that it's an
> angry silence. Is it?"
>
>"You're threatened by my successes" might mean "I'm *worried* that
> you are threatened by my successes and the possibility that you
> are makes me *angry*."

And the wife's statement, "Why are you so angry at me?" might mean
something like:

>"I'm *worried* that you are angry at me. Pressures at work have made
> it so that I've hardly been at home lately and I'm *worried* that
> you might be upset about it. Are you?"

This type of "mindreading" is an incomplete statement. Rather than tell
this wife "don't mindread," I would want to help her to complete the
statement.

So here is my revised mindreading rule:

1. Know the dangers of mindreading, so that when you do it, you
   won't be surprised by the effect; namely, your partner getting
   angry or defensive.
2. Realize that mindreading may be an incomplete statement and
   use it to discover the complete statement.
3. Recognize that certain types of "mindreading" are expressions of
   your fears put in the form of assertions about someone else's
   feelings or motives.

Communication rule 6: *Stick to one topic.*

Juanita and Jose were already having trouble discussing Juanita's
mother. Shifting the subject to Jose's brother and then to Juanita's sister
made it now *three* unmanageable issues to deal with rather than just the
one. It's understandable, therefore, that communication skills trainers would
offer the rule "Stick to one topic."

But let's look at why people *don't* stick to one topic. They don't
because they feel that the topic being discussed places them at a disadvantage.

Juanita feels at a disadvantage in discussing her mother. She thinks that Jose might be right that her mother visits too often. So she shifts the topic to Jose's brother. Jose can hardly complain about her mother's visits, she figures, if he takes into account how often his *brother* visits.

Jose feels at a disadvantage in discussing his brother's visits. So he shifts to a topic—Juanita's sister—that he feels might enable him to regain the advantage.

Juanita and Jose aren't changing the subject simply because they have bad communication habits. They are doing so because they are jockeying for position.

So here is my revised "stick-to-one-subject" rule:

1. *Know* that shifting topics will complicate the situation, frustrate your partner, and make your partner even less likely to listen to you.
2. Know *why* you are doing it; that is, (a) to put yourself in a better position in your argument with your partner, (b) to move away from a point your partner made that you fear may be valid, and (c) to amass further evidence in your effort (futile though it may be) to convince your partner that you are right.
3. *Know* that your efforts to convince your partner are futile. You're in an argument, and in an argument, the point is for each of you to *refute* what the other says.

Communication rule 7: *Don't dig up old grievances.*

In complaining about the time ten years ago when Juanita's sister came for dinner and stayed for several months, Jose is digging up an old grievance.

"The grudges that partners have *now* are difficult enough to deal with," communication skills trainers say. "Why complicate matters by bringing up sensitive and unresolved issues from the past?"

Communication skills trainers may fail to appreciate, however, that grievances from the past often *are* about the present. People frequently bring up past events when they have difficulty justifying complaints they have in the present.

Jose feels that Juanita pays more attention to other people's wishes than she does to his. It's a subtle feeling, however, and he has difficulty pointing to anything specific. In fact, Jose himself can often feel that his complaint is invalid. He has to go back *ten years*—to Juanita's choosing her sister's needs over his—to find a clear example of what he is experiencing in more subtle form now.

Jose's bringing up the past is unfortunate. It makes Juanita even less interested in listening to what he has to say. But he may be lucky to have at least *this* means of representing the feelings that he is having now.

So here is my modified version of the "Don't dig up grievances from the past" rule:

1. *Know* that your bringing up grievances from the past is likely to offend your partner and make him or her even *less* likely to listen to you.
2. *Realize* that you may be going to the past because your partner just criticized you and that you are in great need of evidence— even if it requires bringing up something from long ago—to defend yourself.
3. *Realize* that what you may be going to the past to find is a dramatized version or clearer form of an important concern that you have now.

Jose's complaint *has* a grain of truth. Juanita *isn't* attending to many of his most important needs. And he isn't attending to many of hers.

Communication rule 8: *Don't get sidetracked*

Juanita and Jose's argument about her sister's visit contains another communication skills error. It doesn't *matter* whether this sister stayed two months, as Juanita claims, or three months, as Jose claims. The main point—that Juanita's sister overstayed her welcome—holds in either case. Juanita and Jose are getting hot and bothered over nothing.

So, it's understandable that communication skills trainers would offer the rule: "Don't get bogged down arguing about irrelevant issues."

Juanita and Jose's argument looks so ridiculous, in fact—we can so easily think that they are acting as children and should just stop—that we may forget to consider *why* they are having it. And they are having it because, as things exist between them at the moment, any and every issue is:

> A place to make a stand against what each sees as the other's unreasonable, disagreeable, or provocative behavior.
>
> An opportunity to react against what each sees as the other's unyielding, know-it-all, or self-righteous attitude.
>
> A chance to give expression to the general displeasure that each feels toward the other.

Juanita and Jose feel so aggravated that neither has any wish to go along with *anything* the other says. In such a situation, there is no such thing as an "irrelevant" issue.

So here is my revised "Don't get sidetracked" rule:

> Whenever you and your partner get bogged down discussing "irrelevant" issues, *realize* that the argument is no longer about issues (if it ever was), but is about your general frustration with one another.

And realize that whatever sense of good will (or willingness to give the benefit of the doubt) may have existed between you and your partner before has, for the moment at least, disappeared.

Communication rule 9: *Don't label or name-call.*

Juanita responded to Jose's complaint about her sister's long visit by saying: "It was ten years ago. You've got to be crazy and paranoid to hold a grudge that long."

Juanita's calling Jose "crazy" and "paranoid" destroyed whatever possibility might still have existed for useful conversation. It is understandable, therefore, that communication skills trainers would offer the rule: "Don't name-call."

Instead of telling people not to name-call, however, I would want to tell them:

> 1. *Know* that, when you name-call, you are momentarily feeling *so* frustrated, hurt, stung, put upon, or unlistened to yourself *that you are willing to resort to almost anything*, even to statements

that a moment's reflection would tell you will do the *opposite* of what you want. They will just get your partner *angrier* and *even less* likely to listen to you.

2. And *know* that, at such times, you may not *have* a moment to reflect and that, at such times, you may not *care* whether your partner becomes angrier and less likely to listen to you.

3. *Use* the fact that you are name-calling as a clue that the intensity of your feelings has temporarily exceeded your ability to sort out, think through, and talk about these feelings.

Our ability to sort out and think through our feelings is often imperfect even in calm moments. The result at such times is a kind of *quiet* name-calling. We don't yell, and we don't seem angry, but what we say about our partners is essentially name-calling. We use words like "egotistical," "hostile," "irresponsible," "babyish," "dependent," and "controlling."

Communication rule 10: *Don't dump out stored-up complaints.*

Jose is so angry at Juanita's calling him "crazy" and "paranoid" that he blurts out:

JOSE: I'll tell you who's crazy. It's someone who tells me to be ready to leave in time for a party and then keeps me waiting half an hour [this happened *twelve* days ago]. It's someone who says she wants sex and then, when I'm raring to go, changes her mind [this happened *seven* days ago]. And it's someone who can worry about a stray dog [this happened *three* days ago], but pays no attention to her husband.

Jose had been holding these things back because he didn't want to hurt Juanita's feelings or start a fight. He blurts them out now because, at the moment, he doesn't *care* if he hurts her feelings or starts a fight. In fact, his main concern is that what he says won't be powerful enough to make an impression on Juanita. This is the opposite of his usual concern, which is that what he says will be *too* powerful, will make too much of an impression on Juanita, and will blow her away.

We *all* store up complaints. We do it all the time. And we do it often without knowing it.

We are told to be polite, respectful, tactful, and considerate. In fact, "be polite, respectful, tactful, and considerate" is an *eleventh* rule that communication skills trainers often tell us. But being polite, respectful, and considerate requires *suppressing* complaints. And suppressing complaints means *storing* them up. And storing them up leads to *dumping* them out.

So here's my suggestion. Instead of telling Jose that he shouldn't dump out stored-up complaints, I recommend that he and Juanita use his "dumped out" complaints as clues.

> In complaining about Juanita's keeping him waiting, changing her mind about sex, and paying more attention to a stray dog than to him, Jose is saying, in essence, that he feels *neglected*.

Ironically, Juanita has been trying to tell Jose that *she* feels neglected. That's what her complaint, "You never talk to me anymore," is all about. Accordingly, instead of just telling Jose that he shouldn't dump out stored-up complaints, I would want Juanita and Jose to use what he does "dump out" to discover that they both feel neglected.

So here is my revision of the "dumping out" rule:

1. *Expect* that you and your partner will dump out stored-up complaints. The suppression of complaints is too automatic a process to be able to eliminate entirely.
2. *Appreciate* that such "dumping out" serves a necessary function. If these things are not "dumped out," they might never get out. And it's important that they get out—that is, that they be brought to the surface—so that they can be talked about.
3. *Use* what you and your partner dump out as clues to these important hidden feelings.

TWO NEW RULES

In addition to the common communication rules just described, I propose two others: the recovery rule and the prefacing rule.

Mr. Skeptic: Two *more* rules. I'm beginning to get tired of them.
Wile: Not *too* tired, I hope, because *these* two are really important.

The recovery rule.

As I have said, obeying the ten classic communication rules is impossible. Everyone repeatedly:

Makes "you statements."
Says "always" and "never."
Interrupts.
Fails to paraphrase.
"Mindreads."
Changes topics in the middle of an argument.
Brings up resentments from the distant past.
Gets sidetracked.
Name-calls.
And stores up complaints.

So I recommend that you *expect* to make such "errors" and that you devote yourself to *recovering* from them. By "recovering," I mean becoming familiar enough with how you and your partner make these "errors" and with the effect that these "errors" have, so that later, when the dust has settled, you and your partner will be able to sit down together and figure out what happened.

Here is an idealized version of how Juanita and Jose might sit down and try to figure out what happened:

JUANITA: I guess my saying "You never talk to me anymore" wasn't a great way to start a discussion. And we never *did* get to what I wanted to talk about. (Juanita recognizes that the discussion got off on the wrong foot because she criticized Jose; that is, she made a "you statement.")

JOSE: I didn't know there was something you wanted to talk about. I just thought you wanted to criticize me. So I started defending myself and attacking back. (Jose acknowledges that he got defensive and stopped listening to her.)

JUANITA: You did a good job. I got really upset when you started talking about my mother. That's why I brought up your brother. (Juanita recognizes that she changed topics.)

JOSE: And then we got into that ridiculous argument over whether your sister stayed *two months or three.* (Jose acknowledges that they got sidetracked.)

JUANITA: And I got so frustrated that I started calling you names, which I'm upset about doing. (Juanita admits name-calling.)

JOSE: Well, I didn't like your calling me "crazy" and "paranoid," but if I keep bringing up stuff from ten years ago, like about your sister staying with us that time, I guess I've got to expect that you're not going to be too happy about it. (Jose recognizes that he dug up an old grievance.)

JUANITA: Of course, you got in a few good licks yourself. All that stuff about my being late, about sex, and about that dog.

JOSE: Yeah, I suppose it was a lot to hit you with all at once. (Jose acknowledges having dumped out stored-up complaints.)

JUANITA: I couldn't tell whether you were just angry at me or whether you really meant all those things. (Juanita takes this opportunity to find this out.)

JOSE: Well, I did sort of mean them. I guess what they all point to is the fact that I've been feeling neglected lately. (Jose uses his dumped-out complaints as a clue.)

JUANITA: Well, that really shocks me because *I've* been feeling neglected. That's what I wanted to tell you about in the first place. That's what my saying "you never talk to me" was all about.

In this interchange, which admittedly is idealized, Juanita and Jose would thus be:

Recovering from their communication errors by having a follow-up conversation;

Using their communication errors as clues to uncovering important hidden issues in the relationship;

Beginning to have the conversation that Juanita had originally wanted them to have and, as it turns out, Jose wanted them to have also.

The prefacing rule.

"Recovering" is what partners can do *after* a fight. "Prefacing" is what can be done *before* a fight. Juanita had a vague sense that her original statement—"You never talk to me anymore"—wasn't going to go over well. But she gritted her teeth and said it anyway. Things might have gone differently if, before saying it, Juanita were to have told Jose how she *felt* about saying it.

"I'm worried that this may make you mad or hurt your feelings, but it's so important that I want to try to tell you anyway."

Or, "I'm angry about this, and I've been sitting on my anger, so it's probably not going to come out in a very good way, but. . . ."

Or, "I feel awkward in making this complaint because I don't think it's justified, but. . . ."

The typical effect of such prefacing remarks is to make what the person then goes on to say easier to hear. The listener is less likely to be angered by his or her partner's complaint if he or she knows that:

The partner is having difficulty making the complaint.

The partner, *himself* or *herself*, is worried that the complaint might be provocative.

The partner feels at least partly unjustified in having the complaint.

The complaint is coming out in an exaggerated way because the partner has been holding it back.

The complaint is coming out in an awkward and provocative way because the partner feels uncomfortable about having it.

Shifting from the content to the overview level.

"Recovering" and "prefacing" have something in common. And to show what this is, I'm going to talk about Johnny Carson.

There are certain comedians and comediennes—Johnny Carson is the best recent example—whose humor appears to be based not only on good jokes but also on recovering from bad ones. The masterful way in which Carson deals with a difficult situation—telling a joke to a room full of people and having it fall flat—is often more entertaining than if the joke had been good. It is possible to suggest, in fact, that Carson would lose much of his effectiveness if all his jokes were good.

Carson is having two relationships with the audience. The first is on the content level. He tells a joke and waits for laughter. The second is on the overview level. He interacts with the audience *about* his joke—noting how and why they might have liked it, jokingly threatening them if they don't laugh, making humorous excuses for particularly poor jokes, and so on. It is the overview level that, at least for Johnny Carson, is the critical one.

Applying the example of Johnny Carson to couple relationships, I suggest that the overview level—having a relationship about the relationship and making partners observers of their own interactions—may be a major part of the solution to partner difficulties.

And that's what prefacing and recovering are: ways of shifting from the content to the overview level.

> In prefacing, the person shifts to the overview level *before* the conversation. Juanita describes her feelings, fears, hopes, or reservations about what she is *about* to say.
> In recovering, the partners shift to the overview level *after* the discussion. They step back from the argument and try to figure out what happened.

Recovering is prefacing that occurs at the end. Prefacing is recovering that occurs at the beginning.

It is possible, although difficult, to shift to the overview level right in the middle of an argument. In the course of their argument, Juanita or Jose could have said, for example:

> "You're probably making a good point, but I'm too angry at how you're saying it to listen."
> Or, "I'd like to find a way out of this argument, but I can't seem to stop wanting to make just one last point."
> Or, "I'm saying a lot of things that I don't really mean because I'm so angry at what *you're* saying."

In each case, the speaker is shifting from arguing to talking *about* the argument. If there is any chance to end the argument while still in it, this is how to do it.

So here are my recommendations:

1. Make good use of the communication rules; they can point out ways that you are provoking your partner without knowing it.
2. Make good use of your communication *errors*; they can reveal unrecognized elements in your feelings.
3. Develop skill in *recovering* from your communication errors; that is, become adept in shifting to the overview level and having a conversation *about* these errors (and about your fights).

III

SOMETHING IS WRONG WITH THE WAY WE THINK

*A*t the heart of this book is a distinction between accusing ways of thinking that I see as causing or compounding our problems, and *non*-accusing ways of thinking that I see as potentially solving our problems.

> The accusing ways of thinking are described in Chapters 8 and 9 and the *non*accusing ways of thinking in Chapter 10. All the examples of effective talking discussed in this book are based on using *non*accusing forms of thinking.
>
> In Chapters 11 and 12, I discuss certain effects that the accusing ways of thinking have on the way we view ourselves and relate to one another.

8

Feelings We Think We Shouldn't Have

So far in this book, I've discussed how to use our relationships to solve problems, to fill gaps in our personalities, to learn to love ourselves, to become skillfully dependent, and to become *in*dependent. But the question remains:

> Why don't we do these things already? Why do we need a book to tell us how?

And my answer has been: because they all require skillful talking, and *something is wrong with the way we talk*. Many couples have their bitterest fights when they sit down to talk about their relationships.

> **Mr. Skeptic:** Oh, so *that's* what it is—a communication problem. Is that what you're trying to tell us—that *everything* would be solved if only we became skillful communicators?

> **Wile:** Well, skillful communication would certainly help, but there's a deeper problem. Something is wrong with the way we talk because *something is wrong with the way we think*. Our thinking continually breaks down. We go along fine, thinking more or less logically, when—zap—we start accusing ourselves, or our partners, and useful thinking comes to a halt.

For example, while driving over to see his girl friend Louise, Mel realizes that he isn't looking forward to seeing her. This puzzles him because for the entire two months of their relationship he has always looked forward to seeing her.

> MEL: I know what it is. *I'm afraid of intimacy*. Every time I get close to a woman, I get scared and have to back away.

93

And *zap*—Mel has stopped thinking and has started accusing. "I'm afraid of intimacy" sounds like a neutral and objective statement that will help him understand his behavior. But it isn't. Instead, it's name-calling. It's name-calling in the same way as "I'm a boob," "jerk," "wimp," "idiot," or "baby" is name-calling. In saying that he's afraid of intimacy, Mel means:

That he *shouldn't* be afraid of intimacy.
That something's wrong with him for being afraid of intimacy.
That being afraid of intimacy is a bad thing.
That he's really hung up.
That he's really immature.
That, in some way, he's a failure as a human being.
That he'll never be able to have a real relationship with a woman.
And that, in some sense, he *is* a boob, jerk, wimp, idiot, or baby.

Telling himself that he's afraid of intimacy brings an end to useful thinking. He just feels gloomy. It makes it impossible for Mel to realize that he's hesitant to see Louise because:

He's worried that, as Louise often does, she'll want to cook him a big meal. He feels that he doesn't have the right to tell her that he's on a diet and would prefer cottage cheese. He's afraid that doing so would hurt her feelings.
He's worried that, as Louise sometimes does, she'll suggest that they visit her parents. He feels that he doesn't have the right to say that he'd rather that just the two of them go to the park.

Mel believes that being in an intimate relationship means sacrificing his needs and wishes to those of his partner. He thinks it means being uninterruptedly giving and accepting. It's not intimacy in itself, but what Mel thinks intimacy requires that makes it threatening and that makes him want to withdraw from it. And *anybody* who defines intimacy as completely sacrificing his or her needs to the needs of the partner would find it scary.

Mr. Skeptic: But what about the fact that Mel has *always* had this problem. He's had it in all his other relationships. Doesn't that prove that he has an irrational fear of intimacy?

Wile: That just proves that in *all* his relationships he sacrifices his needs and wishes to those of his partner. And "fear of intimacy" is only one of a number of commonly used ideas or explanations that are accusations and that bring an end to useful thinking. Others include "dependency," "selfishness," and "jealousy."

Mr. Skeptic: Well, if we have all these accusing ideas you say we do, where do they come them?

Wile: Our upbringing. As soon as we begin to learn anything, we start learning these ideas:

> We are told that it's bad to be selfish and that we should learn to share.
>
> We are told that it's bad to be jealous and that we should learn, instead, to love our baby brother.
>
> We are told it's babyish to be dependent and that we should be a "big boy" or "big girl" and "learn to do things for ourselves."

Ideas such as these become so ingrained in our thinking that they can be thought of as a new set of Commandments. In addition to "Thou shalt not kill" and "Thou shalt not steal," we would now have:

1. Thou shalt not be dependent.
2. Thou shalt not be self-centered (selfish).
3. Thou shalt not be jealous.
4. Thou shalt not be boastful.
5. Thou shalt not be withdrawn or withholding.
6. Thou shalt not be afraid of intimacy.

We feel we simply shouldn't be these things. That's what I mean when I say they're *Commandments*. They're like natural laws. No one would even think to question them. Of course, I've been talking about these Commandments all along, although without referring to them as such. The New Commandments are the laws that our internal prosecutors accuse us of violating and that we accuse our *partners* of violating.

Included on the list of New Commandments are fears and vulnerabilities that we think we shouldn't have. *Thou shalt not*:

7. Be depressed.
8. Be overly sensitive.
9. Be anxious; worry about things you can do nothing about.
10. Wallow in self-pity.
11. Run away from your problems.
12. Be unwilling to take risks.

Included in what I'm calling the New Commandments are discredited ways of relating. *Thou shalt not*:

13. Be a nag.
14. Be a wimp.
15. Be bossy (aggressive, domineering, controlling, manipulative, pushy).
16. Be defensive.
17. Feel turned off by your partner.

People differ in which Commandments affect them the most. Women with a traditional upbringing are relatively more afraid of being selfish, bossy, and angry than they are of being dependent, whereas men with a traditional upbringing are relatively more afraid of being dependent than they are of being selfish, bossy, and angry.

Three thou-shalt-nots are of special interest because they imply general attitudes toward life. *Thou shalt not*:

18. Have unrealistic or unrealizable expectations; be perfectionistic.
19. Fail to take responsibility for your actions.
20. Have a negative attitude-or be unfriendly, irritable, grouchy, a drag, a party pooper, a wet blanket, a poor sport, or a killjoy. Thou shalt always look on the positive side.

Some thou-shalt-nots contradict other thou-shalt-nots. Victorian women lived by the Commandment: Thou shalt not enjoy sex. Post-Victorian women lived by the opposite Commandment:

21. Thou shalt not be frigid.

A modified form of the Victorian Commandment persists, however:

22. Thou shalt not be promiscuous.

Men have a parallel set of contradictory Commandments:

23. Thou shalt not be a dirty old man.
24. Thou shalt always be eager and willing to have sex.

Each generation adds its own special thou-shalt-nots. Here are three from ours. *Thou shalt not*:

25. Fail to fulfill your potential. (Thou shalt have it all.)
26. Be a workaholic. (Thou shalt learn to relax and be well-rounded. Thou shalt not be a *Type A* person.)

27. Suppress anger (because it will just build up).

This last coexists with the long-time Commandment: Thou shalt not:

28. *Express* anger (because it will just cause problems). In fact, thou shalt not *be* angry.

Since these Commandments are so binding, we try to find ways to excuse ourselves. We feel that certain of these otherwise forbidden reactions might be okay under certain restricted conditions. For example:

It's okay to be angry if you can point to a clear injustice such as your partner coming home two hours late. But it's not okay if you can't.

It's okay to feel depressed if you can point to a clear reason such as being jilted. But it's not okay if you can't. And even then, it's only okay if the depression doesn't go on "too long."

It's okay to be jealous if your partner gives you cause such as flirting with other people. But it's not okay if he or she doesn't.

And it's never okay to be jealous of your own child. A husband is supposed to be charmed by his newborn infant and not feel jealous of his wife's intimacy with it.

The effect of all this is to make life a minefield:

Phil gets along fine until he transgresses the Seventh Commandment (Thou shalt not be depressed). It's the middle of breakfast and, suddenly, he feels a little depressed. He would have been all right if he had something to point to that would justify feeling depressed. But he doesn't. Everything seems to being going well. It's Saturday, the sun is shining, and he and his wife Ellen have been getting along fine. In fact, she is being particularly cheerful and bubbly this morning.

What makes it even worse is that this is the kind of Saturday that is supposed to make all his hard work worthwhile. He and Ellen are going on a picnic. He isn't looking forward to it, however. In fact, he suddenly wishes that it were Monday and he were going to work. And now he is *really* worried. He feels in violation of Commandment Twenty-Six: Thou shalt not be a workaholic.

Phil doesn't know that it's Ellen's cheerfulness and bubbliness that are depressing him. He has no way of knowing this because he thinks cheerfulness and bubbliness are good things. He thinks *he* should be cheerful and bubbly. And the fact that he *isn't* sets off another mine: Commandment Twenty (Thou shalt not be grouchy).

> Breakfast isn't even over and Phil has already violated three Commandments.

Everyone's subjective life is such a minefield. And the mines are the feelings that people think they shouldn't be having.

Phil is so quick to blame himself that he's unable to see that Ellen's cheerful mood is forced and hollow, which is why he is turned off by it. Since it was Ellen's idea to go on a picnic (she isn't sure how much Phil really wants to go), she feels responsible for making it fun. Being bubbly and cheerful is her way to try to make it fun. And as often happens with such forced attempts to be cheerful, they ring hollow. Not just Phil, but *anyone* sitting at the table might have been put off by them.

The effect of the New Commandments is to prevent Phil from thinking and talking usefully about the situation. In fact, he stops thinking entirely. He believes that he should simply stop being the way he is, and that's all there is to it.

Even if Phil were to tell Ellen what he was feeling (and, as I said, he is unlikely to do so), the situation wouldn't necessarily get better. Ellen might simply agree with him that he *is* a grumpy and depressed workaholic. After all, she too believes in the New Commandments.

The partners are thus unable to discover the important needed information that:

> Phil's reactions make sense. It's understandable that he would be put off by Ellen's pressured behavior.
> And Ellen's reactions also make sense. She is talking in a pressured way because she is oppressed by a feeling of responsibility for the success of the picnic.

If Ellen and Phil are ever to have conversations in which they make such discoveries, they will need to develop a new way of thinking. After describing the principles underlying our old way of thinking (Chapter 9), I shall present this new way of thinking (Chapter 10).

9

Accusing

*T*he New Commandments interrupt thinking by interposing *accusatory judgments.*

> Fran goes to the refrigerator and is about to eat the last piece of cake when she suddenly remembers, "Hey, I was saving this for Dave [her husband]. I almost ate it. How selfish of me."

Labeling herself as "selfish" (and thus in violation of Commandment Two) ends Fran's thinking about the matter: "I shouldn't be selfish like that. That's all there is to it." This self-accusatory judgment prevents Fran from seeing that there *is* more to it. If she hadn't stumbled into a Commandment, Fran might have been able to realize:

FRAN: Since I *didn't* even think about whether Dave might want the cake, and since I'm almost never like this, then I must really have been feeling pretty empty and I must really be needing something pretty badly. And, now that I think about it, I have been and I am. And what I have been feeling most empty about is our relationship and what I am needing most is hopefulness that we'll be able to work things out.

Fran's "selfish" wish (to eat the last piece of cake) isn't a violation of a Commandment. It's a clue. And that's my main point: our quickness to judge our wishes and feelings prevents us from using them as clues.

My purpose in this chapter is to demonstrate the negative effects of the New Commandments and, in particular:

To show that, because of these commandments, we unknowingly and
continually make accusatory (and particularly *self*-accusatory)
judgments that interrupt our thinking and prevent us from using
our feelings as clues.

People approach situations with certain conclusions already in mind.
They are set to see particular things. They have "mental rules of thumb."
There are at least five mental rules of thumb or habits of thought that may
lead to accusatory conclusions. Most of them are based on the New Commandments.

I shall demonstrate these five rules of thumb by means of the following
parable. I expect that you will recognize some of these rules as ones that
you use. That is my purpose: to show how these rules of thumb, which
distort our reasoning, are ingrained in our thinking.

A PARABLE: FIVE ACCUSING TYPES OF REASONING

Judy and Tom are a married couple in their mid-twenties. Tom is a lawyer
in a small firm, and Judy is a buyer at a department store. In her distress
over an argument with Tom the evening before, Judy asks the advice of
five people, each of whom uses one of the five accusing rules of thumb.

Character Flaws

Judy visits her upstairs neighbor Lucille and pours out a sad story:

JUDY: I'm terribly upset. I got furious at Tom. I like to go out a lot, and
Tom mostly likes to stay at home and watch TV. Last night, Tom did
something unusual for him—he took me out to dinner. There was
dancing at the restaurant, and Tom didn't ask me to dance. And when
I asked him, he said he didn't have the right shoes for dancing. Well,
I told him that he didn't need ballet slippers just to bump around the
floor a few times. But still he said no. And when we got home, I called
him names that I didn't even know I knew. And he just sort of sat
there looking glum. I really blew it. And I'm terribly upset with myself.

LUCILLE: I hate to tell you this, honey, but you're married to a jerk. He's
got to be a jerk, for crying out loud, if he takes you dancing and
doesn't dance with you. He's selfish. Doing something to please some-

one else never even occurs to him. My first husband was just as self-centered. Getting rid of him was the best thing I ever did.

How did Lucille arrive at this conclusion, and so quickly, and with such little evidence? She did so by using the character-flaws rule of thumb. She scanned what Judy told her in search of character flaws. If Tom refuses to grant Judy's reasonable request, that means he's selfish.

> The character-flaws rule of thumb is closely connected to the New Commandments. In fact, the New Commandments are in essence a list of possible character defects from which a person using the character-flaws rule of thumb can choose. Here Lucille invokes Commandment Two (Thou shalt not be selfish).

The character-flaws rule of thumb can be applied at all times and to all people. If *Tom* were to have told Lucille the same story, she might have told him:

LUCILLE: I hate to tell you this, my friend, but you're married to a nag. She's got to be a nag, for crying out loud, to make such a big deal over such a little nothing. I know her type. You take her out for dinner, which is what she says she wants, and all she does is find something else to complain about. And she's neurotic and spiteful. She would have gotten along fine with my first husband.

No matter what a person does, his or her character can be impugned. Not getting married can be viewed as fear of commitment. Getting married can be seen as fear of being alone. Going to college can be viewed as irresponsibility and laziness—an unwillingness to get a real job. Not going to college and going to work can be seen as irresponsibility and laziness —a lack of ambition.

One effect of the character-flaw rule of thumb is to foreclose useful thinking. Lucille says in essence:

> The problem is Tom's selfishness and Judy's nagging. That's all there is to it. And there's only one thing to do about it: they should stop behaving that way.

Perhaps Judy's mistake is that she's seeking advice from a nonprofessional. Perhaps she should be talking, instead, to a psychotherapist. Although that's a good idea, there's no certainty that the results will be better since there are some psychotherapists who agree with Lucille's style of thinking. They just use different terms. Instead of "selfish," they say "narcissistic." Instead of "clingy," they say "symbiotic." Instead of "stubborn," they say "anal retentive." And instead of "sneaky," they say "passive-aggressive."

Some of these psychotherapists have misgivings about their tendency to see everything as character defects. They tell the following joke on themselves:

> If patients are early to their appointments, that means they are "anxious." If they are late, that means they are "hostile." And if they are on time, that means they are "compulsive."

You Must Have Wanted It That Way

But let's continue the parable. Since her talk with Lucille doesn't make her feel much better, Judy tells the same story to her office mate Lucifer during a coffee break later that morning.

LUCIFER: I tell you, Judy. Something's fishy. Why would Tom take you where there's dancing and then not dance with you? He must *want* to frustrate you. Otherwise, why would he behave the way he did?

Lucifer came to just as quick a conclusion as did Lucille, but to a *different* conclusion. That's because he has a different mental rule of thumb. According to Lucifer's way of thinking, no one ever does anything without a reason. If Judy is upset by Tom's behavior, he must have *wanted* to upset her.

A person who uses this "you-must-have wanted-it-that-way" rule of thumb sees people as obtaining secret gratification from their problems.

> "People think they don't want the bad things that happen to them," such a person says in effect, "but they really do. People always get what they want. There are no victims. There are only perpetrators."

Judy must also have gotten what she wanted, Lucifer thinks. She may have set up the whole thing. Tom's refusal to dance may be just the excuse she needed to do what she may have wanted to do in the first place—have a tantrum, give Tom a piece of her mind, and show him who's boss. (Lucifer doesn't tell Judy about this part of his idea, however. After all, he has to work with her, and he doesn't want to offend her.)

Returning from the coffee break, Judy continues to mope around the office. Lucifer is disappointed that what he told Judy didn't cheer her up. He concludes:

> Judy must *want* to be miserable. Depression is the ultimate self-indulgence. She's having a wonderful time wallowing in self-pity.

Anything can be seen as serving a secret purpose. When a paralyzed woman failed to rise from her wheelchair after the laying on of hands, the faith-healer said: "Some people don't want to be cured. They need their sickness to get attention." When a wife didn't immediately leave her physically abusive husband, her friend thought: "She must want to be beaten up. Maybe she likes knowing that she can get a rise out of him whenever she wants to. Or maybe she enjoys the fact that she can remain mature while her husband acts like a child."

While Lucille accuses people of having character flaws, Lucifer accuses them of having secret motives. But the secret motives that Lucifer sees people as having are often also character defects. They are violations of the New Commandments. He sees people as selfishly controlling others (Commandment Two), for example, or as manipulatively getting others to take care of them (Commandment One), or as wallowing in self-pity (Commandment Ten).

The you-must-have-wanted-it-that-way rule of thumb has a particularly chilling effect on thinking: it disqualifies the person as an observer of his or her own motivations. "People aren't going to want to admit their unconscious motives," the person who adopts this way of thinking believes. "That's why these motives are unconscious in the first place: because people *don't* want to admit them. Judy's never going to admit that she set up the argument so that she could show Tom who's boss. And she's never going to admit that she prefers to wallow in self-pity rather than to be cheered up. You can't talk to people about their secret motives."

Here again we might recommend that Judy talk to a psychotherapist rather than to a nonprofessional like Lucifer. But, again, that's not a sure-fire guarantee that the results will be different since some psychotherapists agree with Lucifer's style of thinking. These therapists employ some of the terms used by Lucifer: "wallowing in self-pity," "doing it for attention," "manipulation," "you're doing it to yourself," and "you don't want to be helped." But they go even further and talk about "self-destructive drives," "secondary gain," "masochistic gratification," "hidden agendas," and "vindictive enjoyment in defeating people who try to help you."

In *Heartburn*, an autobiographical novel about her husband's divorcing her, Nora Ephron describes how her friend Vera told her that she, Nora, set things up so that they would happen the way they did. Here is what Ephron wrote in objection to her friend's way of thinking:

I love Vera, truly I do, but *doesn't anything happen to you that you don't intend?* "You picked him because you knew it wouldn't work out." "You picked him because his neuroses meshed perfectly with yours." "You picked him because you knew he'd deprive you the way your mother or your father did." That's what they're always telling you . . . "You picked the one person on earth you could have problems with." "You picked the one person on earth you shouldn't be involved with." . . . Robert Browning's shrink probably said it to *him.* "So, Robert, it's very interesting, no? Of all the women in London, you pick this hopeless invalid who has a crush on her father." Let's face it: *everyone* is the one person on earth you shouldn't get involved with.

Not only will therapists tell you that "you picked him because you knew it wouldn't work out," Ephron says, they will also tell you that "your problem is fear of intimacy; that you're connecting to your mother, or holding on to your father."

Therapists who say that "you're connecting to your mother or holding on your father"—that is, that your problem is unresolved issues from the past—are using the back-to-childhood rule of thumb.

Back-to-Childhood

But let's continue the parable. Judy came away from Lucille feeling awful. She comes away from Lucifer feeling worse. So she calls her old school friend Rosebud and tells her the story of the night before. Rosebud uses the back-to-childhood rule of thumb.

ROSEBUD: Well, I'm not the least bit surprised. Tom's spoiled. He doesn't know what it's like to try to do something for another person. His mother waited on him hand-and-foot. It wouldn't even occur to him to try to please you by dancing with you. And I can see how you'd have a hard time when he didn't. You were always being disappointed by your parents. Remember how your dad promised to come to the senior play you were starring in and he didn't show up. And the same with your mom. She was always promising things and she never came through.

According to the back-to-childhood rule of thumb:

> People have unfinished business (emotional baggage) from childhood that they're dragging into the present.
> Just bringing it to their attention may be all that's necessary to free them from it.
> On the other hand, these patterns may be deeply ingrained and difficult to change.

In explaining the present in terms of the past, Rosebud is trying to be sympathetic. It's not Judy's fault, after all, that her parents never came through for her. Listening to Rosebud, Judy begins to sympathize with herself a little. But even though Rosebud's comments do, at first, make Judy feel a little better, their ultimate effect is to make her feel worse. That's because Judy can't imagine how she and Tom are going to be able to change such long-term, deeply ingrained character defects as "selfishness" and "oversensitivity to rejection." And, of course, that's what Rosebud is saying about her and Tom—that they have these character defects.

> Tracing their problems to childhood can provide Judy and Tom with a more long-range and, at times, a less self-accusing view. But it can also cause them to feel even more neurotic and hung up. They may now see themselves as having problems that are difficult to change.

A problem with childhood explanations, ironically, is that they are so convincing. They drive out all other explanations. It's so clear that our problems *do* go back to childhood that it's easy to see such explanations as the complete and final answer. Once Judy and Tom trace their problem to Tom's being spoiled by his mother and Judy's being rejected by her parents, that's all they see: a spoiled little boy and an insecure little girl. It becomes difficult for them to consider the possibility that Tom might have a valid reason for not wanting to dance and that Judy might have a valid reason for getting upset because he didn't.

So once again, we might wish that Judy were talking to a psychotherapist rather than to a nonprofessional such as Rosebud. And once again we must acknowledge that doing so would not be a guarantee of different results, since it's not unusual for therapists to use Rosebud's rule of thumb.

Bad Habits

The more Judy hears, the worse she feels. She worries that what her friends are saying might be correct:

Maybe Tom *is* selfish, as Lucille says, and can never give me what I really want.

And maybe I *am* a nag.

And if, as Lucifer says, Tom *is* trying to frustrate me, he's certainly doing a good job.

And Rosebud may be right that he has been ruined by his parents.

And maybe I've been ruined by mine.

Maybe we're just two screwed-up people who deserve each other.

Furthermore, Judy's car won't start and has to be towed. Although people usually don't talk to their mechanics about personal matters, Judy feels so upset that she tells hers about her difficulty with Tom.

JACK (the mechanic): I don't think it's a serious problem. You and Tom just have some bad habits—sort of like riding the clutch. You and he have just gotten a bit sloppy over the years. He needs to realize that he has to extend himself a little. Dancing once in a while isn't going to kill him. And you've got to learn to give a little, too. If he doesn't dance, it doesn't mean that civilization will come to an end or that General Motors will stop making cars.

On the other hand, you do have one serious problem. You *have* been riding the clutch. And you're going to need a new one.

Jack doesn't believe that Tom and Judy have anything as serious as character defects. In fact, attributing the problem to bad habits is Jack's way of trying to see them as *not* having character defects. As Jack sees it, Tom and Judy have just gotten a little careless. They've just got to learn to try a little harder to make things work out.

Listening to what Jack says, Judy begins to feel better. Maybe Jack's right and the problem isn't as serious as Lucille, Lucifer, and Rosebud had led her to believe.

Judy feels just a *little* better, however. Although Jack's being easy on her, he's still being critical. He says that she has bad habits ("You've gotten a little sloppy over the years"; "You need to learn to give a little").

As in the case with the first three rules of thumb, the bad-habits style of reasoning brings a premature end to thinking. "There's really nothing to think about," Jack says in effect, "it's just a bad habit." Whatever thinking *is* done is limited to figuring out what the bad habit is and how to change it. Judy doesn't get a chance to consider the possibility that the reactions that she and Tom are having might be an important and understandable response to something that is happening in the relationship.

So once again, we might wish that Judy were talking to a psychotherapist rather than to a nonprofessional such as Jack. And once again we must acknowledge that doing so would not be a guarantee of different results, since some therapists apply a professional form of the bad-habits rule of thumb.

Unrealistic Expectations

By this time, Judy is really upset. So when she runs into her friend Marlene while taking the bus home, she spills out her story.

MARLENE: Your problem is that you think a marriage is dancing, romancing, love, and flowers. That's not a marriage. That's a honeymoon. A marriage is compromise, sacrifice, aggravation, and diapers. Let me give you some good advice. Just be glad that you have a husband who comes home at night. He doesn't like dancing? So it's not the end of the world. You've got to accept him the way he is. You can't change people. And you've got this phony view of marriage in which Tom is supposed to satisfy all your needs. No one can satisfy all of a person's needs.

Marlene uses the unrealistic-expectations (or stick-to-reality) rule of thumb for understanding what she sees.

While Lucille looks to see what character defects are being revealed,
And Lucifer looks to see what secret wishes are being fulfilled,
And Rosebud looks to see what early relationships are being repeated,
And Jack looks to see what bad habits are being fostered,
Marlene looks to see what unrealistic expectations are being expressed.

The unrealistic-expectations rule of thumb is based on Commandment Eighteen (Thou shalt not have unrealizable expectations). According to this rule of thumb, all problems stem from perfectionism.

> Show me someone who is forever being disappointed, and I'll show you someone with unrealistic goals. Show me someone who is always depressed, and I'll show you someone who expects too much. Show me someone who carries a grudge, and I'll show you someone who is unwilling to compromise.

Although there is some truth to these statements, the implicit suggestion is that you should just stop having these unrealistic expectations, *which itself is an unrealistic expectation.* A person's expectations don't just come out of the air, but often represent wishes and goals that he or she has considerable stake in.

According to the unrealistic-expectations way of thinking, ninety-nine percent of divorces are caused by unrealistic beliefs. These beliefs are that people who love each other:

> Should be able to maintain the honeymoon feeling throughout marriage.
> Should be able to satisfy all of the other person's needs.
> Should always want to do everything together.
> Should know what the other wants without having to be told.
> Should never have major disagreements.

These beliefs can be burdensome. If you believe that the honeymoon feeling should last throughout your marriage, you may worry that something is seriously wrong when you find that it doesn't. You may be relieved to hear, accordingly, that you have "unrealistic expectations." You may be relieved, that is, until you realize that giving up these wishes and expectations might not be so easy.

As Judy gets off the bus, she feels discouraged. She doesn't see how she's going to get rid of her "unrealistic expectations" for greater intimacy, involvement, and romancing.

Like the previous rules of thumb, the unrealistic-expectations rule of thumb limits thinking. There is thought to be nothing you need to think further about. You're just supposed to get rid of these "unrealistic expectations."

So once again, we might wish that Judy were talking to a psychotherapist rather than to a nonprofessional such as Marlene. And once again we must acknowledge that doing so wouldn't provide absolute assurance of better results, since some therapists agree with Marlene in tracing a person's problems to unrealistic expectations.

Judy comes away from these five people feeling bad. They have accused her, among other things, of being a nag, of having a wonderful time wallowing in self-pity, of being oversensitive to rejection, and of having bad habits and unrealistic expectations.

Mr. Skeptic: Sure, Judy's upset by what these people said, and I feel sorry for her. But not *everyone* who is accused of such things would feel as bad as she does. In fact, some might even be elated. They'd feel inspired by their determination, for example, *never* to nag or be oversensitive again.

Wile: Yeah, but their elation is likely to be temporary, since they'll soon find out that it's not going to be *easy* never to nag or be oversensitive again. It's like parishioners reacting to a hellfire-and-damnation sermon. Some leave such a sermon feeling sinful and hopeless, whereas others leave inspired by their personal pledge never to sin again. But, of course, they're *going* to sin again; their inspiration, determination, and elation are only temporary.

WHO ARE THESE PEOPLE
AND WHY ARE THEY SAYING THESE THINGS?

My point in this chapter is that we all have Lucille, Lucifer, Rosebud, Jack, and Marlene within our minds. And their effect is to interrupt constructive thinking. We attribute our problems to character defects, bad habits, unrealizable expectations, and so on, and we leave it at that. We are unable to use our feelings as clues.

What is needed is a whole new way of thinking that allows us to use our feelings as clues. That is what I shall talk about in the next chapter.

But let's return to the parable. Judy started the day feeling down-in-the-mouth. She ended the day feeling down-on-the-floor. Everyone she talked to made her feel worse. Walking home from the bus stop, she imagined what the evening would be like. Tom, in his usual way of not dealing with situations, would act as if nothing had happened. He would give her a peck, ask how her work went, and not have much more to say. He would probably spend all night watching television. She, in her usual way, would answer his question about work only briefly, since she would think that he wasn't really interested. She'd ask how *his* work went and expect to hear "Oh, pretty good" and nothing more. And she'd probably spend all night reading in the bedroom and feeling lonely.

But Tom was waiting at the door. "I've been doing a lot of thinking about what happened last night," he said. "And I could hardly wait for you to come home to talk about it." Judy couldn't believe what she was hearing:

> Tom had just said more in the first ten seconds than he usually said throughout a whole evening.
>
> And he was confronting a problem.
>
> And he seemed lively and engaged.

"What's gotten into him," Judy thought. "Who *is* this strange man?"

10

Not Accusing

What has gotten into Tom is that he has spent an hour with people who are *non*accusing.

The five accusing rules of thumb are built into everyone's thinking. They are built into my thinking, despite the fact that I'm writing this book about them and thus might be thought to be free of them. These five accusing rules of thumb are automatic and reflexive. At any moment I, or any of us, can become Lucille, Lucifer, Rosebud, Jack, or Marlene.

If we are to protect ourselves from becoming these people and from succumbing to the almost irresistible tendency to accuse, we need an alternative to these accusing mental rules of thumb. My alternative is to adopt the following *non*accusing mental rules of thumb.

SEVEN NONACCUSING TYPES OF REASONING

While Judy was upstairs talking to Lucille, Tom was on his way to work. As he picked up each person in his car pool, Tom told him or her about his argument with Judy. He picked up seven people, each of whom uses one of the seven *non*accusing rules of thumb.

Hidden Appropriateness and Ordinary Feelings

The first riders Tom picked up were Cloe, who uses the hidden-appropriateness rule of thumb, and Joe, who uses the ordinary-feelings rule of thumb. Tom told them the story.

TOM: I don't understand why I didn't just dance with Judy. Everything would have been all right if I'd only gotten out on the floor and stumbled around a little.

Tom thought that his refusal to dance was out of line, off the wall, and inappropriate to the situation. Cloe believes that things that appear out of line, off the wall, and inappropriate often turn out to make a lot of sense once you get to the bottom of them. So Cloe tried to get to the bottom of Tom's not dancing with Judy:

CLOE: Suppose you *had* danced. What would have happened?
TOM: Nothing much. That's the point. Why did I have to make such a big deal about it? It wouldn't have cost me anything to dance.
CLOE: I don't know. Maybe it *would* have cost you. Sometimes things are more expensive than they seem. Do you and Judy do much dancing?
TOM: We've only gone once or twice. I'm not much of a dancer and I sort of make a fool of myself. Judy gets upset about my stepping on her toes and being a klutz.
CLOE (feeling pleased because she believes she has already found the hidden appropriateness in Tom's behavior): Well, there you are, Tom. You had a good reason for not dancing. In fact you were really stuck. You could either dance and make a fool of yourself and get Judy upset with you or *not* dance and get her upset with you.
TOM: Well, maybe.

Tom feels better hearing this explanation. But just a *little* better. He feels he's being let off too easily:

TOM: But it's not just last night. Judy's right about me. I think about *my* needs, not about hers. I don't do enough to try to please her. I'm just selfish.

At this point, Joe, the second passenger, snaps into action. Joe uses the ordinary-feelings rule of thumb. Whenever he hears anyone accuse himself or herself of having a "childish" or "bad" reaction (Tom's calling himself "selfish"), Joe immediately thinks that there's got to be an ordinary, adult, innocuous, garden-variety feeling underneath somewhere.

JOE: Are there *ever* times when you *do* try to please Judy?

TOM: Well, sometimes. I guess that's why I took her out to dinner in the first place. I know she likes fancy restaurants. So we went there, even though places like that make me uncomfortable. And as usual, it didn't work out. I keep trying to show her the good time I know she deserves, but something always goes wrong.

Joe is pleased. He thinks he has found an ordinary feeling already:

JOE: Okay, so what ended in what you see as your "selfishness"—your unwillingness to dance—started as an effort to be *unselfish*. You took Judy to a place you didn't even want to go just to try to please her.

For a moment Tom agrees:

TOM: I guess I got in over my head. Going to a fancy restaurant was already extending myself. Dancing was way beyond what I had in mind. Something like this always happens. My plans hardly ever work out.

The hidden-appropriateness and ordinary-feelings rules of thumb can be applied at all times and to all people. Let's imagine what would have happened if it were *Judy* rather than Tom who was telling Cloe and Joe about the previous evening.

JUDY: It was babyish and inappropriate of me to get so upset.
CLOE (looking for a hidden appropriateness in what Judy believes to be her "inappropriate" behavior): Okay, Judy. You say you shouldn't have gotten so upset. But maybe it wasn't as inappropriate as you think. You just mentioned that you are almost always disappointed in Tom. What's that about?
JUDY: I'm ashamed to say because it's all so petty. Tom seems like a good husband—he does a lot of loving things—but somehow things aren't what I thought they'd be. Tom agreed to help with the housework, and he sort of does. But somehow I'm the one that always ends up with the really dirty jobs like cleaning the toilet. I thought that raising kids would be something we'd do together, and Tom does help a lot. But somehow I'm the one who has the major responsibility, who makes all the arrangements, and who does all the planning. By the time we get together at night, I'm tired and I'm irritated with him and I don't feel very romantic. I thought that getting married was having a live-in person to share intimate feelings with. But lately I've even

been able to have more intimate conversations with my mechanic. I feel like I'm in it all alone.

If Lucille were there, she might say, "Judy, you're too demanding." If Lucifer were there, he might say, "Judy, you're only happy if you've got something to complain about." If Rosebud were there, she might say, "Judy, you're really angry at your father." If Jack were there, he might say, "Judy, you've just never learned how to compromise." If Marlene were there, she might say, "Judy, you're expecting too much." But Cloe is there and she says:

CLOE: I think that getting upset may have been *just the thing to do*. What happened last night perfectly represents all these things you're saying. You're saying Tom goes through the motions of being a good husband, but he doesn't really come through for you. And that's what happened: he took you out and then didn't dance with you. It makes sense that you got upset.

Cloe has found a hidden appropriateness in Judy's behavior.

CLOE: And there's another thing. You want Tom to be really there with you and fully participating. But if he's taking you to a place that he really doesn't want to go, then he *wouldn't* be engaged and he *wouldn't* be participating. So here again it makes sense that you'd get upset.

Judy would feel better if she were to hear this explanation. But just a *little* better.

JUDY: Well, maybe. But it was still childish of me to get so upset.

Joe, who uses the ordinary-feelings rule of thumb, would now snap into action:

JOE: You say that it was childish of you. But there's an understandable feeling underlying what you say is your "childish" reaction. *Anyone* —adult or child—would get upset when faced with such an immediate and dramatic example of the thing that most bothers her, which in your case is your feeling that Tom goes through the motions but doesn't really come through for you.

It's obvious that Judy would have had a better day if she had talked to the people in Tom's car rather than to the ones she did.

Point-Not-Gotten-Across

But let's return to Tom on his way to work. He is already feeling better when he stops to pick up a third car pool member, Camille. Camille uses the point-not-gotten-across rule of thumb. According to her, people get upset when there is something important that they are unable to get across.

Tom tells Camille what happened at the restaurant, relates what the other passengers said about it, and asks for her opinion.

CAMILLE: If Judy got as angry as you say, and kept getting angrier, maybe it was because she wasn't able to say what she needed to say. Maybe what she needed to say was something like: "This is like our whole marriage—you're taking me where there's dancing and then not dancing with me. I feel you just go through the motions of being a good husband, but you don't come through for me. And I can feel really angry about it. But I can also feel really sad. I don't think you know—since I've never told you—how lonely and abandoned I can feel sometimes, even when we're together."

Let's say Judy feels this but is unable to say it. She thinks it would upset you too much. So, instead, she tries to say something milder about your not dancing with her. But she ends up saying it in a wildly angry way. She makes up in intensity what she loses in accuracy.

Tom thinks it's pretty nervy of Camille to say all these things. But he thinks she may be right. He's painfully aware that Judy does see him as inadequate. And it's true, as Camille says, that Judy rarely says anything about it. Maybe she *is* trying to spare his feelings. And it hadn't occurred to him that Judy might feel sad and lonely. But maybe that's true, too. In fact, he begins to think that he has been feeling sad and lonely much of the time himself.

TOM: Well, yeah, but I don't know what to do about it. I try to do things to please her—like taking her out last night—but nothing seems to work.

CAMILLE: Well, maybe you're in the same spot Judy's in. Maybe there's something important you're unable to say to her. Maybe you never get the chance to tell her that you're upset that you never seem to be able to satisfy her. Instead, you *try* to satisfy her—like taking her out last night—even though you know it never works out.

Tom's surprised that he's not more offended by what Camille is saying about him. Discussions like this usually embarrass him. But there's something relieving about being able to make sense out of his own and Judy's behavior.

Universal Issues

Tom picks up a fourth car pool member, Stan. Stan uses the universal-issues rule of thumb. According to him, partners who are having problems are simply experiencing clearer and more intense forms of difficulties that every couple has.

Stan is the opposite of Lucille, who, as you might remember, uses the character-flaws rule of thumb. While Lucille combs through normal behavior looking for an underlying abnormality, Stan combs through abnormal behavior looking for an underlying universality.

STAN: It sounds as if you and Judy ran into the common problem in which one partner—in this case Judy—holds back a complaint in order to avoid a fight. But that just leads to a worse fight later on because by the time the person finally says something about it, he or she has become *really* angry. You and Judy are experiencing a clear example of a problem that we all suffer from.

Although Tom likes the sound of what Stan says, he doesn't see what Stan is getting at:

TOM: Okay, so Judy and I have a universal couple problem. So what? How is knowing that going to help?
STAN: Well, it's easier to deal with a problem if you don't think there's something wrong with you for having it. You won't have to take it so personally. You'll see it as a problem that *every* couple has rather than as a sign that there's something uniquely wrong with your relationship. As a result you might be able to deal with it more calmly and more matter-of-factly.

A Clue to an Underlying Reality

The next car pool member Tom picks up is Carl. Carl uses the hidden-clue rule of thumb. Carl agrees with Cloe, who uses the hidden-appropriateness rule of thumb, that a person's seemingly inappropriate behavior has a hidden appropriateness. Carl goes further, however. He believes that this seemingly inappropriate behavior may be *useful*. It may reveal an important hidden reality in the relationship.

Tom tells Carl about the events of the previous night, relates what the others said about it, and asks for his opinion.

CARL: I don't think your fight with Judy last night was such a disaster, Tom. In fact, I think it might have been *useful*.

TOM: You've got to be kidding.

CARL: I'm not kidding. In fact, I'll go further and say that you might have been *lucky* to have that fight.

TOM: Like I said, you've got to be kidding.

CARL: Think of it this way: the fight gave you a chance to bring up something that you haven't been able to discuss with Judy before.

TOM: What?

CARL: That you're worried that Judy feels that you don't come through for her. It might be a real relief to be able to get that in the open.

TOM: Well, sure, but then the fat would be in the fire. And it would be *my* fat. I don't think it's such a good idea to get Judy started talking about how I don't come through for her. She might go on all day and say a lot of things I don't want to hear.

CARL: Possibly.

TOM: On the other hand, it *would* be a relief to get it all into the open.

CARL: And since you'll be bringing up a problem that Judy herself is having difficulty bringing up, you'd be coming through for her. You'd be doing what she is upset about your not doing. So just raising the problem might already be beginning to solve it.

TOM: Yeah, that does sound good.

CARL: And the ideal would be for you and Judy in the future to be able to use *all* your fights as clues.

Tom feels like turning the car around and going directly home so he can talk to Judy. Unfortunately, there are five people in his car expecting him to drive them to work.

And, anyway, Tom almost immediately has second thoughts. He doubts that he could have a conversation with Judy that would actually work out. It's going to take more than what these people in his car said to convince him otherwise.

Special Sensitivities

Tom picks up the sixth and seventh members of the car pool. It's getting kind of tight in the car, but Tom doesn't mind. Everyone who gets in makes him feel a little better.

> Cloe showed Tom that underlying his and Judy's seemingly inappropriate behavior was a hidden appropriateness.
>
> Joe showed Tom that underlying his and Judy's "bad" reactions were ordinary feelings.
>
> Camille showed that his and Judy's "bad" reactions were the result of their inability to say what they really needed to say.
>
> Stan showed that his and Judy's "bad" reactions were simply particularly clear expressions of common couple issues.
>
> Carl showed that these "bad" reactions were clues to an important hidden issue in the relationship.

Now Amy and Jacob get into the car and each has his or her own mental rule of thumb:

> Amy uses the special-sensitivities rule of thumb. She shows that Judy's "bad" behavior is the result of a childhood-caused special-sensitivity to a present reality.
>
> And Jacob uses the solutions-become-problems rule of thumb. He shows that Judy and Tom's problem is how they handle the problem.

Amy's special-sensitivities rule of thumb provides a nonaccusing alternative to Rosebud's back-to-childhood rule of thumb. Rosebud traces all problems to childhood. Amy agrees that a person's past may produce a special sensitivity. He or she may react in intense ways to things that other people hardly notice. Amy insists, however, that there's a grain of truth in the person's response. He or she is reacting in an intense way to things that are actually happening.

In fact, the sensitivity produced by a person's childhood may make him or her a good observer of certain areas of reality. Like a dog picking up high-pitched sounds that humans can't hear, a person's childhood-caused special sensitivity may enable him or her to detect subtle events that others don't notice. For example, the rejection that a wife suffered as a child may make her a sensitive observer of the subtle ways in which she and her husband slight one another. This wife and husband may wish that she *didn't* have her childhood-based special sensitivity to rejection. It's a nuisance how she gets upset at even minor slights by her husband. Her sensitivity has one important benefit, however. She and her husband will never wake up one day as some people do and find themselves in a detached, withdrawn relationship without knowing how they got there. She's their protection against that. She's an expert at detecting the subtle and often unnoticed slights and rejections that regularly occur between people.

Tom tells Amy what happened the night before, relates what everyone else said about it, and asks for her opinion.

AMY: If Judy suddenly started acting upset, she must have been sensing something. You told us that she said: "You won't dance with me. You won't do anything with me." It sounds as if Judy was feeling a little abandoned.

TOM: Well, that's a problem she had a long time before she ever met me. She's sensitive to abandonment. She felt her mother and father rejected her.

AMY: Okay, she's sensitive to abandonment. But that means that she was reacting sensitively to the fact that in some way she was being abandoned at the moment. Not being danced with could have left her feeling that way. But I think it's more than that. . . . I think I know what it is. You said that the restaurant made you uncomfortable. Judy might have felt, then, that you weren't really with her in enjoying it, that you weren't sharing her enthusiasm, and, in this sense, that she was all alone in it.

TOM: Well, what do you want me to do? Here I do something for Judy that I know she likes and then, because my heart isn't completely in it, she gets upset. It doesn't seem fair.

AMY: Yeah, well. . . .

Solutions Become Problems

At this point, the seventh passenger, Jacob, breaks in:

JACOB (to Tom): I think it's even more "unfair" than you know. And I think you've hit on the real difficulty. Here you are trying the best you can to solve the problem. You take Judy out in an attempt to please her and to make her feel less abandoned. But the fact that you didn't feel completely comfortable in the restaurant and can't fully enter into the spirit of the occasion leads Judy, instead, to feel displeased and *more* abandoned. And this is what's so unfair then: your efforts to try to solve the problem, and to make things better, made things worse.

Jacob, who uses the solutions-become-problems rule of thumb, is in some ways the opposite of Lucifer, who uses the you-must-have-wanted-it-that-way rule of thumb. While Lucifer sees people as successfully (and secretly) trying to keep their problems, Jacob views people as *unsuccessfully* (and secretly) trying to solve them. The idea that solutions become problems was developed by Paul Watzlawick, John Weakland, and Richard Fisch in their book, *Change*.

JACOB (to Tom): The problem is how you and Judy handle problems. Since you were unable to tell Judy that you were upset because you didn't seem able to please her, you were forced to engage in long-shot efforts to try to please her—like taking her to that fancy restaurant.

TOM: I guess maybe it was a long-shot. Something does always seem to go wrong whenever I take her someplace like that. But don't tell me about trying to talk to Judy. I've already tried that. And it doesn't work.

ALL THE PASSENGERS IN THE CAR: *Yeah, but did you ever try to talk to her in the ways that we've been talking here?*

THE CONVERSATION

Tom, of course, never *has* talked to Judy in the ways his car pool mates had been talking. That's because his thinking is dominated by the same five accusing ideas or rules of thumb that Judy's is. These accusing ideas *block* useful talking.

Lucille, who attributes problems to character defects, says there's nothing much to think or talk about. It's just a matter of admitting your defects and correcting them.

Lucifer, who attributes problems to hidden motives, says that thinking and talking won't help. People don't want to admit the real truth. They won't admit that they really want to keep their problems.

Rosebud, who attributes problems to childhood, says that the only thing you need to think or talk about is how your childhood caused your problems.

Jack, who attributes problems to bad habits, says there's nothing much to think or talk about. It's just a matter of changing your behavior.

Marlene, who attributes problems to unrealistic expectations, agrees that there's nothing much to think or talk about. It's just a matter of facing reality.

The five accusing rules of thumb block useful talking by imposing negative judgments and by insisting that the person simply start shaping up. The seven nonaccusing rules of thumb block these negative judgments and direct the person toward useful talking. The person looks for:

1. A hidden appropriateness in his or her seemingly inappropriate behavior.
2. An ordinary feeling that is being expressed in indirect and offensive forms because the person feels uncomfortable with it.
3. An understandable point that the person is having difficulty getting across.
4. A common couple issue that the person is experiencing in a particularly intense form.
5. A hidden reality for which his or her behavior is a clue.
6. A present reality to which the person has a childhood-based special sensitivity.
7. An ordinary problem that has become worse because of the way the person is trying to solve it.

Let's imagine the kind of conversation that Tom might have with Judy if he were to use the nonaccusing rules of thumb that his car pool mates taught him instead of the accusing rules of thumb that he and Judy ordinarily use.

Tom tries to call Judy at work and tell her what he has just learned, but she's at the garage talking to Jack and getting a very different kind of advice.

So as Judy straggles in after her distressing day, Tom tells her that he has a lot of new ideas about what happened to them last night:

TOM: You know, maybe what I should have done last night, rather than take you to that restaurant, is to tell you that I'm upset that I always blow it when I try to please you.

Tom is using the fight last night as a clue to an important issue—that he feels it never works out when he tries to please her. He's using the hidden-clue rule of thumb.

Judy is flabbergasted. She's not used to hearing Tom talk in such a nondefensive and nonaccusing way. But since she has spent the whole day talking to people who think in *accusing* ways, she's suspicious. She thinks that Tom may be making excuses or setting her up. So she says, sarcastically:

JUDY: Well, if you want to please me, one thing you might start doing is dancing with me.

Tom is crushed. This isn't the way that the people in his car had been talking to him. In fact, what Judy says makes him forget everything they said. His mind stops working. He is about to do what he usually does in such situations: defend himself.

But then he remembers Camille's point-not-gotten-across rule of thumb. "If Judy's being sarcastic," he imagines Camille saying to him, "then she must be feeling that she hasn't gotten her point across. And it's possible to *help* her get it across." So that's what Tom tries to do:

TOM: Yeah, that's what I can think too—that I should have danced with you. And I'm upset that I didn't give it a try. And I'm also upset about a lot of other things. I've been feeling that I'm always letting you down and that I'm always displeasing you.

By agreeing with Judy—by admitting that *he too* thinks that he should have danced with her—Tom shows Judy that her point *has* gotten across. And Judy does what people typically do when they feel their point has gotten across. She softens. She feels less critical of Tom:

JUDY: Well, I must admit that's nice to hear because you're right, I have been displeased. And I've been feeling really bad about it. I think there's something really wrong with me—that I'm unforgiving and impossible to please.

In saying that "there's something wrong with me" and in calling herself "unforgiving" and "impossible to please," Judy is using the character-flaws rule of thumb on herself. Tom rescues her from the clutches of the character-flaws rule of thumb by invoking the hidden-appropriateness rule of thumb. He shows Judy that her reactions are appropriate:

TOM: You're forgetting that you have good reason to be displeased. I *do* abandon you. Sure, I do a lot of things to try to please you, but I never talk about how these things never work out. And that's how I abandon you. And that's how you abandon me, since you never talk about how things never work out, either. Think of all that we've needed to be able to say to one another but haven't been able to say. I'm just glad we're finally talking about it now.

Conversations like this one are not just a means for solving Judy and Tom's problem. They *are* the solution. For most people, having a husband who talks this way is more important than being taken dancing. By talking this way, Tom is coming through for Judy. He is providing the thing that Judy is really wanting—his involvement in the relationship—of which dancing is only a surface expression.

JUDY: I don't know why it is, Tom, but suddenly I'm no longer feeling dissatisfied or abandoned.

People are at a severe disadvantage in dealing with their problems to the extent that they think the way that Lucille, Lucifer, Rosebud, Jack, and Marlene think. These accusing rules of thumb block useful thinking and talking. They are responsible for giving talking its bad name. People who employ them run into trouble and quickly conclude that talking is useless.

People who adopt the kind of thinking that Cloe, Joe, Camille, Stan, Carl, Amy, and Jacob employ will be able to:

Talk usefully about their problems.
Use their feelings as clues.
Collaborate in ways that will give talking a *good* name.

A lot depends on which theories you have, which theories your friends have, and, perhaps also, who's in your car pool.

11

Makeshift Solutions

Mr. Skeptic: Okay Wile, I've gotten your point. You're saying that the five accusatory rules of thumb block thinking and talking. . . . But wait a minute. Why does that really have to be such a terrible thing? There are *plenty* of people who never talk to their partners about anything important—and who don't even think much about their relationships— and yet they still get along.

Wile: But let's look at *how* they get along. In fact, let's look at how we *all* get along, since we *all* are at least partly blocked in our ability to think and talk about our problems. What we're all left to do is to engage in *makeshift solutions*: efforts to solve our problems despite the fact that we can't think or talk about them. And these makeshift solutions cause a lot of trouble.

There are three types of makeshift solutions—action-solutions, slogan-solutions, and fantasy-solutions—all of which are demonstrated in the following example.

Katie and Burt are a couple in their early fifties. They have been married twenty-five years and have three grown children. Katie is unable to think or talk about certain problems in their relationship. Here is what Katie needs to be able to say to Burt:

KATIE: I'm afraid to say this because we usually don't talk about such things but I'm missing the fun we used to have. We seem to take each other for granted. At least I feel taken for granted and I think there's lots of times that I take *you* for granted. And we don't seem to have much to say to one another anymore. And I'm worried and discouraged about all of this.

Since Katie can't talk about these problems, she tries to deal with them in another way. She engages in a fantasy:

> She thinks longingly back on the days when the relationship *was* fulfilling. She and Burt used to party, dance, and stay up all night talking and making love.

This fantasy does, at first, solve the problem. For a moment, Katie is back in the old days, passionate and full of life. But her memory of how it used to be makes her all the more aware of how it isn't now. She worries that her lack of romantic feeling means that they have a bad marriage. In an attempt to talk herself out of this worry, Katie tells herself:

> It's unrealistic to expect the honeymoon feeling to last forever.

Katie is engaging in a slogan-solution. She is using a slogan—a familiar saying—to try to convince herself that there's nothing to worry about. And then she engages in an *action*-solution. She tries to get Burt to *do* something that might snap them back into their early romantic feeling.

KATIE: Let's go rowing on the lake.

Katie's having a positive fantasy. She thinks rowing on the lake under a full moon will revive their romance. But Burt's having a negative fantasy. He thinks rowing will show how unromantic they've become. So he says, "Let's talk about it later." He hopes she'll forget about it.

Katie doesn't forget about it, but she doesn't bring it up again either.

Here in miniature is the heart of their problem. Burt's indirectness (he says "let's talk about it later") and Katie's withdrawal (she doesn't press the matter) are typical of the way that they (and a great many of us) interact. Being indirect and withdrawn is a solution to one problem that leads to another problem. Katie and Burt no longer have the distressing fights that they used to have. But their means of avoiding these fights— by being indirect and withdrawn—are largely responsible for the lack of spark in their marriage.

Remembering the spirited and playful conversations she and Burt had at the beginning of the relationship, Katie tries to think of questions that might get one going. And she thinks she finds one. She asks Burt:

KATIE: If you could be any animal, what would you be?

Burt can't figure out what's gotten into Katie. He compliantly answers her question, even though he was about to go out and mow the lawn. He says "I'd be a goat because I could eat and, at the same time, mow the lawn, which reminds me, I've got to mow the lawn."

With Burt outside taking care of the lawn, Katie says to herself, "We're in a rut." She remembers reading a magazine article that recommended spicing up your marriage by doing dramatic, unpredictable things. She decides to try out one of the article's more daring suggestions. So the next day, when Burt comes home from work, she does what the article recommends:

She greets him at the door with nothing on but a smile.

Now Burt feels really on the spot. He read the article too, and he knows he's supposed to find her nakedness enticing and to want to have sex with her. In fact, according to the article, he's supposed to want have sex with her right there in the hallway. But he doesn't feel like it. The hallway floor looks hard and dusty, and Katie doesn't seem very appealing standing there self-conscious and shivering. (The magazine doesn't talk about self-consciousness and shivering.) Fortunately for Burt, a neighbor rings the bell and Katie scurries to the bedroom to put on her clothes. There in the bedroom, putting on her skirt and feeling foolish, Katie has an even more upsetting thought:

KATIE: Burt didn't grab me like the magazine says he's supposed to. Maybe he doesn't find me attractive.

But quickly she reassures herself:

KATIE: Who am I kidding? Why should seeing me naked turn him on? He's seen me naked every day for twenty-five years.

And then she wonders:

KATIE: Why am I getting so upset in the first place? I should be happy with what I've got. All my friends' marriages are worse than mine.

This thought reassures her for a moment. It's an attempt to talk herself out of her worry. But it's soon replaced by the opposite thought:

KATIE: But I'd better not make the mistake my parents did and remain forty years in an unhappy marriage.

So now Katie is back where she started: worried about the situation, thinking that something needs to be done, but not knowing what:

KATIE: Maybe I'm thinking about this all wrong. Maybe I'm being selfish. Instead of trying to get Burt to be more caring of me, maybe I should try to be more caring of *him*. If he felt that I really cared about him, maybe he'd be more caring of me.

So Katie begins doing lots of special things for Burt. She buys his favorite foods. When he's working on the bills, she brings him coffee. She gardens with him. She goes through *TV Guide* and notes the times of the football games so that she can tell him about them and watch them with him.

And then, when there has been very little positive response, she reacts against the whole effort. She is sick of forcing herself to watch football and garden, both of which she hates. She grasps at another slogan-solution:

I can't expect my marriage to satisfy all my needs. I have to look elsewhere.

This slogan-solution sets the scene for a series of action-solutions. Katie thinks of ways to broaden her life:

She signs up for a class in Japanese print-making. She calls several old friends and arranges lunches with them. And she begins to talk more with her neighbors.

And a new fantasy-solution emerges. One of the neighbors is a divorced man who has had a crush on Katie for a long time. Unlike Burt, this neighbor doesn't take her for granted. In fact, he's super-attentive.

Katie finds herself having romantic daydreams about him.

And now Katie has a new problem. She can't stop thinking about this man, and she feels terribly guilty about it. She engages in a slogan-solution to try to talk herself out of her feelings. She tells herself:

KATIE: I've got to remember that men always look better before you start living with them. I've got to be careful that I don't throw away all I have with Burt for just a fling.

It's hard to remember, however, just what she does have with Burt and to believe that things wouldn't be better with her neighbor. And so she shifts from a talk-yourself-*out-of*-a-wish type of slogan-solution into a talk-yourself-*into*-a-wish type. She tells herself, "You only live once."

She dresses herself up in the sexiest dress she has and pays her neighbor a surprise visit on a day when no one else is around. However, he turns out not to be around either. Disappointed, and perhaps also a little relieved, she goes to a movie.

And when she returns, she finds Burt cleaning the garage, something that Katie had wanted him to do for six months. And he has brought her some flowers. Katie's earlier plan was working after all. Burt finally was responding to all the gardening, football watching, coffee bringing, and special meals.

And all these things that Burt was doing made a difference. They gave Katie more of a feeling that they were in it together. She felt a little more inspired about their marriage, at least for a while. She stopped thinking so much about her neighbor.

Katie has engaged in the following fantasy-solutions:

1. Recalling the excitement of the early part of her relationship with Burt.
2. Engaging in romantic daydreams about her neighbor.

And the following slogan-solutions, telling herself:

1. It's unrealistic to expect the honeymoon feeling to last forever.
2. I can't expect his seeing me naked to turn him on when he's seen me naked every day for twenty-five years.
3. I should be happy that the relationship is as good as it is.
4. I mustn't make my parents' mistake of remaining in an unhappy marriage.
5. Instead of expecting things from Burt, I should do things for him.
6. I can't expect my marriage to satisfy all my needs.
7. I've got to remember that men don't look as good when you begin to live with them.
8. You only live once.

And the following action-solutions:

1. Asking Burt to go rowing on the lake.
2. Asking what animal he would like to be.
3. Meeting Burt at the door without any clothes on.
4. Doing special things for Burt.
5. Taking classes, calling friends, meeting her neighbors.
6. Trying to have an affair.

One of the action-solutions did work, at least partly. Doing thoughtful things for Burt did eventually lead to his doing thoughtful things for her. And she began to feel a little better about the relationship. However, her way of getting Burt to behave in this different way was not one that she could use very often. There was just so much football and gardening that she could stand.

So that's what Katie, Burt, and the rest of us do when the accusing rules of thumb block our thinking and talking. We engage in action-solutions, slogan-solutions, and fantasy-solutions. I'll discuss action-solutions in this chapter, slogan-solutions in the following chapter, and fantasy-solutions in Parts 5 and 6.

TRYING TO AVOID FALLING OUT OF LOVE

Let's use two related situations—feeling less sexually attracted to your partner and fearing that you are falling out of love—to suggest the range of action-solutions that people use.

Claude suddenly feels sexually turned off by his wife Beth. If he were able to think and to talk about this feeling, he might realize that it is *appropriate* to the situation. It is a reaction to an argument he had with her the day before. He *can't* think or talk about feeling sexually turned off by Beth, however, because he just thinks he *shouldn't* be feeling this way. He thinks there's something wrong with him. He feels in violation of Commandment 17 (Thou shalt not feel turned off by thy partner).

So what does Claude do? He engages in an action-solution. He deals with his inability to think or talk about the problem of feeling sexually turned off by Beth by engaging in an action that he hopes might solve the problem. He asks Beth to put on a sexy dress and to go out to dinner with him. He hopes that seeing her in that sexy dress will rekindle his passion.

Beth is upset by the fact that *she* suddenly feels sexually turned off by Claude. If she were able to think and talk about these feelings, she might be able to trace them to the fight they had the day before *and* to Claude's strange behavior tonight. He keeps insisting that she wear this stupid dress and that they go out to this fancy restaurant. If Beth were able to think and to talk about these feelings, she'd see that they were, in a way, *appropriate* to the situation. But Beth is unable to do so. She, too, believes that she just shouldn't be having them.

So what does Beth do? She engages in an action-solution. She asks Claude if he loves her. She hopes that hearing him say he does will bring back her positive feelings for him and counteract her present doubt whether he loves her and whether she loves him.

Dean Delis, a psychologist in San Diego, lists a number of common action-solutions that people use when they find themselves falling out of love. In an effort to make their partners more appealing, they try to:

Get their partners to act and to dress in ways that might attract, intrigue, or turn them on.

Get their partners to eliminate mannerisms and habits that turn them off.

Turn their partners into more interesting and intelligent people. They urge their partners to take night courses and to read more books and newspapers.

These people are worried about the fact that they are losing interest in their partners. They don't want to be losing interest. They feel guilty about it. They dread the prospect of having to deal again with the singles scene. They wonder whether they have unrealizable expectations and think that they should be happy with the relationships they've got. They wonder whether they're incapable of long-term relationships. And they have no effective way of talking or thinking about any of these feelings. So they engage in these action-solutions.

And their partners are even more upset. Noticing that their lovers are falling out of love with them, but feeling too threatened to talk or think about it, they engage in action-solutions in an effort to rekindle their partners' love:

They engage in what Delis calls hypercourtship behavior. They try to impress their partners with their intelligence, wit, attractiveness, sexiness, charm, and achievements. Or they do the opposite. They try to be good listeners and to engage their partners by letting these partners impress them.

They make themselves more available. They go along with everything their partners want and try to show how warm and loving they are. Or they do the opposite. They make themselves less available and try to show how independent they are. They try to intrigue their partners by playing hard to get and by making their partners jealous.

They seek reassurance. They ask, "Do you love me?" Or they do the opposite. They play it cool. They try not to make complaints or demands or to ask for reassurance. And they try not to act hurt or jealous.

Mr. Skeptic: This list makes me nervous. I've done almost all these things myself.

Wile: Well, I'm not surprised. These are things that just about everyone does. And they can be at least *partly* successful, although often they are extremely *un*successful:

Attempts to be impressive often come across as boorishness and self-centeredness.

Attempts to please your partner by going along with everything he or she wants can make you boring to be with.

Attempts to play hard-to-get often fool nobody and just prove how totally available and easy-to-get you are.

Reading a few books rarely turns anybody into a fascinating conversationalist.

AN ACTION-SOLUTION THAT WORKED

Everyone uses action-solutions. The words of advice that people give each other and that they give themselves are essentially action-solutions. Women who wish to spice up their marriages or who are worried about losing their husbands are instructed by self-help books to be more mysterious and unpredictable. The wife isn't advised to talk with her husband about her worries. Instead, she is told to *do* something.

I'm not against action-solutions. I use them all the time myself, and I've gotten a lot of mileage out of them. Relationship problems are difficult to deal with and any way of getting an edge on them is fair game. Since they are makeshift solutions, however, they often don't work.

Here is an extended example of an action-solution that *did* work.

Gloria tries to talk herself out of her complaint that her husband George doesn't help with the housework. She's worried about being a nag (Commandment 13) and about being pushy (Commandment 15). And despite all that is said these days about husbands doing fifty percent of the housework, she thinks the idea that a man might actually make a major contribution to the housework is an unrealistic expectation (Commandment 18).

Accordingly, instead of making a general complaint about George's not helping with the housework, Gloria talks herself out of the complaint. In its place, she makes a simple request. She asks him to take out the trash. Taking out the trash is something that she thinks George won't object too much to doing, although it is only a very small part of the help that she really wants.

Gloria's request is an action-solution. It's a way of not making a complaint while, at the same, producing a change that will resolve the complaint. She hopes that his taking out the trash will decrease her feeling that she's the only one doing anything.

And Gloria's action-solution works, at least partly. George responds positively to her request:

He takes out the trash immediately.

And he does it cheerfully.

And on the way to doing it, he gives her a sexy squeeze.

And he does a particularly good job of taking out the trash. He even puts new plastic liners in the wastepaper baskets.

And he adds a little something extra. He rinses out the trash can.

And then, instead of continuing to watch TV, he balances their checkbook.

Gloria had wanted some sign that she wasn't the only one doing things. And that's what she got. And it was a solid sign, since George did such a good job of it. And the cheerful way he did it reassured her that he didn't feel nagged. And the spontaneous hug he gave her made her feel that they were in it together. And his turning off the TV and balancing the checkbook reminded her that George has his own ways of contributing to the household. And they are real contributions. She hates balancing the checkbook.

So, without their even having to talk about it, the problem was solved. Or was it? To her surprise, Gloria continued to have nagging feelings about it. While she no longer felt all alone in the housework, she wasn't sure that in a few days the feeling wouldn't return. And while George had taken out the trash, he hadn't thought to do it himself; it was still she who had to do all the initiating. And after all was said and done, it was still she who did most of the housework.

But she was feeling good at the moment and dismissed these doubts as quibbles.

TOKENS

In trying to get George to take out the garbage, Gloria is asking for a *token* of what she really wants, which is full participation in the housework. She hopes that this token will snap her into a less lonely and less resentful frame of mind.

Getting our partners to engage in token acts is a common type of action-solution. Life is in some sense a search for tokens that will snap us into better frames of mind. Everyone has wishes and feelings that can't be talked about or even fully thought about. And everyone is forced to deal with these wishes and feelings in indirect and symbolic ways, that is, by means of tokens.

Jennifer doesn't have a good way to talk to her husband Alan about her feeling of being taken for granted. They have never learned how to discuss such things. And she doesn't have a good way to think about it. She simply feels that she shouldn't have such complaints. So instead of such thinking or talking, *she just suddenly finds herself wishing that Alan would bring her flowers.* And as people often do, she expresses this wish as an accusation: "Why don't you ever bring me flowers anymore?" Jennifer hopes that if Alan were to engage in this token act, that is, if he were to bring her flowers, this might revive some part of the early excitement of the relationship and make her feel less taken for granted.

And it does. Two days later, Alan dutifully brings home a dozen roses. And Jennifer melts. She feels loved. She think it's the most beautiful bouquet that anyone has ever been given. And she feels this way even though the flowers are rather ordinary and even though Alan isn't doing it out of a feeling of love. He's simply trying to prevent Jennifer from complaining about him in the future.

Mr. Skeptic: Well yeah, women are overly sentimental. They're forever complaining that their husbands aren't demonstrative enough; at least, my wife is. And they place all this importance on tokens of affection.

Wile: But men do too; it's just not as obvious. Alan thinks it's silly for Jennifer to place such importance on flowers, although he is willing to provide them to keep the peace. He doesn't think it's silly, however, for *him* to place such importance on Jennifer's having his dinners ready when he gets home. Alan thinks that he wants his dinners ready simply because he's hungry. He doesn't realize that an even more important reason is that it makes him feel loved. It gives him the feeling that Jennifer really cares about him and wants to do things for him.

Having his dinners made is as much a token to Alan as getting flowers is to Jennifer. If Jennifer is sentimental about flowers, then Alan is sentimental about dinners. And Alan is as easily pleased as Jennifer is. Jennifer isn't much of a cook. But just as Jennifer feels that Alan's flowers are the most beautiful bouquet that anyone has ever been given, Alan thinks that Jennifer's dinners are the best meals anyone has ever had.

And having his dinners made isn't the only token that Alan seeks. He's touched when Jennifer agrees to watch Monday Night football with him. He melts. He feels really loved. He thinks that they have a terrific relationship.

And sex is another important token for Alan. Alan believes that he is always wanting sex with Jennifer because he is just a horny person. He doesn't think it has anything to do with how he feels about her. And that's what Jennifer thinks too. And that's what turns her off.

Alan *is* always horny. But what he is always horny for is reassurance that Jennifer cares about and will accept him. Sex is as much a token for Alan as flowers are for Jennifer.

SNAPPING INTO A BETTER FRAME OF MIND

Everyone has a set of potential tokens that can snap him or her into better frames of mind.

> Some people melt when they are given flowers. Others feel nothing at all. Or they feel *unloved*. They wonder what the giver might be trying to atone for. Or they notice that one of the flowers seems wilted. And they wonder whether these are week-old flowers sold at a reduced price.

> Some people melt when they are given compliments. It makes their day. Others, given the same compliment by the same person,

feel nothing at all. Or they wonder what the person wants. They
get a creepy feeling about how the world is full of operators.
Some people melt when others want to have sex with them. It raises
their spirits. They feel desirable. Others feel degraded. They feel
treated as sex objects.
Some women melt when their husbands take out the trash. They
suddenly feel close to them. Other women may just become
more aware at such times of all the things their husbands *aren't*
doing.

If people are to use their partners' token acts to snap themselves into
better frames of mind, they must get their partners to engage in these acts.
Some people require very little on the part of the other. They need only
a token of a token. For such a person it might be enough that:

The partner brings him or her a wilted dandelion from the lawn.
The partner simply notices that he or she got a haircut. It's not necessary that the partner say that he or she likes the haircut.
The partner is willing to sit in the same room reading during just the
first quarter of the Monday Night football game.
The partner, after three reminders, halfheartedly empties one wastepaper basket.

Other people require more wholehearted efforts from their partners
to snap themselves into better frames of mind. Two weeks after the occasion in which George took out the trash and then came back and balanced the checkbook, Gloria again became resentful about being the only
one doing housework. This time when she asked George to take out the
trash, however, he put off doing it. He was watching an exciting baseball
game on TV.

George's putting off taking out the trash ruined everything. "I got
irrational," Gloria said the next day to her friend Anne. "I felt like a nag.
George said that he'd take out the trash later, but for some reason I needed
him to do it right away. So I asked him again, and he got upset. He said
he'd be happy to take out the trash, but that he wanted to be able to
decide for himself *when* to take it out. He said I was trying to control him.
And he's probably right. Why else would I insist on his taking out the trash
right away?"

What Gloria and George fail to see, however, is that:

Gloria's needing the trash taken out right away makes sense. In a hidden way, it *is* appropriate to the situation. Gloria has limited what she is asking of George to a fraction of what she really wants. The fact that he hesitates to do even this is understandably upsetting to her.

Gloria *is* uncompromising, but that's only because she has already compromised so much. There's an ordinary adult feeling—her resentment about having to do all the housework—underlying her seemingly "childish" and "uncompromising" attitude. She wishes that *she* had the luxury of being able to sit down and watch a TV show once in a while. And maybe she would if George would help out a little more.

Gloria *does* need complete control of George's trash-emptying behavior, but that's only because she feels she has such little control of so much else in the relationship.

A large part of what passes between partners consists of action-solutions. People try to get one another to provide tokens that will enable them to snap into better frames of mind. Taking out the garbage can be such a token. So can giving flowers. And tokens are the currency of relationships.

Anthropologists say that a lot can be told about a people by the nature of their garbage. I suggest that a lot can be told about a couple by the way they *take out* the garbage.

12

Slogans

Slogan-solutions are attempts to deal with feelings, wishes, complaints, worries, or problems that we are confused, uncertain, or conflicted about:

1. By talking ourselves *into* them; that is, by trying to convince ourselves that maybe it's okay or justified to have these feelings, wishes, complaints, worries, or problems after all.
2. Or by talking ourselves *out of* them; that is, by trying to convince ourselves more fully that we shouldn't be having them.

Slogan-solutions are self-propaganda. Slogan-solutions, like other types of makeshift solutions, are efforts to solve problems despite the fact that we can't think about them. *Un*like other types of makeshift solutions, however, slogan-solutions give the *impression* of thinking.

In the following example, a wife uses an action-solution. And then, when that doesn't work, a slogan-solution: she tries to talk herself out of her worry.

A wife feels bad about her loss of sexual interest in her husband. She is too worried about it to be able to talk or think clearly about it, however. She fears it means that she has a bad marriage. So she engages in an action-solution. She tries to get her husband to behave in ways that might revive her sexual interest in him. She asks him to dress more stylishly.

When this doesn't help, she engages in a slogan-solution. She tells herself that "passion always mellows over time" and that she shouldn't take her loss of sexual interest as meaning that she has a bad marriage.

This wife is using an *idea* to try to solve a problem. She isn't really thinking, however; that is, she isn't conducting an unbiased inquiry into her loss of sexual interest in her husband. Instead, she's trying to *convince* herself of something. She's trying to prove to herself that her loss of sexual interest is nothing to worry about. She's engaging in self-propaganda.

In the following example, a woman attempts an action-solution and then uses *both* types of slogan-solution: she tries to talk herself *out of* her complaint and then tries to talk herself *into* it.

> A woman feels unjustified in her complaint that her husband doesn't help around the house. She improvises a solution. She tries to convince him to make a token contribution such as clearing the table after dinner. Her hope is to reduce her feeling that it's all up to her. Her husband clears the table, but this just makes her more aware that she's doing practically all the work.
>
> So she engages in a slogan-solution. She appeals to the traditional idea that "housework is woman's work." Her effort here is to try to talk herself *out of* her complaint. However, she can't talk herself out of her complaint, and she continues to feel resentful.
>
> So she invokes the opposite slogan-solution. She appeals to the contemporary idea that "husbands should share housework." Her effort here is to try to talk herself *into* her complaint. If she feels sufficiently justified in her complaint, she might be able to state it to her husband and stand behind it: "Marriage is a 50-50 proposition. I've just vacuumed my 50 percent of the rugs. Here's the vacuum cleaner. Now you can do yours."

Much of our mental life is devoted to trying to talk ourselves into or out of our feelings.

THINKING AS AN EXERCISE IN SELF-PROPAGANDA

Where do the slogans come from that people use in slogan-solutions? They come them from the general culture, that is, from folk wisdom, kitchen philosophy, street talk, pop psychology, locker room wisdom, and so on. The following shows how ideas can be pulled in from these various sources.

A man is uncomfortable with his attraction toward his best friend's wife. He sees this as an act of disloyalty to his wife and to this friend. In an attempt to talk himself *out of* this feeling, he tells himself "the grass is always greener on the other side of the fence." This old saying helps him feel that his attraction for his friend's wife is an illusion.

A few minutes later, this man again finds himself preoccupied with sexual feelings toward this woman. This time he tries to talk himself *into* his feelings. He seizes upon a cultural belief that helps him feel *more* justified in having these feelings. "Men are basically polygamous," he tells himself. "Feeling turned on by my friend's wife doesn't mean that I'm disloyal to my wife. It just means that I'm having the polygamous feelings that all men have."

But the reassuring effect of this belief is just as short-lived, and a little later he again feels distracted by sexual feelings toward this woman. He engages in another slogan-solution. In an effort to talk himself *out of* these feelings, he turns to an idea from pop psychology. "I want a committed, meaningful, intimate, and authentic relationship and not just casual affairs." But this idea doesn't get him very far. He is not sure that his relationship with his wife is all that meaningful. And if he is going to be authentic, he could just as easily be authentic with his friend's wife.

He appeals next to male locker room wisdom and he starts putting the blame on her. He sees her as playing with him. "She's just a cocktease," he tells himself. "She doesn't have the good qualities that my wife has. And she's like all flirts. She looks sexy enough, but she's probably cold as hell in bed." But watching the sultry way his friend's wife moves, he has a hard time believing that she really is cold in bed.

And for a moment he gives up trying to talk himself out of his sexual feelings. Instead, he feels angry at his wife. "If she were sexier, I wouldn't be longing after such women."

This man probably believes he's thinking. But "thinking" is an unbiased attempt to figure out what's going on. And what he's doing, instead, is applying slogan after slogan in an effort to find something that might ease his mind.

CULTURALLY SANCTIONED COMPLAINTS

What do people do when they have feelings, wishes, or complaints that they think they shouldn't have and don't know how to talk about?

Max feels neglected by his wife Liz. He doesn't know *why* he feels neglected. In fact he doesn't know *that* he feels neglected. No one in his family ever thought or talked about himself or herself in this way—certainly none of the men. Feeling neglected is an experience Max never learned how to have.

So Max is in a lot of trouble when he is suddenly faced with this feeling that he never learned how to recognize. He takes advantage of Liz coming home a few minutes late to justify a complaint. He says:

MAX: Why are you always so late?

Max is unable to say "I've been feeling neglected." But he *is* able to say, "Why are you always so late?" It's a complaint that people in our culture (and in Max's family) feel justified in making. People are supposed to be on time. And if they are not, others are allowed to complain about it. Liz's lateness provides Max with a culturally sanctioned way of saying that he feels neglected.

Max's complaint may be culturally sanctioned, but it doesn't make much sense. Liz *isn't* always late. In fact, she's almost never late. If there is anyone who is usually late, it's Max himself. Liz can't understand why Max is angry at her. And she doesn't like the fact that he is. She tells him:

LIZ: I'm *not* always late. And the only reason I'm late tonight is that I was waiting in line at the butcher getting a steak for your dinner.

Max doesn't have an answer for this. And so he just mutters to himself. If complaining about Liz's lateness is a stab at saying (and maybe discovering) that he feels neglected, then it's monumentally unsuccessful. How can Max justify feeling neglected when Liz turns out to have gone out of her way to get him a steak?

Remember, a complaint is a clue to a feeling. Max's complaint that Liz is late is a clue to the fact that he feels neglected. But if it's to be used as a clue—that is, if Max and Liz are to *discover* that Max feels neglected—then he may need to be able to think about the problem differently and be able to say something like the following:

MAX: Yeah, you're right. You're hardly ever late. And I feel really foolish since it turns out you were doing something for me—getting a steak. I don't have a leg to stand on. But, for some reason, I still didn't like your being late.

Mr. Skeptic: It's hard to imagine Max saying anything like that.

Wile: Yeah, and that's too bad, because If Max *were* able to make this ideal response, then Liz might be able to say:

LIZ: Well, I think you're onto something. With our tight schedules, our jobs, and our kids, we don't have much time for one another. I've been neglecting you and you've been neglecting me. In fact, my getting you a butcher's steak was my attempt to do something special for you. So maybe you're feeling neglected. And maybe that's what's behind your not liking my being late?

Liz has used Max's complaint about her being late as a clue to discovering that he feels neglected by her.

TRADITIONAL HUSBAND AND WIFE COMPLAINTS

Liz and Max are unable to have this conversation, however. In fact, they hardly talk at all. Instead, Max makes complaints. When they sit down to dinner, he complains that the steak is overcooked. His hidden message is that Liz's overcooking the steak indicates her neglect of him.

His message is *too* well hidden, however. Not even Max knows that this is what he is saying. And complaining that your wife has overcooked a steak that she has gone out of her way to get would strike most people as pretty ungrateful.

After dinner, when Max goes upstairs to change his clothes, he criticizes Liz for putting his socks in his underwear drawer. This complaint is another ineffectual way of saying that he feels neglected.

Again, Max's complaint doesn't make much sense. Max is lucky that Liz put his socks away at all. It's supposed to be *his* job to do the laundry.

These complaints are slogan-solutions. They are appeals to cultural slogans to justify feelings or complaints. They enable Max to justify (to explain) to himself, and to express to Liz, a feeling that he is having difficulty discovering, justifying, and expressing: that he feels neglected.

Complaints about steak and socks are traditional *husband* complaints. They are slogans that husbands call upon when they are having difficulty justifying certain wishes and feelings. They are complaints that husbands feel that they can stand behind, that they are justified in making, and that they have an unquestionable, almost God-given right to have. Husbands have difficulty saying, "I feel neglected" or "You don't seem to love me anymore." But they are able to complain about their wives being late, their meat being overcooked, and their socks being put in the wrong drawer.

Wives, of course, have a set of traditional *wife* complaints that they feel they can stand behind.

Traditional Wife Complaints	Traditional Husband Complaints
You're always late for dinner.	Dinner's never ready on time.
I wish you'd dress in a more stylish way.	I wish you'd dress in a sexier way.
You're too strict with the kids.	You spoil the kids.
You never spend any time with the kids.	You're overinvolved with the kids.
You love your work more than you do me.	You just want a meal ticket.
You're insensitive.	You're oversensitive.
You don't listen to me.	You're always nagging me.
You never want to talk.	You always have to talk about everything.
You don't appreciate what it's like to be with the kids all day.	You don't appreciate what it's like to work all day.
You don't help enough around the house.	You criticize it when I do.
The only time you kiss me is during sex.	You never want to have sex.
You don't bring me flowers anymore.	You don't fix yourself up anymore.
You leave the house a mess.	You keep the house a mess.
You never support me when your mother criticizes me.	You always have to argue with my mother.
I wish you'd be nicer to my parents.	Why do we have to see your parents so often?

Traditional Wife Complaints	Traditional Husband Complaints
You're like another child I have to take care of.	When I come home tired from work, I expect a little consideration.
You want a mother, not a wife.	You're just like my mother.

Husbands have no parallel for the following important complaints that many wives are able to make:

You don't love me anymore.
You're not affectionate enough.

There is also a set of traditional *partner* complaints. These are complaints that *both* husbands and wives feel relatively free to make:

You never want to go out anymore.
You never think of anybody but yourself.
You always have to have the last word.
You always have to have things your way.
Nothing ever satisfies you.

Traditional husband and wife complaints are based on male and female roles. When in doubt many people revert to such traditional complaints. These traditional complaints provide a more solid place from which to make a stand. And husbands and wives employ them even though they may not entirely believe them.

Max feels uncomfortable complaining about his steak and his socks. He doesn't like the image he presents of himself as an old style dictatorial husband. He feels neglected, however, and has no way to talk about it. And, as many people do when they have feelings they don't know how to talk about, he gravitates toward traditional complaints.

BORROWING THE OTHER SEX'S COMPLAINTS
AND THE OTHER SEX'S ANSWERS
TO THESE COMPLAINTS

In the stereotype, the husband comes home and watches TV. The wife, who wants a little contact, complains about his not talking to her. The husband replies that he's tired and that he just needs a little peace and quiet. This conflict can be difficult to resolve.

And it is just as difficult if it's the *husband* who feels neglected and the wife who wants a little peace and quiet. The husband may come home raring to go and the wife may need time to herself after a day taking care of preschoolers. Or, as is common these days, it is the wife who comes home tired from work. Many husbands don't have very direct ways of saying they feel neglected and uncared for. Since traditional husband complaints do not provide very good ways of doing so, husbands may appeal at such times to traditional wife complaints.

After dinner, Max washes the dishes and then goes into the living room to watch TV. He expects Liz to join him. She stays in the dining room, however, catching up on work from the office. Max had been feeling pretty neglected all evening. Now he *really* feels neglected.

If it were Liz who was feeling neglected, she might be able to say something about it. As I said, because of their social training, women have an easier time talking about such feelings, although it is difficult even for them. But Max is totally unable to do so. So he casts around for complaints that he *does* feel comfortable in making.

MAX: You shouldn't do work from the office. You're neglecting your children.

Max can't talk about Liz neglecting him. But he can talk about her neglecting their children. Max's comment doesn't get very far. Liz is upset by it, but she doesn't know what Max is talking about. And neither does Max. The kids are outside playing and they clearly don't care what *either* of their parents is doing. So Max quickly skips to something else:

MAX: The problem is that you don't know how to relax.

This is a traditional *partner* complaint. It is sex-role neutral. It can be used equally well by husbands *and* wives. And it is more to the point than his previous comment. Sensing that he is now on the right track, Max takes it one step further:

MAX: You're a workaholic.

This is a traditional *wife* complaint. However, it's one that husbands can employ also without feeling too uncomfortable. Max continues:

MAX: You're married to your work.

This is another traditional wife complaint. And it's one that men generally feel much too threatened to make. Or at least they would if it were stated in its usual form: "you're married to your work *rather than to me*." Omitting the "rather than to me" enables Max to say it. Even then it makes him a little uneasy.

It's not an accident that Max finds himself using traditional *wife* complaints. Because of their social training, wives have better ways of talking about feeling neglected than do husbands.

Liz responds to Max's traditional wife complaints by making a traditional *husband* complaint:

LIZ: Why do you always have to nag? I wish you'd *support* my working rather than giving me a hard time about it. I'm doing it for the family, after all.

Liz caps it off with particularly powerful traditional wife complaints:

LIZ: You want a mother, not a wife. You're like another child I have to take care of.

Why do Max and Liz pick the particular accusations they do? They pick them because they are culturally sanctioned. Everyone immediately sees them as irrefutable. No one even thinks of replying, "What's so bad about being a nag" or "What's so bad about being a workaholic" or "What's wrong with wanting a mother rather than a wife?" We all just accept the fact that being these things or wanting these things is bad.

And everyone immediately thinks that people accused of such things are guilty, even the persons themselves. How does a woman answer the charge that she's a "neglectful parent"? How does a man answer the charge that he "wants a mother, not a wife"? Although people so accused might try to defend themselves, they secretly worry that these charges might be true.

Max scans his past relationships looking for evidence that he might really be looking for a mother. And he's upset because he thinks he finds some. And of course he finds some. When people scan their pasts looking for such things, they often think they find them; that is, their worries distort what they see. What Max had previously felt to be good, healthy relationships with his previous girlfriends, he now suddenly sees as his "simply looking for a mother."

Similarly, Liz anxiously tries to figure out whether she is a neglectful parent. And she has a hard time completely convincing herself that she isn't. Of course she has a hard time. Parents can easily worry that they are not doing everything they can for their kids.

The problem with such traditional complaints is that they are *too* powerful. They wipe out the partner. They put the partner on the defensive and make it impossible for him or her to listen to what the other wants to say.

At the same time as they are too powerful, they are not powerful enough. They don't say what the partner really wants to say. Max doesn't get to say that he feels neglected. And Liz doesn't get to say that she feels hurt by Max's accusations. These traditional complaints wipe out the other person, and they don't even get across what the partner wants to get across.

But slogan-solutions are also opportunities. Practically everything that Max said was a clue to the fact that he felt neglected:

Why are you always late?
You overcooked the steak.
You put my socks in my underwear drawer.
You're neglecting your children.
You don't know how to relax.
You're a workaholic.
You're married to your work.

And practically everything that Liz said was a clue to the fact that she felt criticized and unsupported:

Stop nagging.
I'm working late for the good of the family.
You want a mother not a wife.
You're like another child I have to take care of.

Ideally partners will be able to use their slogan-solutions not just as solutions but also as clues.

In this chapter and the previous one, I have tried to show the extent to which action-solutions and slogan-solutions dominate our thinking and behavior:

We engage in action-solutions and slogan-solutions to solve what
    appear to us to be unsolvable problems. (A wife who doesn't

know how else to deal with her resentment about having to do all the housework engages in an action-solution: she asks her husband to take out the garbage. And then she engages in a slogan-solution: she tries to talk herself out of her resentment. She tells herself, "Housework is woman's work.")

We seek tokens from our partners to snap us into better frames of mind. (The wife hopes that her husband's taking out the garbage will help her feel less resentful.)

We appeal to cultural slogans to talk ourselves into or out of our feelings, wishes, and complaints. (The wife appeals to the cultural slogan "marriage is a fifty-fifty proposition" to convince herself that she has the right to complain about her husband's not helping more with the housework.)

We engage in such action-solutions, slogan-using (self-propaganda), and token-seeking because we are unable to accept our feelings and thus to think and talk about them. (The wife doesn't realize that feelings are their own justification; that is, she doesn't see that her feelings of resentment are important—they are deserving of her and her husband's attention—simply by virtue of the fact that she has them.)

We are unable to think and talk about our feelings because we are possessed by the five accusing inner voices. (The wife thinks that her feelings are unjustified because she believes that they are the result of her "character defects;" that is, her "need to control," her "predisposition to nag," and her "tendency always to make a big issue out of everything.")

This is how we operate. And we are at a great advantage if we appreciate this fact. We are at a great advantage because it can be useful to realize that:

Our partners are continually struggling to make sense of their feelings, which is why they say some of the weird things that they do.

We are continually struggling to make sense of *our* feelings, which is why *we* say some of the weird things that *we* do.

Our partners are trying to get us to engage in token acts, which is why they get into some of the arguments with us that they do.

We are trying to get our partners to engage in token acts, which is why we get into some of the arguments with them that *we* do.

This information will allow us:

> *Not* to take these tokens and slogans so seriously. They're *just* slogans and tokens, after all.
>
> To *take* these tokens and slogans seriously. You can get a lot of satisfaction and reassurance out of tokens and slogans, after all. And you can use your own or your partner's token-seeking and slogan-using as clues to important, often hidden, issues in the relationship.

*F*IGHTING **IV**

*I*n every chapter so far—whether discussing

> Building your relationship on a problem,
> Using the relationship to cure,
> Becoming skillfully dependent,
> Having the conversation that's been missing,
> Avoiding conversational booby traps,
> Using communication errors as clues,
> Seeking tokens and using slogans,
> Using accusing versus nonaccusing rules of thumb—

the question has been how to talk with your partner without just getting into a fight.

Solve the problem of fighting and you've solved the problem of relationships.

Mr. Skeptic: That's what I've been trying to tell you.

Wile. Of course, the major way we *try* to solve the problem of fighting is what creates many of the worst problems. We try to keep from saying anything that might offend our partners.

Mr. Skeptic: What's wrong with that?

Wile: It can lead to *loss* of love and *decreased* intimacy. And it can lead to even worse fighting when the suppressed resentment finally does break through. People in the encounter group movement of the 1960s attempted to deal with this problem by scrupulously *expressing* all anger. Whereas before it had often been thought a sin to express anger, the encounter group people felt it was a sin *not* to express it. In Chapter 13, I discuss the relative advantages of the "letting it all hang out" and "keeping it well tucked in" approaches.

Mr. Skeptic: I've always been a great believer in "keeping it well tucked in."

Wile: I'm going to show how *both* of these common approaches have serious problems. And in Chapter 14 I'm going to present a new way of thinking and talking about fighting.

By fighting, I mean *verbal* fighting. Physical fighting introduces new elements that require a book in itself to understand.

13

To Fight Or To Withdraw

When people think of couple problems, they usually think of *fighting*. "We had a bad week," partners might say. "We fought the whole time." Or, "We had a good week. We didn't fight at all."

If fighting isn't the couple's main problem, then *withdrawal* often is. "We lead basically separate lives," the partners might say. Or, "We hardly ever have anything to say to one another anymore." Or, "There isn't much spark in the relationship. Things are boring."

Fighting and withdrawal may seem like very different problems. They are intimately related, however. Each leads to the other:

> Partners suppress anger (they withdraw) in order not to fight. At some point, however, their anger breaks through, sometimes resulting in worse fights than if the anger had been expressed in the first place. Distressed by their fights, the partners rededicate themselves to suppressing anger; that is, they again withdraw.

Thus, withdrawal leads to fighting and fighting leads to withdrawal just as dieting leads to binging and binging leads to dieting. Fight-withdrawal cycles are occupational hazards of being a couple:

> Even couples who appear *uninterruptedly* withdrawn have fights. But their fights, limited as they are to looks and innuendoes, are easy to miss.
>
> Even couples who appear *continuously* in battle withdraw. But their periods of withdrawal, overshadowed as they are by the dramatic nature of their fights, are easy to miss.

Fight-withdrawal cycles are unavoidable. Couples differ only in which of the elements—the fighting or the withdrawing—predominates and the extent of the damage wrought. For some these cycles are merely major nuisances, for others they are lethal blows to the relationship.

I said that fighting is a major *problem*. But it can also be a major *solution*. Fighting can clear the air. A husband and wife who begin an evening feeling withdrawn and grumpy can feel connected and cheerful following a fight. "We needed that," they might say.

Mr. Skeptic: That never happens in *my* house. When my wife and I fight, at least one of us always ends up feeling *worse*.

Wile: Well yeah, if fighting *is* to clear the air, both partners need to feel that they have gotten in important licks, and both need to be able to tolerate the licks the other gets in. And that usually doesn't happen. What usually *does* happen is that one or even both partners come away from the fight feeling verbally beaten up.

The give-get ratio is delicately balanced. If one partner feels he or she hasn't gotten his or her point across, or feels particularly stung by something the other said, then the result can be further embroilment rather than a clearing of the air.

> "You should be like me," a husband tells his wife. "I get over fights quickly. I'm angry and then it's over. You *nurse* your anger. You hang onto it for days."

The reason this husband "gets over" his anger, of course, is that he gets his licks in. And the reason this wife "hangs onto" her anger is that she *doesn't* get hers in and, instead, feels verbally trounced by her husband.

So here's the problem of fight-withdrawal cycles: people can fight, which too often leads to one or both partners feeling verbally beaten-up, or they can avoid fights, which, as I shall now show, leads to boredom, loss of love, *and* to fights.

BOREDOM

Long-Term Relationships Are Boring.

At least that is what everyone assumes. The classic picture is of a middle-aged couple watching television together, yawning, and saying little. "In order to keep your relationship alive," the women's magazines say, "you must work at it. Spice up your marriage. Break out of your routine. Become unpredictable. For example, greet your husband at the door one evening wrapped in Saran."

I'm not against breaking out of routine or standing in doorways wrapped in Saran. I think this misses the point, however. The question is not whether partners have routines, but whether these routines are *satisfying*. Boredom is the result not of routines but of *unpleasant* routines. It's the result of unexpressed feelings, held-back complaints, and suppressed anger.

Carol and Fred have been married 20 years. She is a computer programmer and he is an electrician. They are bored by their life of watching television nightly and going out once a week to a restaurant, a movie, or bowling. The problem is not this routine in itself, although this is what they believe, but what happens while carrying out the routine.

> It's Saturday night, their night out. Carol suggests that they see a movie. Although she would like to see a tear jerker, she mentions an action film, which she thinks Fred might prefer. Although Fred really wants to go bowling, he agrees to the movie. He has said "no" to several of her recent suggestions for movies and thinks he owes her a "yes."

To start with, then, neither is doing what he or she really wants to do. Fred doesn't want to go to a movie and Carol wants to see a different movie. Each feels a little resentful. Neither says anything about it, however. Each is trying to be considerate of the other—an example of the unspoken compromises and self-sacrifices that everyone continually makes.

So Fred drives them to the movie. On the way there, Carol is upset by the way Fred cuts in front of another driver. But she keeps this criticism to herself, knowing that Fred hates her back-seat driving. (In fact, she hates it in herself. She doesn't want to be like her mother, who's an inveterate back-seat driver.) Although Carol says nothing about it, Fred senses her criticism. She is tense in the way she usually gets when she is disapproving. But he, too, says nothing about it.

Later in line, waiting to get into the movie, they stand slightly apart, dispirited, not talking. Whatever enthusiasm or good will they might have had at the beginning of the evening is gone. They notice a young couple arm-in-arm, laughing, talking, and involved. Carol and Fred think to themselves, "We used to be like that. What's become of us? We've become a tired and bored middle-aged couple in a rut. Look what twenty years have done to us."

What has become of Carol and Fred is not twenty years, but twenty years of evenings like the one they are having. Boring evenings, which lead to a boring relationship, are the consequence of sitting on your feelings.

Let's try to imagine the conversation that might rescue Carol and Fred from their boring evening (and boring relationship).

CAROL: That young couple laughing and talking and holding hands makes me a little jealous. Things have gotten so humdrum and boring between us lately.

There are hazards in this statement, which is why Carol hesitates to make it. Fred, who might not be used to thinking of their relationship as "boring," might deny that it was. Carol would then feel *more* lonely. She'd feel that Fred wasn't *even* with her in feeling bored. Or Fred might think he's being *criticized* for making their life boring, for not laughing and talking enough, and for not holding hands with her. If so, he's likely to defend himself:

FRED: I'm just not in the mood for holding hands.

But let's imagine that Fred *doesn't* become defensive and instead says:

FRED: Yeah, I'm feeling the same way. They remind me of how we used to be. It makes me sad that we've lost all that.

It's an intimate moment, even if Carol and Fred are expressing the worry that they are *not* intimate. It's an opening. Their worlds temporarily interlock.

Mr. Skeptic: Yeah, but what are they going to say next?: "I guess things are hopeless; maybe we should get a divorce." I don't see where this conversation's going or how it could possibly lead to anything useful.

Wile: Well, if this conversation *is* to go somewhere and if it *is* to lead to something useful, Carol and Fred need an important piece of information. They need to know that their boredom isn't just something that has happened over time, but is continually being recreated in the present.

Here is what Carol might say if she were to have this important piece of information:

CAROL: You know, I think a lot of the problem is trying to be so nice to one another. For one thing, I didn't even really want to see this movie.

I only suggested it because I thought *you* wanted to see it. What I really wanted to see was *An Affair to Remember* playing across town. So I've already bored myself even before we got here, by bringing us to a movie that I didn't even want to see.

It could be a big relief to Carol to tell Fred how she really felt about the movie. She would be taking a major step toward *unboring* herself. And Fred might then be able to say:

FRED: Well, I've bored myself even before we got here, too, because I didn't tell you that I didn't want to see *any* movie.

Having said this, Fred, too, might feel better.

CAROL: I can't believe this. Here we are coming all the way across town to stand in this long line to see a movie that neither of us wants to see.

FRED: It's pretty funny when you think about it.

CAROL: Remind me, the next time I drag you to a movie, to drag you to one that *I* like. At least, then, *one* of us will be happy.

FRED: Well, what are we doing standing on this stupid line? Let's go get an ice cream and forget this movie.

And as Carol and Fred walk down the street laughing, the young couple in line who are holding hands say to themselves, "Wouldn't it be wonderful if we were still that much in love when we got to be their age?"

FALLING OUT OF LOVE

Relationships get boring—and people fall out of love—when they are unable to say what they need to say. Here's an example.

Joseph and Karen are a couple in their thirties. Joseph is a dentist. Karen left her job as a surgical nurse to take care of their three small children.

Joseph comes home tired from work. Karen meets him at the door and barrages him with problems from the day. She says that the kids behaved terribly and that he will have to speak to them, that the refrigerator is on the fritz and that he will have to fix it, and that the bank messed up their account and that he will have to straighten it out.

Joseph *feels* like telling her, "Can't you even wait until I take off my coat? I don't want to hear about *anything* until I've had a chance to sit down with the paper and relax a little. And, anyway, can't you take care of anything by yourself?''

I said that Joseph *feels* like saying this. But before he gets a chance to do so, his internal prosecutor takes over:

JOSEPH (to himself): Wait a minute, Joseph. Before you say anything, think about it. If you want to get into a fight and ruin the evening, go ahead and say what you're about to say. But if you want to have any kind of decent evening at all, cool it. Don't be such a baby. You don't even mean half of it, anyway. You're just mad. Getting angry isn't going to help. Look at it from Karen's point of view. She clearly has had a difficult day. Show a little consideration. A little tact never hurt anyone.

Mr. Skeptic: Joseph's internal prosecutor is someone after my own heart. I hope Joseph listens to him.

Wile: He does. Joseph bites his lip. He says that he'll speak to the kids after dinner, look at the refrigerator when the kids go to bed, and take care of the bank in the morning. He then does what he wanted to do in the first place. He fixes himself a drink and sits down with the paper.

Joseph's internal prosecutor is pleased:

JOSEPH (to himself): Isn't that better? You avoid a fight, you avoid hurting Karen's feelings, and look, you even get what you wanted in the first place: a chance to sit down and read the paper undisturbed.

Unfortunately, Joseph *doesn't* quite get what he wants, even though he and his internal prosecutor think he does. He wants to sit down with the paper, and he gets that, but he wants to do so feeling contented with his wife, and he doesn't get that. He feels distant from her.

No one realizes that anything is wrong. Joseph is sitting there as always reading the paper. The kids wander through and they don't see any difference. Karen comes out to water the plants and she doesn't see any difference. And Joseph himself, sitting there, doesn't think there's any difference either. There are clues that something is wrong, but they are easy to overlook:

Clue one: Joseph isn't enjoying the paper as much as he usually does, a clear sign that he hasn't recovered from feeling barraged at the door. But he dismisses this sign. He just thinks the *Tribune* is particularly dull that day.

Clue two: Joseph doesn't feel like doing what he usually does: get up from the paper after a few minutes and wander into the kitchen to chat with Karen. Joseph figures that it's probably because he's tired. And Karen figures that it's probably because Joseph has found an interesting story in the paper.

Clue three: Joseph doesn't have much to say during dinner, which surprises him because there are events at work that he had been looking forward to telling Karen. But he figures that maybe he's just tired of thinking about work.

By this time, however, Karen begins to sense that something's up.

KAREN: You're not saying anything. Is something wrong?

Since by this time Joseph has forgotten what's wrong (that he felt barraged at the door and was unable to say anything about it), he can't tell her. All he can say is:

JOSEPH: No, nothing's wrong. I guess I'm just tired.

Karen is mostly convinced by this. People *do* get tired. She knows she feels tired herself. She prepares herself for an evening with a tired and withdrawn man.

After dinner, and after talking to the kids as he said he would, Joseph goes out and tinkers with the car. Karen, feeling shut out, thinks of going out and talking to him. But she can't think of what she'd say. Instead, she calls a friend. Joseph comes in and, overhearing the call, feels momentarily left out himself. Karen seems so much more spirited and lively talking to this friend than she is with him. After helping Karen put the kids to bed, and after looking at the refrigerator as he said he would, Joseph sits down with her to watch TV. Again, Karen and Joseph find themselves with little to say to one another.

The withdrawal isn't a clearly angry one. If it were, they would at least know what was happening to them. And Karen and Joseph aren't completely silent, since they continue to talk about practical matters such as babysitting arrangements and weekend plans.

In fact, it's easy to miss that these partners are withdrawn at all, since the evening just described is so similar to every other couple's evenings. Even couples that fight a lot are withdrawn much of the time. People continually lose track of their wishes and complaints. And they continually withdraw.

Joseph has avoided getting into a fight or hurting Karen's feelings. The cost, though, is an evening of flatness and withdrawal.

The effect of many unstated complaints over many such evenings is a steadily increasing withdrawal between partners and a steadily increasing loss of energy, interest, love, intimacy, and involvement.

EXPRESSING VERSUS SUPPRESSING ANGER: A DEBATE

Here's my point: expressing anger can lead to a loss of love. But *suppressing* anger can do so too. It's an issue that requires a full-fledged debate. And here are the debaters:

To argue for the importance of *expressing* anger: Camille. Remember her? She's from Chapter 10. She was a passenger in Tom's car. She's the one who uses the point-not-gotten-across rule of thumb. Camille is the natural person to represent this side in the debate, since she believes that problems arise when partners are *unable* to express the feelings they need to express.

To argue for the importance of *suppressing* anger: Mr. Skeptic, the reader who's been arguing with me throughout the book. Mr. Skeptic is the natural person to take this side in the debate, since he believes that problems take care of themselves if you don't always have to talk about them so much.

I'm on Camille's side, since she represents one of the types of reasoning I'm trying to promote. I must admit, however, that Mr. Skeptic has some powerful points of his own to make.

Camille (beginning the debate): Here's why it's important to express anger. If you *don't* express your feelings—if you *suppress* your anger—you're going to pay for it eventually. It will fester and come back to haunt you.

Mr. Skeptic: But wait a minute. It doesn't *always* fester. And it doesn't *always* come back to haunt you. You're forgetting that suppressing anger sometimes works. I was angry at my wife last week for making us late for a party. But I held my tongue and, a few minutes later, I could hardly remember the grudge. I went on to have a grand time. Suppression didn't worl. for Joseph *this* time. But I'll bet there were times in the past when exactly the same thing happened—he felt barraged by Karen at the door—but he overlooked it and went on to have a great evening with Karen.

Camille: But Mr. Skeptic, that's part of the problem. The fact that suppression seems at times to work is what makes it so appealing to try. The thought "why make an issue of it?" and "let sleeping dogs lie" is almost irresistible. It's irresistible even for me. I put aside resentments all the time. It's so easy to think that bringing them up will just ruin the good mood between my husband and me. "Ignore your resentment," I tell myself. "Maybe it'll go away." Sometimes it does and sometimes it doesn't.

Mr. Skeptic: Well sure, suppression doesn't always work. Irritable comments or sarcastic remarks can sneak out no matter how hard you try to hold them back. Totally suppressing them may be impossible, but I'm for trying.

Camille: I don't think it's worth it. Remember, we're talking about how boredom develops and how love is lost. And love is lost because of what people do to try to keep it. They try to keep it by suppressing complaints. And suppressing complaints *weakens* love.

Mr. Skeptic: Maybe it does, but it shouldn't.

Camille: Maybe it shouldn't, but it does. And it's not hard to see *why* it does. How are you going to have positive feelings if you don't get a chance to express your negative ones?

Mr. Skeptic: Yeah, but what usually happens when you express negative feelings is that your partner gets angry and you get into a fight.

Camille: Well, maybe that's so, but it's too bad.

Mr. Skeptic: Well, maybe it's too bad, but it's so. And there's something else. What about people who don't *want* to express their negative feelings? They think it's a good thing to be tolerant, polite, conscientious, considerate, gracious, generous, understanding, and uncomplaining. They're proud of their ability to overlook their resentments and to turn the other cheek. They enjoy seeing themselves as remaining unprovoked and unperturbed no matter what happens. What about them? Are you saying that they have to express their anger even if they don't want to?

Camille: Now wait just a minute . . .

Mr. Skeptic: No. I'm *not* going to wait just a minute. I know your type. You're talking just the way people in the Encounter Group movement in the 1960s used to talk. Before the 1960s, people were told "you shouldn't express your anger." In the 1960s, they were told "you've got to express your anger." People came home from Encounter Group weekends and immediately alienated everyone. It didn't take them long to figure out that they'd better cool it if they wanted to keep their friends and their jobs. I thought we got rid of you encounter group people twenty years ago.

Camille: That's a pretty low blow—associating me with encounter groups. Apparently *you* don't have any difficulty expressing *your* anger.

Mr. Skeptic: Excuse me. I got a little carried away there.

Camille: I'm not telling people that they *have* to express their anger. I'm just saying that people are at an advantage if they know that the loss of love and the increased boredom they feel are a result of suppressing anger or complaints. Partners may know all this and decide to build their relationship on politeness and graciousness, anyway. But at least they'll realize—and they won't be surprised—that the cost may be a weakening of their passions.

IN DEFENSE OF MUTUAL WITHDRAWAL

So what does this debate prove? And who won? Mr. Skeptic correctly warns against the danger of telling people that they *have* to express their anger. As he said, this is the mistake made by some in the Encounter Group movement.

We need to remember that the tendency to suppress anger (and to withdraw) is universal. Every couple does it, and every couple does it a lot. Even partners who have lots of fights, or who continually snipe at one other, have periods in which they carefully try to avoid offending one another. And it's understandable that they might. As Mr. Skeptic said, uncontrolled arguments can lead to big problems.

When you think about it, withdrawn partners are just more successful at doing what everyone else is trying to do. Nearly everyone thinks it's a good thing to overlook petty annoyances and to avoid unnecessarily making issues out of things. And nearly everyone tries to do these things. But whereas most people can do them for just so long before rebelling against the whole effort and becoming angry or sarcastic, withdrawn couples can remain polite and respectful indefinitely. They are penalized for being so good at what we were all taught to do.

They are penalized but they are also rewarded. Partners who can't stop fighting might long for such a relationship in which they are spared the bitter unresolvable arguments and the demoralizing unrelenting bickering that plague so many couples.

CONCLUSION

So here's the situation. Avoiding fighting is impossible for some couples and is unwise for many others: it leads to boredom and loss of love. But the only alternative, fighting, has its own problems: it leads to turmoil and bitterness.

> We can express our anger and get into a fight that ruins the evening. Or we can withhold our anger and become withdrawn, which ruins the evening. The choice is only *which way* to ruin the evening.

What's needed is a new way of thinking about anger and fighting. That's what I'm going to talk about in the next chapter.

14

The Facts of Fighting

*I*f avoiding fights isn't the answer, let's *have* fights, *but do a better job of it*. Let's become skillful fighters. In this chapter, I shall try to describe how to do this. The ideal is to be able to:

1. Express your anger,
2. Without permanently damaging your relationship,
3. And, if possible, *benefitting* from it.

When people discuss skillful fighting, they usually talk about limiting and controlling the fight. Partners are told to express anger in a way that doesn't get their partners too upset. They are told to obey the following *rules of fair fighting*, which parallel the rules of good communication described in Chapter 7 (the idea of "fair fighting" was developed by George Bach in his book, *The Intimate Enemy*):

Don't hit below the belt.
Don't name-call.
Don't dredge up things from the past.
Don't store up complaints and then dump them on your partner.
Express feelings rather than make accusations.
Make only constructive criticisms.
Acknowledge what your partner has just said rather than immediately
    argue with it.
And, in general, cool it.

These all seem like good principles, and I follow them whenever possible. Unfortunately, these rules of fair fighting are hardest to follow just when you need them most.

That's because people aren't interested in fair fighting when they're angry. They are interested in winning, that is, in landing verbal punches and avoiding those of their partners. In the middle of a fight, the rules of fair fighting seem ridiculous, if anyone can even think of them at all.

Feeling stung by their partners' accusations, people have an over-powering need to sting back. Feeling frustrated by their partners' refusal to acknowledge any of their points, they seek ever more powerful, which means ever more inflammatory, means to make these points. Feeling increasingly less understood, they feel increasingly less like providing the one thing their partners need: acknowledgment of *their* points so that *they* can feel understood. So, here's my idea:

If getting people to limit themselves to noninflammatory forms of fighting (by obeying the rules of fair fighting) doesn't work, let's not require it. In fact, let's not require that they necessarily say or do *anything* different than they are already saying or doing. Let's just have them *think* differently.

In fact, let's have them think differently in eighteen ways.

THE EIGHTEEN FACTS OF FIGHTING

People may think that they know everything about fighting, but they don't. There are eighteen things in particular that they don't know or that they forget when they most need to remember.

I shall use the case of Karen and Joseph as a frame of reference. As you remember, these were the partners who spent the evening in mutual withdrawal. Each wished to be greeted by a loving and attentive partner who would make up for the difficult day. It didn't work out that way, however. Karen greeted Joseph not with a Bloody Mary and a smile, which is what he would have liked, but with a request that he speak to the kids, fix the refrigerator, and straighten out their checking account. Here is the argument they might have had if Joseph had expressed his resentment (which may be why he tried so hard to suppress it):

JOSEPH: Can't you even wait until I take off my coat for heaven's sake. I don't want to hear about *anything* until I've had a chance to sit down with the paper and relax a moment. You never think of anybody but yourself. It would never occur to you that I've been working hard all day. And, anyway, can't you take care of anything by yourself? Do I have to do everything?

KAREN: Well you don't have to jump down my throat.

JOSEPH: I'm not jumping down your throat. I'm just telling you how I feel. And, anyway, I'll stop jumping down your throat when you stop ambushing me at the door.

KAREN: I'm not ambushing you. I'm just telling you about the day I had. And, anyway, you've got some nerve saying that *you* do everything around here. You never do anything. You're like another child I have to pick up after.

JOSEPH: Well, I'd do a lot more if you didn't nag me all the time.

KAREN: Well, if you think I nag you all the time, why do you stick around?

JOSEPH: Well, maybe I won't.

KAREN: That's just like you. A little argument and you're talking divorce.

JOSEPH: I'm not talking divorce. *You're* talking divorce. You're the one who said "Why do you stick around?"

KAREN: Yeah, and *you're* the one who said "Maybe I won't."

JOSEPH: This is getting nowhere. (Turns to leave).

KAREN: That's just like you. A little fight and you head for the hills. You don't have the guts to stick around and talk it out.

JOSEPH: But you're a crazy woman. There's no way to talk to you.

KAREN: How would you know? You don't stay long enough to find out.

JOSEPH: This is too much (slams the door behind him).

This is an example of a quickly escalating fight. Three exchanges and the subject of divorce comes up. Five more and Joseph can't stand it and has to leave.

With this interchange in mind, let's go over the facts of fighting. First, here they are listed. People in a fight need to know that:

1. Their fight is unresolvable because neither partner is able to get across the important points he or she needs to get across.
2. Their fight may be a consequence of efforts to keep the peace.
3. What people are saying may be more accusing than they realize.
4. Accusing turns the other person into someone who won't listen.

5. Fighting and discussing don't mix, and it may be necessary to have the fight first. A fight is not a time to expect to work out issues, even though this may be the only time that partners ever bring up these issues.

6. People employ powerful, irrefutable, culturally sanctioned complaints to try to get across points they are having difficulty getting across.

7. Fights lead to predictable spin-off fights that may be as distressing as the original fight.

8. The initial statements of held-back complaints are likely to be exaggerated.

9. The initial accusations may simply be rough first approximations.

10. A fight may be the only entry point to a needed conversation.

11. Fighting can escalate so quickly that partners may fail to realize that the fight is based on a simple misunderstanding. Or they may be so angry by the time they *do* realize it that they no longer care.

12. Making a complaint may be an alternative to withdrawing.

13. Anger drives out feelings; people who are angry don't realize that they aren't talking about any of their feelings and that they have lost awareness of most of them.

14. Your partner is more likely to listen to you if you *report* your anger (that is, say that you are angry) than if you *express* your anger (that is, say angry things). Your partner is even more likely to listen to you if you report the *hurt* or *disappointment* that underlies your anger.

15. Complaints, however inflammatory, are often remnants of forgotten fantasy-expectations.

16. Complaints are often remnants of simple and ordinary wishes.

17. One way to get your partner to listen to you is to discover the ways in which you agree with what your partner has just said and go on from there to make your point.

18. Talking about your partner's contribution to the fight is likely to rekindle the fight.

Let's take these one at a time.

Mr. Skeptic: I'm not sure I'm entirely up to taking *eighteen* facts one at a time. It seems like an awful lot.

Wile: Well, if you like, skip them for the time being and turn to page 180 where I describe how knowing these facts puts you in a better position. You can come back to them later.

Fight fact 1: *people need to know that their fight is unre-solvable because neither partner is able to get across any of his or her points.*

That's what a fight is: two people who are unable to get across their points. Whenever I see a fight (or find myself in one), I immediately assume that *that's* what's happening. People are *unable* to get their points across because:

> They aren't stating them clearly.
> They don't *know* what their points are (and thus have no chance at
> all of getting them across).
> Their partners aren't listening.

And, of course, their partners *aren't* listening. A fight is going on, and the point in a fight is to refute what the other says rather than to listen to it. In a fight, neither participant has any interest in hearing what the other has to say until the other hears what he or she has to say.

> Joseph needs Karen to appreciate that he felt barraged at the door
> before he will have any interest in appreciating that she felt jumped
> on. But that won't happen because Karen needs Joseph to ap-
> preciate that she felt jumped on before she will have any interest
> in appreciating that he felt barraged at the door.
> And Joseph needs Karen to appreciate that he can feel at times that
> everything is up to him before he will have any interest in ap-
> preciating that she felt all day that everything is up to her. But
> that won't happen because Karen needs Joseph to appreciate
> that she felt all day that everything is up to her before she will
> have any interest in appreciating that he can feel at times that
> everything is up to him.

If a fight is two people who are not listening to the other's points, then the way out of the fight is for one of them to begin to listen. As soon as partner A softens a bit and begins to acknowledge a little of what partner B has been saying, partner B might then soften a bit and acknowledge a little of what partner A has been saying.

If Karen were to say "Well, I can see how you could have felt barraged by all the things I asked you to do," then Joseph might soften a little and admit his own contribution to the problem ("Well, I did come down pretty hard on you. It was difficult for me to deal with your requests because I had an awful day") and begin to acknowledge Karen's feelings ("And it looks like you had an awful day, too.").

I don't mean that people should be able to make such acknowledging statements *during* the fight. That's too much to ask. It's certainly more than I want to ask of myself. But knowing this fact of fighting—that is, knowing that your fight is unresolvable because neither you nor your partner is getting across any points—can enable you to feel less bewildered by the fight and can make it easier to pick up the pieces afterwards (to sit down with your partner and figure out what happened).

The following is the inner dialogue of a person (let's say Joseph) who knows this first fact of fighting and is able to make good use of it:

JOSEPH (to himself): Since Karen and I are fighting, that means that we both have a point that we're unable to get across. So let me try to figure out what her point is that she is unable to get across, and let me also try to figure out what my point is that *I* am unable to get across.

Fight fact 2: *partners need to know that their fights may be consequences of their efforts to keep the peace.*

The readiness with which partners accuse one another makes it easy for them to forget that the cause of their fights may be efforts to *avoid* fights. They suppress resentment, which sets the stage for sudden mutual outpourings of resentment—fights.

Partners who recognize that fights may be consequences of their efforts to keep the peace may be protected against the nightmare view that their fights simply are signs that they are incompatible or basically hate one another.

Fight fact 3: *people need to know that what they are saying may be more accusing than they realize.*

In a fight, people tend to underestimate the provocative effects of what they say while fully experiencing the provocative effects of what their partners say. Joseph thinks it's irrational and oversensitive of Karen to get so upset over his saying "This is getting nowhere." He thinks he's just saying what's true. Karen thinks it's irrational and oversensitive of Joseph to get so upset over *her* saying "That's just like you. One little fight and you head for the hills." She thinks *she's* just saying what's true. Neither realizes how provocative these remarks are.

If people believe that they are simply—

Stating facts,
Expressing their feelings,
Responding to their partners' accusations,

and they don't realize that they are doing so in an accusing way, they will be puzzled by their partners' angry or defensive response. They may conclude that there is no way to reason with their partners and that talking doesn't help.

The following rules of thumb can be used to protect against this danger:

If my partner starts accusing or getting defensive for no apparent reason, it's possible that I have just accused him or her without knowing it.

If my partner is surprised by how accusing or defensive I get, it's possible that he or she may have just accused me without knowing it.

Here is the inner dialogue of a person (let's say Karen) who uses this rule of thumb:

KAREN (to herself): Joseph just said an outrageous thing—he called me a "crazy woman"—so *maybe I just accused him without even knowing it.* And now that I think about it, I *did.* I *thought* I was just expressing my feelings, but what I actually did was accuse him of heading for the hills and of having no guts. Those are pretty provocative things to say. Maybe "crazy woman" is mild compared to what he *could* have called me.

In realizing that Joseph was responding to what she now recognizes to be her own provocative remarks, Karen is discovering an appropriateness in what she at first believed to be Joseph's totally inappropriate comment.

Fight fact 4: *people need to know that accusing turns the other person into someone who won't listen.*

We all *sort* of know this. We sense that the more we argue and accuse, the less our partners listen. In the heat of the moment, it is easy to lose awareness of this fact, however, and to feel that we can *force* our partners to listen if only we find the *right* arguments.

> **Fight fact 5:** *people need to know that fighting and discussing don't mix and that it's necessary to have the fight first. A fight is not a time to expect to work out issues, even though this may be the only time that partners ever bring up these issues.*

We often try to express anger (have an argument) and discuss issues (have a conversation) at the same time. We forget that the two are incompatible. The point of a discussion is to listen to and to build on what the other says, whereas the point of an argument is to disregard and to refute what the other says.

The belief that you are having a discussion when you are really having an argument is what has given talking a bad name. Partners come away from such an interaction all the more convinced that talking just makes things worse.

I'm not saying that people *shouldn't* argue with or accuse one another. In fact, it may be important at times to be able to do so. I'm just saying that it's difficult to have a conversation and a fight at the same time and that it's necessary to have the fight first. That's because people who have strong feelings about a matter can't listen or think until they've had a chance to express some of their feelings. Later on, and if the fight provides each a chance to have his or her say, it may be possible to have a conversation.

> **Fight fact 6:** *people need to know that they and their partners employ powerful and, at times, devastating and irrefutable, culturally sanctioned complaints or slogans in an attempt (1) to get across points they are having difficulty getting across and (2) to justify feelings and wishes that they are having difficulty justifying.*

In an attempt to get their points across, people appeal to anything that they think might break through the other person's defenses, as I described in the chapter on slogan-solutions (Chapter 12):

Joseph called Karen a "nag," a powerful insult in our culture, particularly when expressed about a woman.

Karen accused Joseph of "having no guts," another powerful insult in our culture, particularly when expressed about a man.

People use slogan-solutions not only to break through their partners' defenses but also to override their own personal doubts about what they are saying. In an effort *to justify feelings* they are having difficulty justifying, people latch onto whatever complaints they can feel at least a little justified in making. Karen and Joseph did not feel entitled to tell one another that they were disappointed that the other didn't automatically cheer them up from their difficult days. So they had to resort to slogans.

Joseph felt at least partly and momentarily justified in making certain standard, culturally sanctioned husband complaints: "It would never occur to you that I've been working hard all day."

Similarly, Karen felt at least partly and momentarily justified in making certain familiar, culturally sanctioned wife complaints: "You never do anything. You're like another child I have to pick up after."

Such culturally sanctioned complaints are the closest that Karen and Joseph came to talking about their fantasy wishes that the other make up for their difficult days.

Knowledge of the fact that they and their partners use powerful, irrefutable culturally sanctioned complaints will enable people to understand why they are so affronted by what their partners say and why their partners are so affronted by what they say. And knowing this may enable them to feel less affronted.

Fight fact 7: *people need to know that fights lead to predictable spin-off fights that may be as distressing as the original fight.*

Partners will be at an advantage if they establish a joint awareness of the pattern of their fights, and, in particular, the common spin-off fights they can get into. The more partners know about their fights, the better prepared they will be to handle them and the better able they will be to talk about them afterwards.

The following pattern occurs with such regularity with so many couples that it can be considered a standard sequence in a couple fight:

STAGE ONE: *A slashing argument.* For some couples a "slashing argument" is a three-day yelling match; for others it is an exchange of looks. For Karen and Joseph it's two minutes of angry exchange in which both partners feel so stung by what the other says that they lash out with anything that might penetrate what at the moment seems to them the impenetrable defense of the other.

STAGE TWO: *An argument over whether to continue the argument.* Joseph says that it's stupid to continue arguing and that they should each go off alone and cool off. Karen says that they shouldn't run away from their problems but should try to talk them out. A new argument, sometimes more intense then the original one, occurs over this issue.

STAGE THREE: *Sulking.* At some point they do stop. Each goes off and sulks.

STAGE FOUR: *Peacemaking attempt by partner A.* Karen, who cools down quicker and who is made more nervous by the fight, makes a peace overture. Joseph isn't ready, and rebuffs the overture. This enrages Karen who becomes particularly incensed at the fact that she's always the first to try to make peace.

At times, Karen tries to make peace even before *she* is ready; she is still angry but doesn't realize it. Her peace overture has a barb to it, and Joseph responds angrily. Karen, not knowing about the barb, sees Joseph as getting angry at her for no reason and becomes angry herself.

STAGE FIVE: *Peacemaking attempt by partner B.* Joseph has now cooled down and makes a peace overture. But Karen, angered by the rejection of her own attempt, is no longer interested. She rebuffs his attempt.

STAGE SIX: *Cooling down period.* Nothing more is said that evening and they go to bed without a word. Karen sleeps poorly, upset about the fight. Joseph is also upset, but is able to sleep well. Karen resents Joseph for being able to sleep.

STAGE SEVEN: *Sudden end of fight.* They wake up the next morning and go on as if nothing has happened. No one says anything about the fight. They are worried that doing so will just start it up again. They're just glad it's over.

This is the general pattern that Karen, Joseph, and a great number of us continually repeat.

We're in a better position if we are able jointly to construct such a natural history of our fights. The realization that these are common patterns —that is, that a great many other couples go through them—can make them easier to deal with. We won't have to feel that there is something wrong with us for having these patterns.

As the example shows, much of the problem comes from attempts to solve the problem. Karen's efforts to seek a reconciliation before Joseph was ready, or before *she* was ready, led to intensified fighting. Recognizing this irony—that attempts to solve the problem may increase the problem —can help partners deal with this intensified fighting.

> **Fight fact 8:** *people need to know that the initial statements of held-back complaints are likely to be exaggerated.*

If people take their partners' initial wild accusations and angry ulti- matums at face value—as how their partners really feel about them deep down—they may have no alternative but to feel threatened and to respond angrily or defensively. If they realize, however, that their partners' accu- sations and ultimatums are exaggerated and that their partners are soon likely to take a more moderate stance, they will feel less threatened by them, will take them less personally, and may choose simply to wait for the explosion to pass.

Here's what Karen might say to herself if she *were* to realize that Joseph's statements—"You never think of anyone but yourself" and that "I always have to do everything"—were exaggerated:

> Maybe Joseph is coming out with all this stuff in such an angry way because he's been holding it back. Maybe he doesn't really hate me as much as he seems to and, if I wait a few minutes, he'll talk in a more moderate manner.

Karen may still go on to say exactly what she was going to say ("Well, you don't have to jump down my throat"), but she'll feel less upset and less provoked. And any shift in the direction of feeling less upset and less provoked can make a big difference.

Fight fact 9: *people need to know that their (or their partners')*
initial accusations may simply be rough first approximations.

Not only are these initial statements exaggerated, they may not even
be about the right issues. Although partners may know they are angry,
they may not know exactly what they are angry about.

People who realize that their partners' initial accusations are simply
rough first approximations will be able to avoid mistaking these accusations
as the final word on the matter. They may thus be able to avoid getting
into arguments over statements that a few minutes later the person making
the charge may discover that he or she doesn't even really mean. Here is
what Karen might say to herself if she knew this fact of fighting:

KAREN (to herself): I don't like Joseph's accusing me of being selfish. But
　　　maybe that isn't even what he's really angry about. Before I get upset,
　　　maybe I ought to wait to be sure what it is that's really bothering him.

Joseph may need the chance to lay out all the different feelings and
complaints he has in order to discover what his real concerns are. He may
need to say "You never think of anybody but yourself" in order to realize
that what he's really upset about is that he and Karen seem to have drifted
apart; they haven't been talking lately.

What Joseph originally experienced as Karen's not reaching out to
him ("You never think of anybody but yourself"), he now sees as a *mutual*
problem: they had drifted apart. *Neither* had been reaching out to the
other.

It would be a shame if Joseph and Karen were to become bogged
down arguing whether or not Karen thinks only about herself when his
real concern is that the two of them haven't been talking.

Fight fact 10: *people need to know that an argument may be*
the only entry point to a needed conversation.

Everyone knows that people say many things in fights that they don't
mean. And everyone knows that fights may be the only times that people
are able to say certain things that they *do* mean. People don't sufficiently
appreciate, however, how this latter fact can be turned to advantage.

Joseph's complaint that Karen thinks only about herself could lead later on to a conversation in which they discover that:

> Joseph misses their not talking much together anymore.
> Karen does also.
> It's easy for them to get caught up in the rush of everyday activities and forget to talk.
> And they are already feeling much better now that they *are* talking, even though what they're talking about is how they haven't been talking.

Joseph's angry statement that Karen never thinks of anybody but herself could be used as an entry point to this important conversation.

> **Fight fact 11:** *people need to know that, when angry, it's easy to overlook the possibility that the argument may be based on a simple misunderstanding.*

Two teenagers—a boy and a girl—were eating a pizza. There was one piece left. The boy asked "Are you going to eat it?" The girl got enraged, stalked out, and didn't talk to him for two weeks.

What happened? The girl took the boy's question as disapproval of her for eating so much and for being so fat. And that's too bad because the boy wasn't thinking about her being fat at all; he was thinking about *his* being hungry. He was asking her if she wanted the last piece of pizza because if she didn't, *he* did.

Joseph was upset at Karen for failing to turn on the coffeemaker when she got up one morning before he did. (He was the only coffee drinker in the house.) He saw this as showing that she was selfish and uncaring and had no interest in his needs. He got so angry about it, and Karen got so rattled and so angry in return, that they never got the chance to see that the whole thing resulted from a simple misunderstanding. Karen had decided not to turn on Joseph's coffee because she didn't know when he would get up and she thought he would want his coffee fresh. What Joseph took as Karen's lack of concern for his needs was actually an *expression* of concern for them.

I don't mean that people should hold off getting angry until they check out every avenue of possible misunderstanding. I'm just talking about the advantage of getting angry *and*, at the back of their minds, considering the possibility that the whole thing is based on a simple misunderstanding. This would make it easier to sit down together after the fight and to figure out what happened.

And I don't even mean that Joseph was necessarily mistaken in his general point. He is right that many of his important needs are not being appreciated. His complaint about the coffeemaker may be one of the few times that he is able to raise this issue, even though it turns out *not* to be an example of what he is trying to demonstrate. The ideal would be for Karen and Joseph to be able to use his anger as an entry point to a needed conversation about the fact that he, and perhaps Karen also, feels that certain important needs that they are having are not being appreciated by the other.

Fight fact 12: *people need to know that making a complaint may be an alternative to withdrawing.*

Joseph knew that if he failed to complain about feeling barraged at the door, he would probably remain emotionally detached for the rest of the evening. Thus, as ironic as it may seem, Joseph's complaint was a potential *contribution* to the relationship. It was an effort *not* to withdraw. Karen would have felt very differently about Joseph's outburst if she had known about this.

Fight fact number 13: *people who are angry don't realize that they aren't talking about any of their feelings and that they have lost awareness of most of them.*

People who are angry are so filled with feelings that it's easy to miss the fact that they aren't talking about any of them. Joseph isn't saying that he feels overwhelmed and neglected, and Karen isn't saying that she feels hurt and abandoned. The omission of feelings isn't surprising, however. In a fight all the important feelings are left out and that's what causes the fight.

People start spouting accusations when the press of events over-whelms their ability to handle and express the feelings generated by these events.

When Joseph said, "Can't you even wait until I take off my coat, for heaven's sake" and "Can't you take care of *anything* by yourself?," Karen was unable to tell him (or even fully to register within herself) that she felt:

Shocked by how angry he seems to be with her.
Angry at what seemed to her in some way an unfair charge.
Guilty about what she feels in other ways might be a fair charge.
Bad about letting him down.
Hurt and unloved.

Instead of saying any of these things, she said, "Well, you don't have to jump down my throat."

People fight because they can't talk. If Karen had been able to express the feelings just described, she wouldn't have had to snap back in the accusing and ineffectual way she did. Fighting is what people are left to do when they lose track of their feelings. If Karen and Joseph were to realize this important fact about fighting, they would be in a favorable position to try to figure out what their feelings are and, perhaps, to tell the other about them.

> **Fight fact 14:** *people need to know that their partners are more likely to listen to them if they report their anger (that is, talk about the fact that they are angry) rather than simply express it (that is, say angry things). And they need to know that their partners are even more likely to listen to them if they report the hurt or disappointment that may underlie their anger.*

I said that Karen and Joseph weren't talking about any of their feelings. They do appear to be talking about at least one kind of feeling, however: anger. But they aren't. Instead, they are saying angry things. There's a difference. Talking *about* their anger—saying "I'm angry"—would provide at least a possibility of having a conversation. The other person might then ask what he or she is angry about and the two might be able to have a discussion about the matter. *Saying angry things*—such as "You're a nag" and "You don't have any guts"—is inflammatory and ends all possibility of discussion.

Your partner is much more likely to listen to you if you say, "When you showed up late, I got angry," than if you say, "You're an irresponsible jerk." The former is *reporting* your anger and the later is *expressing* it.

And your partner is even *more* likely to listen to you if you add, "And I felt really *hurt* about your being late."

> **Fight fact 15:** *people need to know that their complaints (or their partners' complaints) might be remnants of forgotten fantasy-wishes.*

I said that in a fight people lose awareness of their feelings. A type of feeling that people lose particular awareness of is fantasy expectations. If partners feel awkward or uncomfortable with their fantasy wishes, they are likely to express them as disconnected complaints. Joseph lost awareness of his fantasy wish that Karen rescue him from his difficult day. All that was left were a few disconnected complaints:

"You didn't iron my shirts."
"The meat's overdone."
"There aren't enough potatoes."

Karen was offended by these complaints (she had no way of knowing that they were the result of the disappointment of Joseph's fantasy-wish), and she and Joseph got into a fight.

If Karen and Joseph were to recognize that his disconnected complaints were remnants of forgotten fantasies, they might be able to recover these fantasies. In so doing, they might shift from Joseph's provocative blurted-out complaints to a nonprovocative statement about his fantasy. Joseph could say:

> I just figured out why I've been crabbing at you all evening. I had this fantasy that you would magically do all kinds of wonderful things to make up for the difficult day I just had. I know it's ridiculous of me to expect this. I didn't even tell you that I had a hard day and, besides, you had a hard day of your own.

> **Fight fact 16:** *people need to know that their blurted-out complaints might be remnants (distorted expressions) of simple and ordinary wishes.*

People often feel uncomfortable, not simply about their fantasy expectations, but also about their *ordinary* wishes. Karen and Joseph had rather extravagant fantasies of what they hoped the other might do for them. When it came down to it, however, all they really needed was a kind word from the other to recover from the difficulties of the day. Since they were unable to talk about their disappointment at the frustration of these ordinary wishes, they were forced to express this disappointment in indirect and, as it turned out, offensive ways. Karen complained, "You never want to talk to me." And Joseph complained, "The only person you care about is yourself."

Since Karen and Joseph were unaware that they *hadn't* told the other what they were wanting (reassurance to make up for the difficulties of the day) they were forced to conclude that the other was just unwilling to provide it.

If you don't know that the problem is your own inability to ask, then you may be stuck concluding that the problem is your partner's unwillingness to *give*.

Fight fact 17: *people need to remember that one way to get your partner to listen to you is to discover the ways in which you agree with what your partner just said and then go on from there to make your point.*

What is easy to miss, since Karen and Joseph seem to be defending their positions so vigorously, is how poor a job they're doing. Karen answers Joseph's statement that she ambushed him at the door by saying, "I'm not ambushing you. I'm just telling you about the day I had." This is not an effective way to fight. *Disagreeing* with what your partner just said simply gets him or her angrier. Suppose, instead, Karen had *agreed*:

> Yeah, you're right, I did ambush you. And that's too bad because I had a really awful day today, and so I really wanted things to go well between us tonight.

Joseph is less likely to want to continue the fight after hearing this. Agreeing with your partner (finding the elements in what your partner says that make sense to you) is a good way to get your partner to listen to you.

Fight fact 18: *people need to know that talking about a fight (in an attempt to work it out) will simply rekindle the fight*

if you bring up your partner's contribution to the fight or if
your partner brings up your contribution.

It's the old principle: "It's okay for me to criticize my family, but I won't tolerate your doing so." In this case the principle is: "It's okay for me to talk about *my* part in our fights, but I won't tolerate your doing so."

> If you talk about only *your* contributions to the fight, then the only person you can possibly accuse is yourself. And your partner isn't going to be offended by your accusing yourself. In fact, he or she might want to come to your rescue.

> If you talk about your *partner's* contributions to the fight, however, you *are* likely to start accusing him or her. And your partner *is* going to be offended by that.

Here is an example of Karen and Joseph talking exclusively about their *own* contributions to the fight:

JOSEPH: You know, you're right. I *did* jump down your throat and so I can understand your getting upset about it.

KAREN: Yeah, but we have to remember that *I* barraged you with all those things I wanted you to do.

JOSEPH: Well yeah, but you'd been with the kids all day and I know what that's like. I should be willing to help more when I get home.

KAREN: Yeah, but you've been working hard too, and I should be willing to let you relax a little when you get home.

As long as Karen and Joseph talk this way—that is, as long as they discuss only their own personal responsibility for the fight—they can't possibly start another fight. Each person's admitting things leads the other to feel like admitting things.

But people don't generally talk this way. After saying "You know, you're right. I *did* jump down your throat," Joseph is likely to add:

JOSEPH: But *you* had a part in it, too. After all, you did barrage me with all those things you wanted me to do.

Here, Joseph is talking about *Karen's* contribution to the fight (and, as you may notice, it's an accusation). If Joseph had not come out and said this, Karen would have made this exact comment about *herself* the very next moment. Coming from Joseph, however, she won't stand for it:

KAREN: What do you mean, "barrage" you? I didn't *barrage* you. I just *asked* you. And the only reason I even had to ask you is because it wouldn't occur to you in a million years to offer to help on your own.

And immediately Karen and Joseph would be back in the fight.

Now, you may object that you don't *want* to always have to stick exclusively to discussing your own contribution to the fight and that it's too hard to do even if you wanted to. And my answer is: you don't have to stick to it. This fact of fighting—and the others—are things to *know*, not things you have to *do*.

So here is my recommendation:

Talk about your partner's contribution to the fight if you want to, but *know* about it so you won't be surprised by the effect; namely, your partner getting defensive or angry. The greater danger isn't getting back into fights. It's getting back into fights without knowing *why*.

CONCLUSION

Preventing fights is difficult. There's always going to be something that will set you off or that will set your partner off. So rather than devote yourself entirely to preventing fights, I recommend that you develop skill in *recovering* from them, and even *profiting* from them. By recovering and profiting, I mean getting together with your partner afterwards to *talk* about the fights.

Mr. Skeptic: I'm not sure that talking about fights is such a good idea. Many partners get into their worst fights when they sit down to talk about them. At least, that's what happens with my wife and me. When our fights are over we're just *glad* they're over. We don't want to tempt fate by bringing them up again.

Wile: Well, that's what this list of eighteen facts of fighting is for. It's an attempt to provide enough information about fights so that you'll have a better chance to work things out if you *do* sit down later to try to talk about your fights.

How can these eighteen facts of fighting help you? You still may have a lot of fights and you still may say a lot of angry things, but:

Since you'll *know* that you're saying a lot of angry things, you won't be surprised by your partner's angry or defensive response.

You'll know that you and your partner are *caught* in a stinging back-and-forth exchange that might need to run its course.

You'll know that a lot of things are being said that, since they are exaggerations and first approximations, need not completely be taken at face value.

You'll know that the fight is temporarily unresolvable because neither partner is able to get across what he or she needs to get across to resolve the fight.

And you'll know how, later on when you're not so angry, you'll be able to resolve it; that is, by helping your partner get across what he or she needs to get across.

You'll know that you're in a kind of classic battle that nearly all couples get into, and so the fact that you're in it doesn't necessarily mean that something is wrong with you or your relationship.

You'll know that all the important feelings that could soften the interaction and help make sense of things are being left out.

You'll know that this isn't a time to expect to work out any issues.

Nevertheless, you'll know that there may be important issues somewhere in there among the charges.

And that your present argument, as distressing as it might seem, might serve the useful purpose of bringing up these important issues.

And you'll know that it will be possible following the fight to sit down with your partner to figure out what happened.

And you'll know, when you do sit down, what will lead to a restarting of the fight and what won't.

And because of all this knowledge, your fights will seem very different to you.

V

TWO RELATED PATTERNS THAT DRIVE US CRAZY

As I said, fighting and withdrawing are the major problem in a relationship. But two other problems are almost as major:

Pursuit and distance, which I shall discuss in Chapters 15 and 16.
Bypassing and nonbypassing, which I shall discuss in Chapter 17.

A REVISED MARITAL VOW

Fight and withdrawal, pursuit and distance, and bypassing and nonbypassing occur with such frequency that they deserve to be considered the occupational hazards of being a couple. Hardly anyone escapes them. Couples differ primarily in the *degree* of wreckage wrought. These three problems are so common, and exert such a powerful effect on our relationships, that I wouldn't entirely be against revising the marital vows to read:

Do you, Joseph (Karen), take this woman (man) to be your lawful wedded wife (husband), for better or worse, in sickness and health, *and through inevitable periods of fight-withdrawal, pursuit-distance, and bypassing-nonbypassing.*

15

Pursuing and Distancing

*T*homas Fogarty, a well-known family therapist in New York, describes a couple pattern he calls "pursuit and distance." Here is the pattern in a nutshell:

> One partner, the "pursuer," seeks increased involvement, intimacy, engagement, talking, affection, sex, or time together, while the other, the "distancer," seeks increased separation and privacy.

The pattern is self-reinforcing and self-escalating. The more the pursuing partner pursues, the more trapped the distancing partner feels and the more he or she needs to get away. The more the distancing partner needs to get away, the more deserted the pursuing partners feels and the more he or she needs to pursue.

Pursuer-distancer conflicts are as difficult to resolve as are fight-withdrawal cycles. In fact, pursuit-distance difficulties are often what partners in a fight-withdrawal cycle fight about. In such a fight:

> The pursuer accuses the distancer of being withdrawn, withholding, unavailable, unloving, uncommitted, or afraid of closeness.
> The distancer accuses the pursuer of clinging, nagging, demanding, and needing to control.

AN EXAMPLE OF A COUPLE
IN A PURSUER-DISTANCER CONFLICT

I expect that you will recognize yourself in some aspects of the following extended example. In fact, you're supposed to. One of my goals is to suggest that everyone gets caught up in pursuit and distance at least to some extent.

Paula and Jay are a married couple in their early twenties. Paula is a waitress and Jay, who makes his living teaching tennis, has cut back to half-time so that he can go back to school. Jay can't understand why Paula acts the way she does:

JAY: I'm going to school for us so that I can get a job that pays well enough so Paula can quit her job and we can have children. But instead of helping, she's become my biggest problem. She's jealous of the time I spend studying. She sits around the house and doesn't do anything on her own. And she always has to be the center of my attention. Even when she is, she isn't happy. I take her on picnics and things. And it's unbelievable that it's just those times that she picks a fight. And whenever we have even the slightest little problem, she always has to talk it into the ground. Things would take care of themselves if she didn't talk about them so much.

Paula sees *Jay* as the problem:

PAULA: Jay says he has to do schoolwork, but that's just an excuse. He used to ignore me even before he went back to school. It's just worse now. I think he just doesn't want to be with me. When he does take time off from studying, instead of doing something with me, he plays basketball or goes out for a beer with friends. He's hardly said two words to me in a week. Whenever I try to talk about our problems, he heads for the door. And we haven't had sex in a month. I think he's afraid of making a commitment. It's the old story. I'll support him through school and then he'll divorce me. My mother keeps telling me there are plenty of fish in the sea. Maybe I should go out and get another fish.

Paula is the "pursuer." She feels abandoned by Jay and reacts by pressuring. Jay is the "distancer." He feels pressured by Paula and reacts by withdrawing.

The problem, in part, is their differing character styles:

Throughout her life, Paula has dealt with problems by *engaging*—
that is, by talking to people and by seeking reassurance.

Throughout his life, Jay has dealt with problems by *disengaging*—
that is, by keeping things to himself and by going on long solitary
walks to think things over.

At the source of Paula and Jay's problems is this incompatibility in character
style.

Mr. Skeptic: I think you're missing the point. Their incompatibility
is what brought them together. They probably *wanted* their marriage to
fail, at least unconsciously. Why else would they marry a person who is
so clearly inappropriate?

Wile: That's the you-must-have-wanted-it-that-way style of reasoning, Mr. Skeptic. You're saying that Paula and Jay got married *because
of* their problems. An alternative view, and the one that I believe, is that
Paula and Jay got married *in spite of* these problems—that is, what they
liked about one another outweighed what they didn't like.

Of course, what people *don't* like about their partners is often connected to what they *do* like. In fact, a relationship is, in some sense, the
attempt to work out the negative side effects of what attracts you to your
partner in the first place:

Jay was fascinated by someone who could express feelings and reach
out to others the way that Paula could. One relationship task—
what Paula and Jay may need to do to make the relationship
work—is to find a way for Jay to deal with the aspects of Paula's
reaching out and expressiveness that he doesn't like. A person
may reach out and be expressive in both appealing and unap-
pealing ways, and his or her partner will understandably like the
former and dislike the latter.

Paula was fascinated by someone who could remain self-possessed
and self-reliant the way that Jay could. Another relationship
task—what Paula and Jay may need to do to make the relationship work—is to find a way for Paula to deal with the expressions of Jay's self-possession and self-reliance that she doesn't
like.

While Paula and Jay see the other as unwilling to make the commitment to try to solve their problems, I see them as continually trying to

solve their problems. And that's the problem; that is, the ways these partners attempt to deal with their problem reinforces the problem.

The primary way in which Paula and Jay try to deal with the problem is to downplay it. Each evening, Jay sneaks into the bedroom to do his schoolwork. He hopes Paula won't notice. He worries that she will resent his having to spend so much time on his studies and away from her. Paula does notice, of course. What she notices is that Jay is sneaking away, as if she were the enemy.

What Jay and Paula miss is that she wouldn't necessarily have minded Jay's studying—or, at least, she wouldn't necessarily have minded it so much. If Paula were feeling more secure about Jay's affection for her, she might have been at least partly content to do things on her own: to catch up on her reading, to talk to friends on the phone, to fiddle with the computer, or to redecorate the apartment. But the creepy way Jay slips into the bedroom, as if she were a danger to avoid, causes Paula to feel unloved and to lose spirit for all these other things. She mopes around the apartment waiting for Jay to finish.

> Jay's effort to keep his studying from becoming a problem has turned it into a problem.
>
> Jay's attempt not to abandon Paula leaves her feeling abandoned.

Feeling that Jay already sees her as a burden, Paula pretends she doesn't mind his slipping into the bedroom. And she tries to hide the fact that she's moping around waiting for him to come out and talk to her.

Jay senses what she's doing, of course, and feels pressured. He resents her hanging around waiting for him. He has begun to feel that she is a needy neurotic woman who feels abandoned at the drop of a hat. (In seeing Paula as having these character flaws, of course, Jay is using the character-flaws habit of thought.) By the time he emerges from the bedroom at the end of the evening, he no longer wants to be with her. He slips out for a beer with a friend.

Incidents like this poison the relationship. Jay feels he is continually letting Paula down and that he is a failure as a husband. Being away from her starts to feel like a relief, although he feels too guilty to admit this, even to himself. Returning home from school, Jay hopes that Paula will be out so that he won't have to be with her. Even sex becomes a pressure. Previously, Jay could hardly keep his hands off Paula. Now he hardly ever wants to put them on her.

This whole unfortunate interaction exaggerates the dependence of

Paula and the independence of Jay. It changes Paula from a person who could potentially have made good use of time alone into a person who mopes around. And it changes Jay from a potentially involved person who needs Paula into a detached person who doesn't.

Jay's preoccupation with Paula's needs—his worry that he isn't doing enough for her—prevents him from noticing that his own needs aren't being satisfied. If he didn't have to sneak off because of concern that Paula might resent his studying, he might have said:

JAY: I really don't feel like studying tonight because something kind of upsetting happened at school that I want to tell you about. I guess I'd better study at least a couple of hours, but then maybe we can go out for a beer.

Paula is suffering from not hearing things like this. And Jay is suffering from not feeling like saying them. He is deprived and doesn't know it. Paula, who could have been his major resource in dealing with problems, has become his major problem.

Paula's Private Problem-solving Effort

Paula tries to deal with Jay's unavailability and with the worry that she's "too dependent" by trying to prove her independence. She goes to a movie with a friend and she takes a pottery class.

The movie, however, is about unrequited love and just reminds Paula of her own situation. The pottery class seems filled with lonely people and depresses her. As often happens with such attempts to prove one's independence, Paula comes home feeling even more needy.

And there's a further disappointment. Paula secretly hoped that Jay would worry that she's becoming too independent and would miss her. Accordingly, she's terribly upset when she discovers that Jay hardly notices her absence. If anything, he seems relieved by it. Frustrated by the failure of her plan, Paula throws aside all pretense and insists that Jay should appreciate her more:

PAULA: You're married to your books and not to me. You didn't even notice that I was gone all evening. You never pay any attention to me or think about what *I* might like. I can't even remember the last time you bought me flowers. It was so long ago, in fact, that they hadn't even evolved yet. You had to bring me ferns.

Paula's attempt to be independent and undemanding thus ends in this dependent and demanding complaint.

Jay's Private Problem-solving Effort

Jay engages in his own attempt to make things better. Feeling pressured by Paula's complaint, and in an effort to give her what he thinks she wants, Jay arranges a picnic. He does all the shopping, gets all her favorite foods, brings her flowers *and* ferns, and takes her to the park they went to on their first date.

Jay's plan fizzles. Since it's clear to Paula that he'd really rather be studying, she doesn't get much satisfaction from the picnic. She tries to act pleased in order to reward him for the effort and to avoid disappointing him, but it's evident that her heart isn't in it.

Paula's lukewarm reaction to the picnic is frustrating to Jay. Since he's already overextending himself to go on the picnic, he has little patience with Paula's unenthusiastic response. And when Paula comments that he forgot to bring mustard, it's more than Jay can stand.

JAY: Look at all the trouble I went to, all this food, all the effort, and the only thing you say is: "You forgot the mustard."

PAULA: Ahah. So you went to a lot of trouble. You really didn't want to go on a picnic in the first place, did you? Well, that's fine with me. Next time, don't bother yourself.

JAY: I shouldn't have bothered myself *this* time. If we were at home both of us would have been happy. I could have studied, and you could have had all the mustard you wanted.

Jay's attempt to be loving thus ends in this unloving argument. They go into a ten-minute mental divorce:

Paula's Ten-minute Mental Divorce: I shouldn't have married him. I should have listened to my mother. He doesn't care about me. The whole marriage is a charade. He's married to his books. He only thinks of himself. And I can't stand the way I get so clingy. I hate myself sometimes.

Jay's Ten-minute Mental Divorce: What a mistake to marry a Virgo. She's just too neurotic. No matter what I do she's always going to complain. And I don't need complaints. I need support. I should have married Vicki. But then, I wasn't able to satisfy her, either. Maybe I'm too selfish to be married to anyone.

The rest of the day is spent in a mutual sulk, and neither sleeps very well that night. But at breakfast the next morning, Jay acts as if nothing has happened. He chats in his usual way about interesting things in the newspaper. Paula, grateful that the crisis has passed, also acts as if nothing has happened.

IS THE PROBLEM MERELY A MATTER OF FAULTY COMMUNICATION?

A communication skills trainer might point to the fact that at no instant did Paula and Jay ever really talk. The day of the picnic began with a long period in which both partners tried to act nice in an effort to make the outing work. That was followed in succession by:

A short argument about mustard.
A ten-minute mental divorce.
An afternoon sulk.
A sleepless night.
And a sudden return to "normal."

What Paula and Jay need, this communication skills trainer might suggest, is to sit down and discuss what had happened. But would such a discussion really solve the problem? The following demonstrates the difficulties that a certain type of communication skills training approach can run into. Here is the trainer talking to Paula and Jay:

TRAINER: Let's imagine how things would go if the two of you had tried to talk about things the morning after the picnic. Who would have begun and what would he or she have said?

PAULA: It would have had to be up to me. I'm always the one who has to start everything. And I'd say what I said at the time (turning to Jay): Why did you take me on a picnic when you really didn't want to go?

JAY: I *did* want to go. It was only when you made your mustard comment that I got upset.

PAULA: That's the problem. You always get upset about everything. You're like a fussy child. Like the time in Mexico when. . . .

JAY: You never forget anything. For heaven sakes, we went to Mexico *four* years ago.

PAULA: It wasn't four years ago. It was only three.

JAY: I distinctly remember that we went to Mexico after my brother's wedding and that was four. . . .

PAULA: It wasn't after your brother's wedding. It was after your sister's wedding. And that was three years ago.

JAY: No it wasn't.

PAULA: Yes it was.

In just two minutes, Paula and Jay have broken nearly every communication rule in the book.

TRAINER: I think we need some ground rules.

The following is a condensation. The trainer didn't give all these rules at once. He gave them a few at a time over the course of several sessions.

1. Don't ask "why" questions. Asking "*Why* did you take me on a picnic when you really didn't want to go?" is blaming. And blaming doesn't help.

2. Paraphrase what the other has said so that he or she knows that you have heard. Instead of saying, "I *did* want to go," say, "I hear you saying that you felt that I didn't want to go."

3. Try to stick to one topic. Things went downhill when you shifted from the picnic to talking about Mexico.

4. Don't bog down in irrelevant issues. It doesn't matter whether you went to Mexico three years ago or four.

5. Don't dredge up things from the past. The issue is what is happening now, not what might or might not have happened three or four years ago.

6. Don't name-call or label. Calling Jay a "fussy child" doesn't add anything and just makes him angry.

7. Don't make "you" statements. Statements such as "*You* always get upset about everything" are accusations. Instead, say how you feel.

8. Don't say "always" or "never." Such exaggerations just provoke the other.

9. Don't interrupt. Give the other person a chance to finish.

It's hard to imagine that Paula and Jay, as angry as they are, will be able to apply any of these rules. If, however, the communication skills trainer is somehow able to get them to do so, the result might sound something like the following:

PAULA (attempts to express feelings rather than state accusations with a sidelong glance at the trainer looking for a sign from him whether or not she is doing it right): I feel bad about some of the things I said at the picnic yesterday. I was upset because I felt that you really didn't want to be with me.

JAY (takes a deep breath and conscientiously tries to paraphrase what Paula just said): I hear you saying that you feel bad about what you said and that you felt I didn't want to be with you. I appreciate your saying this. I feel bad about some of the stuff that I said, also. But it's not that I didn't want to be with you. I was just disappointed because we were doing something that I thought you'd like—going on a picnic.

PAULA (effortfully, and with another quick sidelong glance at the trainer, tries to paraphrase what Jay just said): I hear you saying that you were disappointed that I didn't enjoy the picnic. I don't know why I didn't. For some reason the idea of a picnic never hit me right.

TRAINER (speaking with emphasis because he now believes he has discovered the critical communication error): Jay, you were *mindreading*. Instead of asking Paula whether she wanted to go on a picnic, you just assumed that she did. That's where the trouble began. You can never assume that you know what the other person wants. The next time you plan something, Jay, you should *ask* Paula what she wants. In fact, as a practice exercise, why don't the two of you plan something now.

JAY (privately vowing to himself never again to second-guess Paula's wishes): Okay. (To Paula:) What would you like to do Saturday?

PAULA (seems uncertain): I don't know. (Long pause). Maybe it would be nice to go to the beach.

JAY (quickly): Okay, we'll go to the beach.

The communication skills trainer has unwittingly set in motion another problem-solving effort. And the same things happen as occurred on the picnic. Before Paula and Jay even arrive at the beach, Paula senses that Jay really wants to be home studying. She becomes disheartened. Jay, noticing her lack of enthusiasm, becomes frustrated. And when Paula doesn't immediately go into the water, it's too much for him.

JAY (trying to imagine what the communication trainer would want him to say, but then giving up entirely and blurting out): We drive across three counties so you can go to the beach, and you don't even go into the goddamn water.

Since going to the beach was *her* idea, Paula doesn't feel entitled, as she had on the picnic, to complain about his not really wanting to be there in the first place. She is forced to resort to more primitive arguments:

PAULA (completely forgetting everything the trainer has taught her): I don't see a sign anywhere saying that I have to go into the goddamn water. Go into your own goddamn water. I came here to relax. Maybe I'll go in the water later and maybe I won't.

The communication skills trainer has made a gallant effort. But talking by itself is not the whole answer. If talking is to help, Paula and Jay need to have certain information about their relationship that they do not now have. The trainer has taught them to talk politely and respectfully. But he has done so by imposing an artificial and highly stylized verbal etiquette. And preoccupation with this etiquette may make it *more* difficult for Paula and Jay to obtain the information they need to have.

And what is this information? If Paula and Jay are to talk usefully about the situation:

They need to know that they have a severe case of a problem that, to one extent or another, every couple has—a pursuer-distancer problem.

They need to know that what makes the problem so difficult for couples is that almost every attempt to solve it deepens it.

They need to know how Jay periodically plans "duty" outings, just as Paula occasionally tries to become "independent."

They need to know why neither effort ever works out. Jay's effort not to deprive Paula *causes* him to deprive her, and Paula's effort not to pressure him *causes* her to pressure him.

And they need to know that Jay also has relationship needs, but that these needs are crowded out by his worry about not satisfying Paula's needs.

Even if they were to have this information, there's a danger that they wouldn't be able to use it:

Paula might be too alarmed at the thought of being a "dependent, nagging woman" to do anything other than to try to be "independent."

And Jay might feel too guilty about depriving Paula to do anything other than to try not to deprive her, which leads inevitably to other periods in which he gives up entirely, goes off on his own, and tries not to think about it.

Mr. Skeptic: You make it all sound pretty hopeless, Wile. Is that what you really believe—that the problem is just too difficult to expect Paula and Jay ever to work out?

Wile: Well, actually, there are a few principles that Paula and Jay could learn that *could* enable them to work it out.

And here they are.

16

Mastering the Facts of Pursuit and Distance

*P*eople have trouble dealing with their pursuer-distancer conflicts because they can't stand the idea that they have them. Pursuers can't stand the idea that they pursue, and distancers can't stand the idea that they withdraw. Pursuers and distancers see themselves as defective people with defective partners in defective relationships:

> Pursuers are upset by their pictures of themselves as "dependent," "demanding," and "nagging." They often have long painful histories of criticism from others (and from themselves) about such tendencies. In addition, they frequently associate this characteristic with a parent whom, at least in this respect, they don't want to be like.
>
> Distancers often have similar experiences and sensitivities about being seen as "withdrawn," "uninvolved," and "afraid of intimacy."

Pursuit and distance provide a field day for the character-flaws form of reasoning, and that is why it is such a big problem. People in such an interaction have an almost irresistible urge to attribute their own or their partners' behavior to character defects.

Paula and Jay don't realize it, but what they are doing—accusing themselves or one another of being "dependent," "demanding," or "afraid of intimacy"—is name-calling, which brings an end to all serious and useful thinking about the matter. There is believed to be nothing further to think or talk about; you're just supposed to *stop* being dependent or demanding or whatever it is you're being accused of.

A *NONACCUSING* VIEW OF PURSUIT AND DISTANCE

If Paula and Jay are to work out their pursuer-distancer conflict, they need a *nonaccusing* way of thinking about it:

1. They need to know that they have a severe case of a problem that, to one extent or another, *every* couple has. Realizing this will help Paula and Jay feel less that something is uniquely wrong with them.

2. They need to know that the persistence of this problem *isn't* just the result of their failure to try to change. Paula *can't* simply stop pursuing, and Jay *can't* simply stop withdrawing.

3. They need to know that what makes the problem so difficult is that almost every attempt to solve it deepens it. Paula spends most of her time trying not to pursue (and that is part of the problem), and Jay's makes ineffectual and counterproductive efforts not to withdraw.

4. They need to know that they are trapped—they are caught in a difficult dilemma—and that they are not simply the selfish, unreasonable, uncooperative, uncompromising, insensitive, mean-spirited, unfeeling, or self-destructive people they seem to themselves or to one another to be.

5. They need to know that Paula has reason to pursue (she's the only one noticing how lonely, depriving, and empty the relationship is) and Jay has reason to withdraw (he's the only one noticing how dangerous the relationship is).

6. They need to know that both of them have important points to make that they are having difficulty getting across. Paula is right that they need to be able to talk about their problems, and Jay is right that their attempts to do so generally lead to fights that neither of them wants.

7. They need to know that the only way to avoid pursuit and distance is to be completely nonaccusing, which is impossible. When the pursuer reaches out, he or she inevitably does so in a subtly (or not so subtly) accusing way, which causes the distancer to withdraw.

8. They need to know that pursuit and distance exaggerate the differences between partners. Originally, Jay had at least *some* desire to do the things that Paula wanted to do—talk, spend

time together, be affectionate, and have sex. The more he feels criticized by Paula for not doing these things, however, the less he finds himself wanting to do them.

9. They need to know that the pursuer isn't the only person being deprived. The distancer is being deprived too; he or she just doesn't know it. While Paula is deprived of having a husband who'd want to spend time with her, Jay is deprived of having a wife he'd *want* to spend time with.

10. They need to know that each partner's attempts to deal with his or her problem increases that of the other. Paula deals with feeling abandoned by pressuring, while Jay deals with feeling pressured by abandoning.

11. They need to know that pursuit and distance may depend, in part, on situational factors such as who is busier.

For those of you who want more details on these eleven points, here they are (for those who don't, skip to page 210, where I give an example of how partners who have mastered these eleven facts might talk):

Fact 1: *Partners in a pursuer-distancer conflict need to know that they are suffering from an intense form of a universal couple problem.*

Paula and Jay think that people with good relationships don't have the kind of problems they have. They feel that something is uniquely and dreadfully wrong with their relationship. They would feel better about it if they were to realize that pursuit and distance are occupational hazards of a relationship. Every couple has the problem at least to some extent. They just happen to have an extreme version of it. People who view pursuit and distance as a universal couple issue rather than as simply a sign of character defects will be better able to deal with it.

Fact 2: *People need to know that the pursuer can't stop pursuing and that the distancer can't stop withdrawing.*

The main advice generally given to partners in a pursuer-distancer conflict is to *stop* doing what they are doing. Pursuers are advised:

To respect their partners' needs for privacy.
To spend more time doing things on their own.

To be a little more standoffish.

To accept a more separated and detached style of relating.

To not always have to talk about everything.

To stop pressuring, nagging, demanding, and controlling.

To play a little hard to get.

In other words: *stop pursuing.*

If the pursuer stops pursuing, this reasoning goes, than the distancer won't feel so pressured and have to withdraw.

The problem with this advice is that the pursuer *can't* stop pursuing; that is, he or she can't escape the role of pursuer. Although Paula can force herself to stop asking Jay for more affection, she can't force herself to stop *wanting* it. And Jay, knowing that she continues to want it, even though she has stopped asking for it, continues to feel the pressure.

This fact explains why playing hard to get so rarely works. Your partner *knows* that you are playing hard to get, and that, actually, you are still very easy to get. In fact, he or she takes your playing hard to get as additional pressure on him or her to come around and to be more attentive. Playing hard to get may work—your partner may come around—when you are no longer playing; that is, when you really have lost interest. Of course, by that time, you no longer *care* whether or not he or she comes around.

Just as pursuers can't stop pursuing, distancers can't stop withdrawing. Withdrawing is typically the only reliable way that distancers feel they have to deal with the criticism and pressure they are experiencing.

People who see their partners and themselves as caught in a difficult situation rather than as just stubbornly refusing to change are likely to feel more sympathy about their situation.

Fact 3: *People need to know that the pursuer is spending most of his or her time trying not to pursue and that the distancer is making effortful but hardly noticeable attempts not to withdraw.*

Another reason why advising the pursuer to stop pursuing doesn't help is that the pursuer is already trying to stop and that's what's causing much of the problem.

Paula hates the picture of herself as a dependent person who hangs around waiting for Jay to give her some attention. And she hates the position it puts her in. So she makes efforts to go out and do things on her own. But that doesn't help because her attempts to prove her independence—for example, by taking a pottery class and going to a movie with a friend—typically backfire and result in her feeling even more dependent.

And there's another thing that Paula hates. She hates her picture of herself as the type of person who is always complaining about not being given enough attention. So she makes an effort not to complain. But that doesn't help because her efforts to suppress her complaints typically lead to an intense outpouring of complaints later, confirming Jay's view that the complaints have been there all along.

And there's still another thing that Paula hates. She hates the picture of herself as the type of person who always tries to change her partner. So she makes efforts to try to accept Jay the way he is. But that doesn't work because her attempts not to try to change him typically lead to intense demands for change later on.

At the same time that Paula (the pursuer) is trying not to pursue, Jay (the distancer) is trying not to withdraw. Jay hates the picture of himself as a withdrawn, withholding, tight-lipped, and rejecting person. So he makes efforts not to withdraw and, instead, to act in a more interested and engaged way. It's an uphill battle, however, and he quickly gets discouraged. The need for self-protection soon reasserts itself. When Jay does make energetic and concerted efforts to give Paula what he thinks she wants—for example, his taking her on a picnic—these efforts typically backfire.

Pursuers and distancers are generally seen as wholeheartedly behind what they are doing. What now becomes apparent is that, instead, both are devoted to suppressing the very behavior for which they are being condemned:

Paula, who is worried about being too pushy, is spending most of her time trying not to pursue, though sporadically bursting forth with impulsive pursuing efforts.

Jay, who is concerned about being too detached, is continuously —though unsuccessfully—trying to suppress his tendency to withdraw.

If Paula and Jay were to know how hard they were trying to change, they'd have greater sympathy for themselves and for one another.

> **Fact 4:** *People in a pursuer-distancer conflict need to know that their partners are as stuck as they are and that they themselves are even more stuck than they think they are.*

Pursuers and distancers often feel that it would be easy for their partners to change. Pursuers don't see why it would be so difficult for their partners to be a little more forthcoming and affectionate. Distancers don't see why it would be so difficult for their partners to be a little less dependent and demanding.

People in a pursuer-distancer conflict fail to realize that their partners are as stuck as they are and that *they* themselves are even more stuck than they think they are.

> Paula and Jay are each faced with two unworkable alternatives. Paula can pursue or try not to pursue. Jay can withdraw or try not to withdraw. As we can see, neither alternative works out well for either partner.

Paula and Jay will be at an advantage if they realize that both of them are caught in difficult dilemmas and that they are not simply the selfish, unreasonable, uncompromising, insensitive, mean-spirited, unfeeling, or self-destructive people they seem. The recognition that they are both stuck may enable them to increase their sense of sympathy for their shared situation.

> Partners are in a good position, or at least in a better position, when they jointly appreciate how *bad* their position is.

Since Paula and Jay don't realize that they are stuck—they think they could change if they really wanted to—they conclude that:

They must unconsciously want the relationship to fail.
Perhaps they purposefully chose a partner who would mistreat them the way they were mistreated in childhood.

These accusing and self-accusing speculations, since they suggest that Paula and Jay secretly want and unconsciously plan the unpleasant things that happen to them, are expressions of the you-must-have-wanted-it-that-way style of thinking.

Paula and Jay come to these conclusions because they have no other way to understand why Paula doesn't simply stop pursuing and Jay doesn't simply stop withdrawing. They are thus in need of important information. They need to realize that:

> They can't simply stop pursuing and withdrawing. They are stuck (Fact 2).
>
> They are trying to stop, which is causing much of the problem (Facts 3 and 4).
>
> It is understandable that the pursuer is pursuing and the distancer is withdrawing (Fact 5).

Fact 5: *People need to know that the pursuer has reason to pursue and that the distancer has reason to withdraw.*

Since Paula reacts to withdrawal with demandingness, and since Jay reacts to demandingness with withdrawal:

> Paula actually *is* being abandoned. She has reason to pursue.
> And Jay actually *is* being pressured. He has reason to withdraw.

Given the situation with which Paula is dealing, it makes sense that she would pursue. What else can a person do who is:

> Shut out by the person with whom it is most important to be able to talk?
>
> Abandoned by the individual whom he or she most counts on to be there?

Paula is in some sense forced into the position of pursuer. She is the only one noticing how lonely, empty, and depriving the relationship is.

Given the impossible situation in which Jay finds himself, it makes sense that he might want to withdraw. He is in an untenable position of:

> Working hard to give something (affection) that can only be given spontaneously; that is, by *not* working at it.
>
> Trying to feel affection toward a person who, since she is angry at him, is not feeling or expressing much affection toward him.

Jay is in some sense forced into the position of distancer. He is the only one noticing how dangerous the relationship is.

Fact 6: *People need to know that both partners have important points to make that they are having difficulty getting across.*

There is an important grain of truth in both partners' positions. A good example of this can be seen in the typical argument that pursuers and distancers have about talking:

> The pursuer presses for more talking. Paula resents the way Jay leaves the room in middle of their fights. She sees him as never staying around to talk anything through.
>
> The distancer wants to put a clamp on their talking. Jay thinks that Paula always talks everything into the ground. He says, "Talking only makes things worse. Most problems will take care of themselves if only you don't talk about them so much."

Actually, both partners are partly right. Paula is right that there are problems that need to be talked about. And Jay is right that they presently have no way to do so; all their attempts to talk turn into fights that neither of them wants.

Here, as in many ways, partners in a pursuer-distancer conflict take opposite sides on issues on which, in an important way, they agree. In calmer moments—when they are not fighting—Jay might agree that there are issues that need to be talked about (even though it's not his natural tendency to talk), and Paula might agree that their talks rarely work out.

Fact 7. *People need to know that the only way to avoid pursuer-distancer conflicts (or, for that matter, any other conflicts) is to be completely nonaccusing, which is impossible.*

Pursuit and distance are caused by accusations that the partners may not realize they are making.

Pursuers and distancers are caught in a situation in which it is almost impossible not to feel accused:

> The pursuer feels in continuous danger of criticism or self-criticism for being a nag.
>
> The distancer feels in continuous danger of criticism or self-criticism for being withdrawn.

Pursuers become pursuers because they are more likely than their partners to react to momentary tensions, disruptions, disappointments, or disconnections by *engaging*. That's what Paula does. She deals with a momentary feeling of disconnectedness from Jay by saying:

PAULA: You seem quiet tonight.

This looks at first like a reasonable thing to say. To begin with, it's true; Jay *has* been quiet. For another, it's the kind of comment that partners say to one another all the time without thinking about it. And for a third, it seems useful for someone to point out what's going on in the relationship.

But there is a hidden criticism in this statement. "You *seem* quiet" implies "you *shouldn't* be quiet." Jay, sensing the criticism, defends himself:

JAY: I'm just tired. And, anyway, I don't see why we have to spend every night talking.

Paula and Jay, who may have been having identical desires for intimacy just a moment before, are now polarized. That's what accusing can do. Whatever wish Jay might have had for closer contact has been superceded by the more pressing need to defend himself. Paula is stuck defending why it's important to talk, and Jay is stuck defending why it's important not to have to talk.

It doesn't take much to get a pursuer-distancer interaction going. And once it gets going, it can escalate quickly. Since Paula feels she hasn't gotten her point across, she intensifies her charge:

PAULA: Well, it's not just tonight that you haven't talked to me. It's *every* night. It's been *every* night this week.

And then Jay *really* feels criticized:

JAY: Well, I've been *tired* all week. And besides, I *have* been doing a lot of talking.

And then Paula *really* feels she hasn't gotten her point across. And, as people do at such times, she exaggerates:

PAULA: You call saying "Pass the salt" and "Where's the mail?" a lot of talking? Cause that's just about all you've been saying these days.

Paula and Jay could have avoided this pursuer-distancer conflict, but doing so would have required near perfect communication. Instead of "You seem quiet tonight," Paula would have had to say something like:

PAULA: I don't know why—maybe it's because of our busy schedules— but I don't feel as close to you as I used to, *and I miss it.*

Clearly Paula is *not* accusing Jay here. And since he wouldn't be feeling accused, Jay wouldn't have to defend himself. He might have been able to say something like:

JAY: Yeah, me too. I guess I haven't been talking much because I've been worried about school. And for some reason, I've been keeping it to myself. And that's too bad because I think I'd have felt better telling you about it.

Jay is able to talk when he doesn't feel criticized and pressured.

If Paula and Jay could have had this exchange, they would have realized that both were having the same feeling: they were missing feeling close. And since they would be talking about what is on their minds, they would be reestablishing the wished-for sense of closeness.

Since no one can consistently talk in this near-perfect way, however, every couple inevitably gets caught in pursuer-distancer interactions, although generally not to the extent that Paula and Jay do.

Partners are in a better position to work out their pursuer-distancer conflicts if they realize that:

> Between the two, one is always more likely than the other to deal with uncertainty or tension by engaging.
> This engaging almost always has a hidden (or not so hidden) accusing quality that causes the other to defend or withdraw.

It's easier to deal with this pattern of engaging and defending-withdrawing if you see it as inescapable rather than as a sign that there is something basically and uniquely wrong with you, your partner, or the relationship.

Fact 8: *People need to know that pursuers may lose whatever wish they might have had for separation and distancers may lose whatever wish they might have had for intimacy.*

A major point in the story of Paula and Jay is how their relationship deprived them of certain wishes and abilities that they had prior to the relationship:

> Originally, Jay had at least some desire to talk to, spend time with, be affectionate with, and have sex with Paula. The more Jay felt criticized for not wanting to do these things enough, the less he

found himself wanting to do them. He became "withdrawn" and
"afraid of intimacy."

Originally, Paula liked to do many things on her own. The more
rejected she felt by Jay, however, the less she found herself
wanting or able to do things on her own. She became "dependent" and "demanding."

It is important to see a loss of such wishes as a consequence of what
happens in the relationship and not just the result of the partners' personalities.

Fact 9: *People need to know that the distancer is as deprived as the pursuer.*

It is easy to see that *Paula* is deprived. She misses the warmth, affection, tenderness, caring, confiding, and companionship that people seek
in relationships and that she originally entered the relationship with Jay to
obtain. At times she feels trapped in a loveless marriage.

When Jay comes home in the evening, he greets their dog more
enthusiastically than he greets her. Everyone would immediately
sympathize with Paula for taking second place to a poodle.

What Paula, Jay, and nearly everyone fail to see, however, is that
Jay is as deprived as Paula is. While Paula is deprived of having a husband
who looks forward to greeting her in the evening, Jay is deprived of *being*
a husband who looks forward to greeting his wife in the evening.

It's a lot more fun to look forward to seeing your wife than it is to
come home to someone you mostly want to avoid.

And it's a lot more satisfying to be in a relationship in which you feel
warmth, affection, tenderness, caring, companionship, and sexual interest than it is to be in one in which you don't.

Jay is trapped in the same loveless relationship as Paula is. His hopes
for the marriage have been similarly dashed. He is as deprived as she is.
He just doesn't know it. Jay is so focused on what Paula says *she* is missing,
and on defending himself against her criticisms, that he fails to notice what
he is missing.

Fact 10: *Partners in a pursuer-distancer interaction need to know that, for the moment at least, they may be unable to keep from rubbing one another the wrong way.*

Even if Paula and Jay were to realize that their reactions were justifiable, they might still blame themselves for staying in a relationship that has such glaring problems. They need to realize that all relationships have glaring problems. Areas of vulnerability always exist somewhere within a relationship and these areas inevitably come into increasing prominence.

The issues and problems that partners can handle well typically fade into the background. The ones they can't—the sticking points in the relationship—come into increasing prominence. Soon it is only these sticking points that the partners are aware of.

Paula and Jay are resources to one another in many ways. When Paula feels threatened, upset, or discouraged, she can usually count on Jay to come to her assistance. When she has problems with friends, family, or work, she can usually rely on Jay's sympathy, concern, and help. And Jay can count on Paula for the same things.

There are always circumstances, however, in which partners are unable to be resources to one other. This happens when each person's way of responding to his or her buttons being pushed pushes the buttons of the other.

> Paula's buttons are pushed when she feels abandoned; she deals with feeling abandoned by pressuring.
> Jay's buttons are pushed when he feels pressured; he deals with feeling pressured by abandoning.

There are times and places in every relationship in which partners can't help rubbing one another the wrong way. If partners realize that there are always such weak points or sore points somewhere in the relationship, they may be able to commiserate with one another about these sore spots rather than conclude that something is specially and fatally wrong with themselves or the relationship.

People need to know that pursuit and distance cause partners to appear even more incompatible than they actually are. Partners caught in a pursuer-distancer conflict can easily feel that they have completely different wishes, interests, and concerns; so much so, in fact, that they can feel they

are from different planets. This is how Paula and Jay felt in the weeks
before their wedding.

> As their wedding day approached, Jay felt increasingly less desire to
> see Paula. When he did visit, he had little to say, spent most of
> the time watching TV, and found reason to leave early.
> Paula, in contrast, felt increasingly *more* desire to see Jay.

The irony, and it would have helped a great deal if Paula and Jay
had known this, is that they were dealing with a shared concern. Both
had fears about getting married. While Jay dealt with his by withdrawing
and spending more time by himself, Paula dealt with hers by pursuing.
She sought to reassure herself about his love for her, her love for him,
their general compatibility, and the wisdom of their decision to marry by
trying to have continuous contact; long intimate talks; and lots of flowers,
gifts, and sex.

> The problem was self-escalating. The more Jay withdrew, the more
> Paula needed reassuring contact. The more she sought contact,
> the more he needed to withdraw.

The problem was serious and almost caused them to call off the
wedding. They were on the verge of calling it off, in fact, when they went
to see a therapist who showed them that they were both feeling the same
thing (nervousness about getting married) but were expressing it in different
ways.

Paula and Jay's realization that they were worried about the *same*
thing made them feel less at odds. They began to think that maybe they
come from the same planet after all.

Pursuers have a hard time understanding how their distancer partners
can possibly act and feel the way they do. They can't see why it should
be so difficult for their partners to talk a little more and to be a little more
attentive, engaged, and affectionate. It's so easy for them to do these things
that they can't see how it could possibly be hard for anyone else.

Similarly, distancers have a hard time understanding how their pursuer
partners can possibly act and feel the way *they* do. They can't see why
their partners need so much affection and why they can't get along more
on their own. And they can't understand how a hug or a little talking can
mean so much to their partners, since such things mean so little to them.

The first step in understanding how your pursuer or distancer partner
can possibly act and feel the way he or she does is to appreciate
that it's going to be *hard* to understand.

One way to get a sense of how your partner feels is to recall periods
(either in your previous relationships or earlier in your present relationship)
in which *you* were in your partner's position.

When they first met, Jay, who was totally infatuated with Paula, wanted
to spend all his time with her. Paula, who was not as infatuated with Jay,
felt smothered by him. In this early period, *Jay* was the pursuer and *Paula*
was the distancer. By recalling this early stage in their relationship, Paula
can get a sense for Jay's experience now and Jay can get a sense for
Paula's.

In some relationships—although not in Paula and Jay's—the pursuer
in one aspect of the relationship is the distancer in another. That's the case
with Lisa and Bill. Although Lisa is the pursuer and Bill is the distancer in
most areas of the relationship, Bill is the pursuer and Lisa is the distancer
when it comes to sex. He regularly approaches Lisa for sex, and she
regularly puts him off. Lisa and Bill can use their experiences in their sexual
relationship to appreciate what the other feels in the relationship in general.

Fact 11: *Pursuit and distance may depend, in part, on situational factors such as who is busier.*

Two years have passed. Jay has graduated from school, and Paula
has just given birth to twins. In fact, part of the reason that Paula wanted
children had been that Jay was so engrossed in his studies. Suddenly,
Paula becomes the busier; she has to devote all her time and energy to
the twins. Jay tries to help, but since Paula is breast-feeding, Paula is the
main one relating to them. Jay feels left out and neglected. He has become
the pursuer and Paula the distancer.

A few years later, with the twins no longer requiring so much from
her, Paula is ready to spend more time with Jay. By now, however, Jay
has become deeply involved in his work, partly because Paula had been
so deeply involved with the twins. So when Paula reaches out, he is no
longer available. At this point Paula is again the pursuer and Jay the
distancer.

Pursuit and distance are to some degree the result of such situational factors and are not just a consequence of the partners' personalities.

BUT CAN KNOWING THESE THINGS REALLY HELP?

Mr. Skeptic: Well all that's very interesting. I must admit that some of what you say reminds me a lot of my own marriage. But how can these eleven new ideas about pursuit and distance really help. They seem so *intellectual.*

Wile: They can help because it's the old ideas—the thinking that Paula, Jay, and the rest of us ordinarily use—that *cause* the problem. The solution is intellectual because the *problem* is intellectual. There wouldn't even *be* a pursuer-distancer problem if people didn't have the accusing ways of thinking that they have.

Paula and Jay's problem isn't that Jay sneaks into the bedroom to study and that Paula hangs around waiting for him. The problem is that they think that something is wrong with them for having this problem. They don't realize that nearly everyone has at least a mild version of this problem. They think that they should try harder to change; they don't realize that their attempts to change cause much of the problem. They criticize Paula for not being more independent and Jay for not being more intimate; they don't realize that the relationship makes it impossible for them to be these things.

Imagine what it would be like if Paula and Jay were to know the eleven facts I just described. Instead of seeing themselves:

As defective people in a defective relationship,
Who are unwilling to change,
And who may even be wanting their relationship to fail,

they would now see themselves:

As trying to change,
Which, ironically is causing much of the problem,
And as struggling with a universal couple problem,
In which it is impossible for them and their partner not to feel accused,
And as caught in a trap in which each partner's efforts to make things
     better tend to make them worse.

In the old way of thinking, there is no way for them to talk usefully with one another about the problem. They feel there is nothing to talk about. They think that they should simply stop being so selfish, unreasonable, and self-destructive.

In the new way of thinking, there *is* a way for them to talk usefully with one another about the problem, although it's still not *easy* to do so.

Let's say that when Jay had gone back to school, he and Paula were to have seen a psychotherapist who teaches them this new way of thinking. As before, Jay comes home with his arms full of books. Paula's heart sinks, since she wants to talk to him and she knows that Jay won't want to do anything until he finishes studying. So right away Paula is in a difficult spot. All that she can think to do are things that in the past embroiled her in pursuit and distance:

1. Throw caution to the winds and try to talk to Jay anyway. (But this would be pursuing.)
2. Wait until he finishes studying and try to talk to him then. (But this would be trying *not* to pursue, which is part of the pursuit-and-distance pattern.)
3. Decide not to rely on Jay and do something on her own; for example, see a movie. (But this would be trying to prove her independence, which also is part of the pursuit-and-distance pattern.)

When I say that Paula has mastered the facts of pursuit and distance, I don't mean that she'd no longer do these three things. In fact, she might do *all* of them. But—and here's the important point—she'd do them in a *new* way: she'd know what she was doing (or at least be able to figure it out later) and she'd be able to talk with Jay about it.

PAULA (after coming home from the movie): Well, I did it again. It all started when I insisted on talking to you even though I knew that your mind was on your studies. I don't know why I did it. . . . Well, I guess I do. There were so many things I wanted to tell you. I guess my excitement got the better of me.

In talking this way, Paula is no longer pursuing. Instead, she is talking *about* her pursuing. And that makes a difference. Since he doesn't feel as pursued, Jay feels less need to withdraw. Instead, he does what Paula had been wanting him to do all along: he listens to what she says and reacts to it.

JAY: Well, I can see how we got into trouble, then, because when I saw you wanted to talk, I did what I usually do. I pretended to be interested—I wanted to be polite—and then I looked for the first opportunity to slip away. I feel bad about pretending like that. And I don't even know why I did it. It never fools anybody—you always figure it out. And I feel *bad* about doing it.

In talking this way, Jay is no longer withdrawing. Instead, he is talking *about* his withdrawing. And although he is saying things that you'd think might upset Paula, she's *not* that upset. That's because Jay is finally engaged with her, even if it's to discuss how he's been unengaged.

PAULA: Well, I *did* figure it out. And I did what *I* usually do. I told myself, "Who needs you," and I tried to prove I *didn't*. I went to a movie. But I hated the movie; and I hated being there alone. I keep forgetting that trying to prove my independence never works.

JAY: I know what you mean. Trying to prove how caring I am never works either. Remember the time I took you on that picnic?

PAULA: Isn't it something how we keep doing these things?

JAY: Maybe we'd have better luck if *I* went to the movies and *you* arranged the picnics.

This is the kind of conversation that is possible to have if partners have a usable joint overview of their pursuit and distance. Only people who had at least partly forgiven themselves and their partners for being pursuers and distancers could talk about these difficult matters in such a nonaccusing, nonself-hating, and matter-of-fact manner.

So a good way for partners to handle pursuit and distance is to be able to talk about it *afterwards*. And when they have mastered this, they might then go to the next step and try to have such conversations *beforehand*. Here's an idealized example of how Paula and Jay could have done this:

PAULA: I'm worried about tonight. I want to talk, but I see you want to study. And we usually get into trouble when this happens: I end up feeling neglected, and you end up feeling crowded.

Instead of talking to Jay (or trying not to talk), Paula is telling him about her *wish* to talk.

JAY: I know what you mean. That *is* what often happens. And it could *really* happen tonight, because I need to study even more than usual. I'm worried about my math.

Instead of skirting around the problem, which is what Paula and Jay usually do, they are spelling it out. In so doing, Jay is getting the chance to explain that he *really* needs to study and Paula is getting the chance to hear what's on Jay's mind.

PAULA: What's the problem with your math?
JAY: I got my midterms back today, and I got the worst grade in class. I was so humiliated. It made me wonder whether I'll *ever* graduate.

This brief interchange means a lot to Paula. Hearing what Jay feels—particularly since he so rarely tells her—makes her feel closer to him and more included in his life. As a result, she feels more content than usual to do things on her own. In fact, she becomes so engrossed fiddling with the computer that Jay has to tear her away when, after finishing his math, he suggests they go for a beer.

This brief interchange means a lot to Jay also. It makes him feel closer to Paula. That's why he wants to take her out for a beer. It's important to him to be able to tell her his worries about his math.

If partners learn to accept pursuit and distance as a commonplace event rather than as something awful and unacceptable, they'd be better able to think about, talk about, and deal with this occupational hazard of being a couple.

17

Bypassing and Nonbypassing

Partners need a way to deal with the common situation in which one gets caught up in a fantasy while the other is left behind in reality.

When Polly thinks of having a party, she thinks of:

The chance to experiment with exotic new recipes.
Sparkling conversation.
Everyone having a grand time.
The chance to invite friends whom she hasn't seen for months.
Setting the perfect table.
The chance, finally, to use the new serving platter she got last Christmas.
The chance to introduce her neighborhood friends to her work buddies. She's sure they'll really get along.
The chance to introduce her best friend, Maggie, who's single, to the interesting new unattached man at work. She's sure *they'll* really hit it off.
Everyone noticing what a great decorating job she and her husband Mike did on their living room.

And thinking about a party this way—as something wonderful—Polly really wants to have one. She suggests the idea to Mike.

When *Mike* thinks of a party, however, he thinks of:

The expense.
Cleaning up the mess afterwards.
People feeling left out and resentful because they weren't invited.
His neighborhood friends *not* getting along with his work buddies.

People noticing what a lousy job he did wallpapering the bathroom.
Forgetting people's names when he tries to introduce them.
Strained conversation; no one quite knowing what to say.
Food spills leaving stains on the rug that won't come out.
People leaving early because they didn't have a good time.
Or people having such a good time that they stay till six in the morning.
Eating leftovers for a week.

And thinking about it this way, Mike *doesn't* want to have a party.

MIKE: A party's the last thing we need right now. We just finished redecorating the house.

POLLY: But that's just why we *should* throw a party. To celebrate, and to show off what we've done.

MIKE: Yeah, but after all that work, we need a rest.

POLLY: *I* don't need a rest. I need a *party*.

MIKE: But you're forgetting all the effort it will take: the shopping, the preparing.

POLLY: It'll be *fun*.

MIKE: Yeah, what about the cleaning? *That* won't be fun. And what about the expense? Did you see how much we owe this month on our *Visa*?

POLLY: Oh pooh! Why do you always have to be so *negative*?

MIKE: I'm *not* negative. I'm just being realistic. Wasn't it you who said: "Remind me never to throw a party again?" Okay, so now I'm reminding you.

POLLY: Yeah, but I only said that because I was frustrated *at the moment*. We couldn't find the table leaf. We forgot the charcoal. And then I couldn't get the turkey to fit in the oven. But I soon got over it and the party turned out to be a great success.

As this episode demonstrates, there are at least two ways to think about a party:

You can go into *fantasy overdrive*. You can be like Polly and get caught up in a fantasy about how wonderful it will be.

Or you can go into *reverse*. You can be like Mike and think of all the problems.

What's interesting is that Mike wouldn't *inevitably* have been against a party and might even have gotten into the spirit of it. For this to happen, however, he would have needed Polly to appreciate how he felt. He would have needed her to say something like—

POLLY: Yeah, you're right, there *are* a lot of negative things about a party—the expense, cleaning up afterwards, and everything else. I guess when I'm in a mood like this, I *forget* all the problems. I suppose it's ridiculous to have a party at this time. It's just that it'd mean a lot to me.

Hearing this—having Polly acknowledge the grain of truth in what he is saying—Mike might now begin to feel more like having the party—

MIKE: Well, what the heck. Another seventy-five dollars isn't going to sink us. And maybe a party *would* be fun.

Or the opposite might occur. Seeing that Mike has come around—not only has he agreed to the party, but he *even* thinks it's a good idea—Polly might now begin to realize that she had been overglamorizing parties. The fact that they are no longer arguing—she no longer feels the need to defend herself—makes it possible for Polly to *consider* what Mike has said:

POLLY: I don't know. I'm thinking about what you said earlier. Maybe you're saving us from making a big mistake. I'm beginning to re-member now how much work it is to throw a party and how they're never as much fun as I always think they're going to be. In fact, they can be downright awful.

In reacting to an idea, one partner may go on fantasy overdrive and the other may go into reverse. How the partners talk about these different ways of reacting can intensify or reduce their conflict about it.

THREE INSTANCES OF FANTASY OVERDRIVE

Most people would want to be like Polly. It's more fun to have a positive rather than a negative attitude. And it's more fun to deal with a problem by going into fantasy overdrive—becoming enthusiastic—than it is to with-draw, fight, or become depressed, which is what many people do.

But let's go back earlier in the day to see what led up to this con-versation. Polly was getting ready to go out and do some weeding when she said:

POLLY: How come you never help in the yard anymore?
MIKE: You think I'm going to go out there and get dirty and sweaty just

to get nagged? Because that's what always happens. You don't like
the way I prune.

POLLY: I've never criticized your pruning.

MIKE: Oh yeah? What about last spring with the roses?

POLLY: I was just giving you a few pointers.

MIKE: Since when are *you* the great expert? I have my own way of pruning.

POLLY: Hacking a rose bush with a pair of clippers is hardly a "way of
pruning."

MIKE: You see? You *don't* like the way I prune.

POLLY: Well, I don't like your *hacking* my roses.

MIKE: Oh? Since when are they *your* roses? It was *my* idea to get them,
and it ought to be up to me to take care of them.

POLLY: Well, if that's the case, I feel sorry for the roses.

MIKE: And *I* feel sorry for you, because you're not going to get me out
there in the yard.

POLLY: Well, maybe that's a good thing. At least the roses will be safe.

When Polly comes in after working in the yard, she and Mike don't
speak for an hour. And when they do finally talk, they do so hesitantly
and tensely. They don't want to start another fight.

So that was the atmosphere, then, in which Polly went into fantasy
overdrive and suggested that they throw a party. She ignored the tension
between them and pretended that they were getting along so well that
they might even want to give a party together.

Although Polly was discouraged when Mike rejected the idea of a
party, a little later she went into fantasy overdrive again. She approached
Mike with a handful of travel brochures. Her hope, although she was not
thinking of it in this way at the time, was to patch things up by musing
about fabulous vacations trips that they might take together.

While Polly was thinking of having a great time getting away together,
doing exciting things, really getting along, and making love in quaint and
exotic places, Mike was thinking of jetlag, boring guided tours, getting on
one another's nerves, arguing about what to see, and making love in
uncomfortable, unfamiliar beds.

Sensing that Mike was not sharing her enthusiasm about traveling,
Polly gathered up her brochures and put them away.

And a few hours later, Polly went into fantasy overdrive again. She went into the bedroom where Mike was reading and started caressing him. Her hope, although she was not thinking of it in this way at the time, was to patch things up through sex. She was thinking how handsome he was and how sexually giving they could be to one another.

And, again, Mike went into reverse. "What makes her think I'd be interested in sex?" he said to himself. "First she criticizes me, then she doesn't talk to me, then we quarrel about having a party and going on a trip."

> "In response to touch," Bernard Apfelbaum writes, "there is one kind of person for whom all worries and grudges are suddenly forgotten; for another kind of person worries and grudges are just as suddenly remembered."

Apfelbaum refers to the first type of person as a "bypasser" and the second as a "nonbypasser."

> Bypassers can enjoy sex *despite* what is going on in the relationship. They are somehow able to overlook the fact that, for instance, they haven't exchanged a civil word with their partners all day.
> Nonbypassers can't enjoy sex because they *can't* overlook what's going on in the relationship. The thought of physical intimacy with their partners just makes them more aware of the *lack* of emotional intimacy.

The ideas of bypassing and nonbypassing can be applied not only to sex, but to any activity.

BYPASSER-NONBYPASSER CONFLICTS

Bypassing and nonbypassing are mutually incompatible ways of dealing with problems.

> The bypasser's way to solve a problem is to stop talking about it— because that just makes it worse—and to trip off in fantasy.
> The nonbypasser *can't* trip off in fantasy. If he or she is to solve a problem, he or she has to *try* to talk about it—even though talking about it *might* make things worse.

So when Polly, the bypasser, deals with the problem by approaching Mike for sex (she has the fantasy of their having great sex to compensate for the problems of the day), Mike, the *non*bypasser, deals with it by trying to talk.

MIKE: What makes you think I'd be interested in sex? We've been fighting all day. And when we weren't fighting, we weren't talking. And then, when we did begin to talk, you started pressuring me about having a party and going on a trip. And I'm still smarting over what you said about my pruning.

And having said all that, Mike now feels a little better and a little more like having sex. The chance to state feelings and make complaints can have a powerful affection-reviving and love-reviving effect.

But while Mike now feels more like having sex, Polly now feels *less* like having it. It's hard for Polly to think of how handsome Mike is and how sexually giving they could be to one another when he's making these complaints.

POLLY: Why did you have to bring all that up and ruin the mood? I don't even feel like sex anymore.

So here's the problem of bypasser-nonbypasser conflicts: what each partner needs to improve the mood ruins the mood for the other.

In a bypasser-nonbypasser conflict, each partner's way of staying in love interferes with the other's way of doing so. Nonbypassers maintain their feeling of love by talking about their problems. Bypassers maintain their feeling of love by *not* talking about their problems.

Bypassers such as Polly can't understand why their nonbypassing partners can't "relax a little," "take things as they come," "put aside their problems," and "stop having to talk about everything." They don't see why it would cost their partners so much to do the very little they require to keep the fantasy of intimacy going: an "I love you" once in a while, a hug, a card, or a willingness to have sex or muse about romantic vacations. They are forced to conclude that their partners must *want* to frustrate them.

Nonbypassers such as Mike can't understand how their bypassing partners can possibly *want* to have sex or muse about romantic vacations given the problems between them. They don't see why it would cost their partners so much to do the very little they require: to talk about their problems. Getting things off their chests is so relieving to them that they can't understand why their partners don't experience the same relief.

Although Polly is generally the bypasser and Mike is generally the nonbypasser, at times they reverse roles. Mike loves fishing and Polly hates it. If, among the vacation plans Polly had suggested to Mike, she had included fly casting for trout, Mike would have immediately gone into fantasy overdrive. He'd forget about the disagreeableness of the day and, appreciating Polly's willingness to consider such a trip, he'd begin thinking how wonderful it would be—just the two of them alone on the river with all that trout. Polly would never suggest fly casting, of course, since just the thought of fishing makes her want to yawn.

So what do you do if you're trying to deal with a particular problem by bypassing while your partner is trying to do so by nonbypassing? First, you'll need to appreciate that you and your partner are adopting contrasting strategies in dealing with a difficult problem:

> The bypasser, having given up on the possibility of dealing with the problem by talking about it, shifts into fantasy overdrive.
>
> The nonbypasser, having given up on the possibility of dealing with the problem by shifting into fantasy overdrive, tries to talk about it.

And now it's easy to see how bypassing and nonbypassing relate to pursuit and distance, the other major pattern talked about in this section of the book:

> Pursuit and distance refer to *readiness* to engage: the pursuer engages and the distancer doesn't.
>
> Bypassing and nonbypassing refer to *what* the pursuer is trying to engage the partner *in*. The bypasser tries to engage the partner in a *fantasy*. The nonbypasser tries to engage the partner in *talking*.

So, depending on who is trying to engage whom in what, either the bypasser *or* the nonbypasser can be the pursuer.

Recognizing bypassing and nonbypassing as understandable, although alternative, strategies for dealing with difficult problems may enable partners to feel less accusing toward themselves and one another for adopting them.

Polly and Mike could even have talked about their alternative strategies, although since it is talking, it's something that the nonbypasser—Mike—is more likely to want to do:

MIKE: I don't like your not wanting to talk about our problems, but I understand it. After all, talking can make things worse. In fact, in some ways I wish *I* could do what you do and forget our problems and just imagine feeling good about one another.

POLLY: I don't like your not wanting to have sex (or plan a party or muse about vacations), but I understand it. After all, we haven't said a civil word to one another all day. And the fact that *I'm* caught up in a fantasy about sex (or about a party or about romantic vacations) doesn't mean that *you* have to be.

It's clear that Polly and Mike would have an easier time dealing with the situation if they were to think and talk about it in this nonaccusing way.

VI

COMPROMISING AND FANTASIZING

Everyone *hopes* that relationships are based on love:

> While the honeymoon feeling doesn't last (or for some couples, was
> never there in the first place), it is thought that over time a deeper
> although less intense love develops. Or at least we hope it does.
> And this deeper although less intense love lasts even though we
> grow older and less attractive. Or at least we hope it does. And
> the rough edges mellow; the characteristics of our partner that
> we didn't like become endearing to us. Or at least we hope they
> do. And we find ourselves wanting to do things for our partner,
> wanting to please him or her, wanting to spend time with him
> or her, and wanting to do what our partner wants to do. Or at
> least we hope we do. And we find ourselves wanting to remain
> faithful. We're so in love that we don't even think about having
> affairs. Or so we hope.

But everyone is *afraid* that relationships are based on duty:

> A relationship is a set of compromises that have to be made. It's
> having to give when you want to receive. It's being reassuring
> when you don't feel like reassuring. It's being faithful when you
> don't want to be faithful. It's work. It's going bowling when
> you want to go to a flower show. It's going to a flower show when
> you want to go bowling. It's two people doing things they don't
> want to do in order to make the other person happy.

Many people seem resigned to the duty view and are skeptical about
the love view. We tell ourselves to avoid romantic fantasies and unrealistic

expectations and to recognize that a relationship requires compromise, hard work, commitment, and sacrifice.

> "You think that a relationship is glamor, romance, and sex," a person who adopts the unrealistic-expectations way of thinking might say. "It's not. It's diapers, it's scrubbing the floor, and it's 'Sorry, I've got a headache tonight.' "

I shall try to show that:

Compromises are dangerous. They're calculated risks that people don't realize they are making. The calculated risk is that they will be able to get away with doing something they really don't want to do without becoming too resentful and without having to withdraw (Chapter 18).

Although having romantic fantasies causes problems, so does trying *not* to have them. Romantic fantasies are on the cutting edge of the relationship. They're clues to reality. And they're more fulfillable than many people think (Chapters 19 and 20).

18

Discovering the Hidden Compromises

*E*veryone knows the hazards of *not* compromising. My goal in this chapter is to describe the equally dangerous but less well-known hazards of *compromising*. Partners will be at an advantage if they realize that:

1. People make compromises so quickly and so automatically that they are often unaware of doing so.
2. The boredom and devitalization that can creep into a couple's relationship are unrecognized consequences of the continuous flow of compromises and accommodations.
3. What appears to be a partner's unwillingness to compromise may actually be reactions to unrecognized compromises that he or she is already making.
4. Compromises are hidden gambles. People gamble that they will be able to make compromises without becoming too resentful or too withdrawn. Sometimes the gamble pays off and sometimes it doesn't.
5. Beneath the emphasis placed on the need to compromise is the belief that people are basically selfish; they have to be weaned from the childish joys of selfishness.

Not compromising can ruin relationships. But so can compromising.

ALREADY EXISTING HIDDEN COMPROMISES

One danger with the common view about compromises—the view that partners should try harder to make them—is that problems arise from the hidden ways in which they are *already* compromising. Here is an example:

225

Joyce and Claire are a lesbian couple who have lived together for five years. They are in their early thirties. Joyce seems unreasonable and uncompromising because she's unresponsive to Claire's needs for affection. When Claire comes into the kitchen for a hug and a kiss, Joyce turns away. When Claire persists, Joyce says impatiently:

JOYCE: Can't you see I'm stirring the soup?
CLAIRE: These days you're *always* stirring the soup, or studying, or *something*.

What might seem like unresponsiveness to Claire's needs is a consequence of Joyce's *dedication* to her needs. Claire's presence in the kitchen is a nuisance because Joyce is so busy trying to fulfill Claire's needs, or at least what she *thinks* are Claire's needs. Since Claire can't cook but loves to eat, one of the special things that Joyce does for her is to prepare her gourmet meals. And she does so even though she goes to school and has a full-time job. For Joyce, Claire's coming into the kitchen for a hug is simply another demand on her time.

Both partners feel that Joyce is being ungiving and selfish in failing to give Claire a hug when she wants one. They think that people have to extend themselves a little if a relationship is to work out.

An alternative view is that people may appear selfish and uncompromising because of the hidden ways in which they are already compromising. Joyce comes to Claire later that evening and says:

JOYCE: I felt bad about shrugging you off when you came in for a hug. That's not how I want to be.

What makes this the beginning of a conversation rather than the beginning of an argument is that Joyce isn't criticizing *Claire*. Instead, she's criticizing herself.

When one partner admits the ways that he or she might have been wrong, the other partner often feels like admitting the ways that he or she might have been wrong:

CLAIRE: I appreciate your saying that. If you think about it, though, my timing was pretty bad. You'd just come home from work, it was a night you had to go to class, and there you were busy fixing dinner.

By talking about only their *own*, and not their partner's, contributions to the fight, Joyce and Claire are keeping the discussion from turning back into a fight.

Joyce responds to Claire's generous response by making one of her own:

JOYCE: Well it's important to me to treat you well. I know how hard you work at the hospital. You *deserve* a good meal.

CLAIRE: Well, maybe that's what I deserve, but let me tell you what I'd really like. On nights like this when you come home late from work and then have to go to school, I'd like to find you relaxing in the living room rather than scurrying around the kitchen.

Joyce can't believe Claire means it:

JOYCE: Really? Are you sure? You're forgetting how much you like a really decent meal.

CLAIRE: Sure. But there's something I like even more. I like to talk to you a little before you go to school. On those nights, I can find a way to fix my own dinner.

Claire is helping Joyce to stop compromising; that is, to become less concerned with what she *thinks* are Claire's needs. If Joyce were to stop compromising, she might be able to give Claire what she really wants. Claire would rather have a hug from a relaxed partner than a big meal from a tense one.

A CHAIN OF COMPROMISES

People make compromises so quickly and so automatically that they are often unaware of doing so.

Martha and James are a married couple in their mid-thirties. Martha goes to a local college and works part-time as a nurse. James is a general contractor.

On the way home from her job one day, Martha daydreams about vacationing in Italy. Since she knows that James is worried about money and wouldn't even want to think about such a trip, she quickly dismisses the idea and, instead, thinks of their going to an Italian opera. Since she knows that James doesn't like opera, she quickly dismisses this idea and, instead, thinks of their going to an Italian restaurant. Since it's Wednesday and she knows that James doesn't like to go to restaurants in the middle of the week, she quickly dismisses this idea and, instead, thinks of their sending out for pizza.

Martha hasn't even *talked* to James and she's already made three compromises.

When James says that he doesn't feel like a pizza, Martha throws a tantrum and then sulks. James can't figure out what's gotten into her. And Martha doesn't know what's gotten into her, either. Compromises are made so quickly and so automatically that the person often forgets that he or she has made them. James (and Martha too) suddenly sees her as a selfish, unreasonable, and uncompromising woman who gets upset if she doesn't immediately get everything she wants.

What James doesn't know, and what Martha herself has forgotten, is that Martha isn't getting *anything* she wants. She wants to go to Italy, but she'll make do with pizza. And James won't even go along with that.

Martha's tantrum, which both attribute to her demanding, uncompromising attitude, is the result of compromises she has made with James that he knows nothing about. He's unaware of all that's riding on the pizza.

Even so, James's saying no to pizza is a surprise. He loves pizza and typically looks for any opportunity to have one. In substituting a pizza for a trip to Italy, Martha is only asking for something that she has every reason to believe that James already wants.

James's saying no to pizza turns out to be a consequence of unspoken compromises of his own. Since he *is* worried about money, he wants to suggest that Martha quit school and get a full-time job. He doesn't suggest this, however, since he knows how important school is to her. He thinks it's small-minded of him to begrudge her an education and he doesn't want to be seen as a male chauvinist who stands in the way of what his wife wants to do. So, instead, he considers making the more modest request of asking her to cut down on her expenses. However, he doesn't do this either. Martha has gotten upset in the past when he's asked her to spend less because she felt accused of being a spendthrift, which she feels she isn't. So, instead, James decides on the still more modest plan of their jointly cutting down on luxuries such as eating out, going to movies, and sending out for pizza. He doesn't tell Martha about this, however, since he thinks she won't like hearing it; she already thinks he's overconcerned about money.

Martha and James need a conversation in which they sort out what has happened. Here is an idealized picture of how such a conversation might go:

MARTHA : I can't understand why I got so upset about your not wanting to send out for pizza. I don't even like pizza all that much. It's usually the other way around. You're the one who wants to send out for it and I'm the one who says no.

Since Martha isn't blaming him, James doesn't have to defend himself:

JAMES: Well that's true. In fact, I thought getting a pizza was a great idea. I only said no because I was worried about the money.

And now that the issue of money has come up, things could get sticky. James could say something like, "You always spend too much" or "It's hard making ends meet when you don't bring in your share," which would immediately transform the conversation into an argument.

Instead, however, James says:

JAMES: I didn't tell you about this because we always get into fights when we talk about money. But I was thinking this morning that it might help if we didn't eat out so much. Little did I know that the first thing to go would be what I like best—pizza.

MARTHA: Well, you may not have known it, but I *was* economizing. You can't imagine how much money I saved us. I was thinking today of our going to Italy. But then I though, why all that bother when we can send out for pizza.

And Martha now realizes what got her so upset about the pizza:

MARTHA: And I guess that's why I got so upset about the pizza. I had given up so many things I really wanted to do—in addition to Italy, I was thinking about our going to an opera or to that new Italian restaurant. You thought you were just saying no to pizza. You didn't realize all that was riding on a few anchovies.

Hearing what Martha had been feeling, James now feels like trying to do something to please her:

JAMES: Well, what the heck. Let's send out for a pizza. Or better yet, let's go to that restaurant. We'll save money tomorrow.

The problem, it now becomes clear, is that Martha and James had been deprived of the *chance* to compromise. They had been deprived of the opportunity to state what they really wanted and to discover what the other really wanted. And they had been deprived of the feeling of good will that would enable them to *want* to do things for their partner and to *enjoy* compromising.

COMPROMISES ARE HIDDEN GAMBLES

People often think that compromising—putting yourself out a little—is easy to do. All it takes, they believe, is a little maturity and a little willingness to think of someone besides yourself. It's not going to kill a husband to put off tennis and, instead, stay home with the kids so his wife can go swimming. And it's not going to hurt a wife to go with her husband occasionally to the kind of movie *he* likes to see. People make accommodations all the time. Compromising is not hard. It's no big deal.

We don't ordinarily think of it this way but compromises are gambles. In compromising, people force themselves to do things that they otherwise wouldn't want to do. If the accommodation or sacrifice turns out to be more difficult and unpleasant than anticipated and to have less of a payoff, the person may rebel against the whole thing and become angry or withdrawn. The gamble is that people will be able to get the benefits of compromising (pleasing the partner and cementing the relationship) *without* becoming resentful and without withdrawing.

> James takes Martha to the restaurant and, a month later, offers to go to an opera. He thinks he owes it to her, even though he doesn't much care for opera; Martha makes so many compromises for him. She doesn't particularly care for baseball, for example, but she recently suggested that they go to a game when the Red Sox come to town.

But even before the curtain rises on *La Boheme*, James realizes he has made a mistake:

JAMES (to himself): How did I get myself into this? The show hasn't even begun and I already want to go home. I've got to get out of here, but I can't think how. Maybe there'll be an earthquake, and they'll have to cancel the show. Or maybe the star will come down with laryngitis. I wish they'd get it started and get it over with.

James guts it through the opera. On the way home, when Martha criticizes him for driving too fast, he blows up:

JAMES: I've just spent three awful hours being bored to tears so that *you* would have someone to take you to this stupid opera and the first thing you say is, "You're driving too fast." Of course I'm driving too fast. I'm trying to get as far away as fast as I can.

Martha is immediately sorry they ever went to the opera. She blames herself for dragging him there. And she blames *James* for being so nasty about it. She spits out:

MARTHA: Well, don't worry your head about it. We'll never go again.

A month later, at the baseball game, Martha realizes that *she* has made a mistake:

MARTHA (to herself): I can't believe it's just the second inning. It seems like we've been here for years. It's beginning to cloud up. Maybe it'll rain and we can go home. Or maybe the Sox will play badly and James'll want to leave early. Fat chance. He's really enjoying himself. He'll stay no matter what. And it'd be just my luck to have the game go into extra innings. What a horrible thought.

Martha guts out the remainder of the game. On the way home, James says to her: "You seem quiet. Is there something wrong?"

"No. I'm just a little tired," she replies.

This is a classic exchange of partners when they sense that something's amiss but don't quite know what it is or how to talk about it.

James's and Martha's calculated risks didn't work out. James didn't realize the extent to which he would hate the opera, and Martha didn't realize the extent to which she would hate the game. But their gambles *could* have worked out. Other gambles of a similar nature had, at times, worked out in the past:

The previous winter, as a special favor to James, Martha agreed to go skiing with him. The fact that she had such low expectations —she hadn't the slightest hope that she'd enjoy the trip—allowed her to relax and kind of enjoy it. James was so pleased that Martha had come skiing and, in addition, that she seemed to be in such good spirits about it, that he felt like doing something special for her. He suggested they go dancing, which is something she had always wanted them to do. And just as Martha had gotten caught up in skiing, James got caught up in dancing. He found her enthusiasm contagious. And he was touched by how touched she was at his suggesting they go dancing. She was more affectionate than she had been in years, and later that evening they had the greatest sex ever.

What allows people to force themselves to do things they don't really want to do and still have it come out all right? Much depends on how much of a sacrifice it is. Dancing turned out to be much more pleasant than James had anticipated, and the opera turned out to be much more *un*pleasant. Skiing turned out to be much more pleasant than Martha had anticipated, and the ball game turned out to be much more *un*pleasant.

Chance plays an important role. Whatever possibility that James had for enjoying the opera—and there was some—was completely destroyed by the fact that his best friend phoned just before they left and offered him boxing tickets for that very evening. So going to the opera meant he had to give up the fights. Furthermore, traffic was heavy, parking was difficult, and the theater was overheated. To top it all off, Martha didn't seem nearly as grateful and appreciative for his sacrifice as he had expected she'd be. The gamble, which James didn't even know he was making, many unpleasant factors like these wouldn't occur.

People differ in how they react when their hidden gambles fail and when they realize that they have committed themselves to something that they really can't stand:

1. Some immediately *uncommit* themselves. James, for example, might have turned in his seat and announced to Martha that he hates the opera (even though it hadn't even begun), that he's going to the bar across the street, and that he'll meet her afterwards. Martha is unlikely to be very happy about this. And James himself might feel bad about letting Martha down. On the other hand, James would no longer feel trapped at the opera.
2. Some, as James did, force themselves to go through with the activity and *then* express resentment. The common result is to make both partners sorry that they even started the activity.
3. Some, as Martha did, force themselves to go through with the activity (the ball game) and *don't* express resentment. The common result is a subtle withdrawal, which in some ways can be even more disturbing to the relationship. The devitalization that occurs to a greater or lesser extent in all relationships is a consequence of the hidden sacrifices, accommodations, and com-

promises that partners continually make and are unable to talk about.

People who know that their efforts to compromise are gambles will be better able to recover from those that don't work out. Here's the idealized conversation that James and Martha might have had at the opera. James would turn to Martha and say:

JAMES: I know you're not going to like hearing this but I think I made a big mistake coming here. I blew it again. I keep forgetting how dangerous compromises are and I keep making them anyway. Coming to this opera was really chancy although it *might* have worked out if so many things hadn't gone wrong: if Sam hadn't called with tickets for the fights, if the traffic hadn't been so bad, and if we didn't have to park in a tow-away zone. Who knows if the car's even going to be there when we get out? And I'm really disgusted with myself. This is the first thing we've done in our new plan to do more things together and I'm screwing it up already. It's not your fault—I'm the one who suggested we come to this opera—but somehow I'm beginning to blame you anyway.

If Martha responds angrily, they might have a whispery fight right there at the refreshment stand. After their fight, however, and depending on whether Martha and James feel they have gotten their points across, interesting and unexpected things might happen:

The opportunity to say how much he hates the opera, to describe how everything has gone wrong, and to have his feelings acknowledged may enable James to stop hating the opera. He may now be content to stay.

And the chance to say how much she resents his leaving, to say how much she resents his blaming her when it was his idea to come, and to have *her* feelings acknowledged may enable Martha to feel okay about his leaving.

SELFISHNESS

The issue of compromise is important because of its connection with "selfishness." Selfishness is a key element in how we commonly view relationships. People are often seen as basically selfish; that is, as interested only in their own personal pleasure and unwilling to compromise. Selfishness is viewed as the great relationship destroyer.

I have a different idea. I believe that the *inability* to be selfish is the great relationship destroyer. The problem with people whom we generally think of as "selfish" is that they are *limited* in their ability to be selfish. Although they *appear* self-indulgent, they are actually deprived. They are deprived of the major source of personal pleasure and the ultimate form of selfishness: having someone whom you feel so close to and connected with that you really *care* how he or she feels.

The issue of "selfishness" is a complex one that requires a full-scale debate. And here are the debaters:

> Representing the proposition that people are basically selfish and have to learn to compromise: Lucille, from Chapter 9. Lucille, as you remember, uses the character-flaws rule of thumb. Lucille's the natural person to represent the position that people are basically selfish, since selfishness is one of the major character flaws that she's always talking about.

> Representing the position that people who seem selfish are actually deprived: Joe, from Chapter 10. Joe uses the ordinary-feelings rule of thumb. Joe's the natural person to represent this position, since he insists that behavior that we generally see as "childish" and "primitive"—in this case, "selfishness"—is a distorted expression of an ordinary, adult, understandable, garden-variety feeling.

LUCILLE (beginning the debate): Let's face it. People are basically selfish. They think only about themselves. For partners to work out even a halfway decent relationship, they'll have to suppress their selfishness and learn to extend themselves. They'll have to learn to compromise.

JOE: But what about the fact that it's extending themselves and suppressing their "selfish" wishes that *causes* many of these problems. Joyce's effort to extend herself and do something special for Claire—cooking her big meals—had the ironic effect of convincing Claire that Joyce never does *anything* for her. And James's suppressing his wish to complain about the opera led to his tantrum on the way home.

LUCILLE: Well, let's *talk* about James. There are lots of things that he could have done besides suppressing anger and having a tantrum. If he didn't like the singing, he could have focused on parts that he *did* like, such as the costumes or the sets. Or he could have spent the time mentally going over his schedule for the week. Or he could have just enjoyed the fact that he was pleasing Martha and making up for all the things that she's done for him.

JOE: Well yeah, those are good things to try, and, as it happens, James tried them *all*. Unfortunately, there was just so long that he was able to sit there enjoying the costumes. And when he tried to use the time to go over his schedule, the loud singing kept him from concentrating. And when he tried to focus on the pleasure of doing something for Martha, he kept coming back to his *displeasure* in feeling trapped.

LUCILLE: Well, I still think he didn't try hard enough. The world is full of people who are unprepared to work on their relationships and who spend all their time satisfying their own selfish needs.

JOE: You're forgetting that selfishness isn't necessarily that much fun. At least it can be highly overrated. I realize, Lucille, that this differs from your belief that selfishness is so much fun that people have to be weaned from it. But, if you think about it, selfishness—pushing people out of the way and grabbing what you want—is a second rate satisfaction. It's a fallback position. It's what people do when they feel cheated, mistreated, frustrated, disappointed, starved, desperate, lonely, or bored. It's what people do when they do not value, or have temporarily lost the sense of the value, of their relationships with those whom they then push aside. It's the result of a relationship that's not going well. Feeling unfairly treated by her playmate, a three-year-old snatches his toy from him, and he starts crying. Five minutes later, and no longer feeling unfairly treated, the three-year-old shares her candy with him.

LUCILLE: But let's be truthful. We'd *all* be selfish if we thought we could get away with it. Children, at least, are honest about it. They make it clear that they don't want to have to give things; they just want to get them. They say "gimme, gimme, gimme."

JOE: But children *do* want to give. In fact it's hard at times to keep them from giving things to you, bringing you things, trying to help you, and trying to do things for you. Children appear to be like everyone else. They like to get things and they like to give them.

LUCILLE: Well, that's just because their parents have taught them that they *should* give. But let's look at someone who has thrown all that aside. Let's look at the husband who plops in front of the TV and expects his wife to bring him a beer, to make his supper for him, and to wait on him hand-and-foot. He switches to the programs he wants to see and doesn't ask his wife what she wants to watch. Everything revolves around his needs. And when his wife finally does ask for something— she wants to talk a little, she wants a little affection—he says no. You'll have to admit *that's* selfish.

JOE: Maybe so.

LUCILLE: "Maybe so" nothing. This husband is completely committed to his own selfish needs.

JOE: Well, if he is, he's doing a pretty poor job of it. Turning a wife or husband into a servant is like buying a new sportscar and then using it to haul trash. There are much better things to do with a partner. A partner can be used to feel excited about, to have dreams with, to enjoy taking care of as well as to enjoy being taken care of by, to talk things over with, to enjoy giving things to as well as enjoy getting things from, and to feel "in it together" with. This husband is getting none of these things. He's being deprived. He's getting only a fraction of what's possible to get from a relationship.

CONCLUSION

When you think about it, the people whom we generally see as "selfish"—that is, those who exploit their partners—really aren't very good at being selfish. They leave untouched and untapped the major sources of satisfaction that are available in a relationship.

> There are better ways to be selfish than most people realize. And these better ways involve collaboration.

And what would such "collaboration" look like? I've been talking about it all along, of course. It's the kind of interaction that becomes possible when partners adopt nonaccusing forms of thinking, which allow them to:

Build upon (rather than have to defend against) what the other says.

Develop a shared nonjudgmental vantage point for looking at their relationship.

Use their problems as clues.

19

Revealing Fantasies

People have fantasy wishes, and they have them all the time. They hope, for example, that their partners will automatically and spontaneously:

Perform particularly thoughtful or caring acts (bring flowers, cook a special meal, get up with the kids on Saturday mornings, do the vacuuming without having to be asked) that will *really* make them feel loved and satisfied rather than taken for granted.

Engage in sex more enthusiastically, more frequently, with greater abandon, or be willing to engage in a particular sexual act that will *really* make them feel loved and satisfied.

Share a particular interest of theirs that is especially important to them (tennis, camping, gardening) rather than throwing cold water on it.

Take care of tasks that seem particularly burdensome to them at the moment; for example, putting away the baby's toys or calling the washing machine repair shop for the third time.

Greet them at the end of difficult days in a loving and comforting way that will make it all seem worthwhile.

Share their high spirits rather than bring them down.

Snap them out of their low spirits rather than bring them down further.

Mr. Skeptic: People who have such fantasy hopes are just asking for trouble.

Wile: If so, then we're *all* asking for trouble, because we *all* have such hopes.

RECOVERING OVERLOOKED FANTASIES

Everyone knows about the hazards of fantasy expectations:

People who expect the honeymoon feeling to last throughout the marriage may end up with lots of marriages (and lots of honeymoons).

People who wait for perfect partners to come along may end up without any partners.

People who expect their partners to know what they want and how they feel without having to be told are likely to end up continually disappointed.

People who believe that they and their partners should want to spend all their time together may soon end up wanting to spend very little time together.

People who believe that partners who truly love each other never exchange cross words may end up exchanging practically no words.

Few people are aware, however, of the hazards of trying *not* to have fantasies. In fact, this is *the* great hidden hazard in couple relationships.

Loretta is an eighth grade teacher. Her husband, Fred, manages a bakery. They have been married twelve years and have three children. It's Loretta's 40th birthday, and she insists that she doesn't want a party. So, Fred arranges a celebration for just the two of them. He takes her to a hot springs for a sauna and massage, which has always been a special treat for her. Then he takes her to her favorite restaurant. When they get home, he opens a bottle of fancy champagne, and gives her a special gift: a sexy nightgown.

But something is wrong. The sauna and massage don't feel as good as Loretta remembers them. The restaurant doesn't seem as elegant. And when they get home, champagne and nightgown notwithstanding, Loretta just feels sad.

Loretta's problem is a fantasy wish she doesn't know how to deal with. On the way to the hot springs, she realized that she really wanted a party after all. And she hoped that Fred had ignored her instructions and had secretly arranged one for her.

She imagined her friends coming from all over the country. People would even write songs for the occasion. It would be a grand affair lasting till three in the morning. She'd feel so close to everyone.

That's how she wanted to turn forty—in style. And that's why she felt dissatisfed at the hot springs and impatient at the restaurant. And that's why she was disappointed when they got home and found no party. She was disappointed and she was angry. She was angry because she felt that Fred didn't want to give her a party. She felt that he had been secretly relieved when she had told him a month earlier that she didn't want one.

Mr. Skeptic: I'm afraid that Loretta's not going to get much sympathy from me. She's being egotistical to want such a fuss made over her birthday—even if it *is* her fortieth. And it's childish of her to get angry at Fred because he's unable to guess that she wants a surprise party. Talk about unrealistic expectations.

Wile: But *everyone* has unrealistic expectations, and everyone has them all the time. In fact, the fantasy of being given a surprise party is a particularly common one. It's a *standard* fantasy wish. Almost everyone has had it at one time or another.

Mr. Skeptic: Yeah, but Loretta doesn't just expect Fred to know she wants a party. She expects him to know she wants one *even though she tells him she doesn't*. People like that are doomed to disappointment. And they deserve what they get.

Wile: Yeah, that's what Loretta believes too, and *that's* the problem. Her self-criticism and embarrassment about her fantasy prevent her from confiding in Fred about it. And that's too bad because it could be a significant relief if she were able to tell him:

LORETTA: I told you that I didn't want a party, and I didn't. But suddenly today I did. And I was disappointed and even a little angry when we got home just now. I know it's ridiculous and unfair of me, but I had the magical hope that you might have arranged a surprise party even though I told you not to.

A surprise party would have been nice. But the lack of one—the disappointment of Loretta's fantasy wish—is not her major problem. Disappointment is an everyday, even an hourly, event. People are used to being disappointed, and they learn to take it in stride. Loretta's major problem is her *shame* about having such a fantasy wish and the *disconnection* she feels from Fred because she is unable to talk with him about it. Confiding in him could be a good way to deal with this embarrassment and disconnection.

Loretta needs a new way of looking at this fantasy wish. She needs to be able to say to herself:

1. My wish for a surprise party is an *ordinary* wish and not a selfish one. Everyone has wishes like this.
2. It's okay to change my mind. The fact that I told Fred that I didn't want a party doesn't mean that I shouldn't wish that he threw one for me anyway.
3. True, if I were to tell Fred about my fantasy wish, he might feel criticized for not throwing me a party. But I can do my best to make it clear that I'm *not* criticizing him.

People would be less embarrassed by their fantasies if they were to see them as inevitable accompaniments to life. Where they had been saying "What's wrong with me that I'm having this fantasy," they would now be able to say: "Amazing! I'd never have predicted *this* fantasy showing up."

FINDING FANTASIES IN UNEXPECTED PLACES

Mr. Skeptic: I'm not convinced that fantasies are so inevitable. Maybe Loretta has them, but lots of people don't. I'll bet that a person like *Fred* doesn't have them, for instance.

Wile: But he *does*. It's just that his are harder to notice. At the same time that Loretta was hoping for a surprise birthday party, Fred was having a fantasy of his own.

At first, Fred planned Loretta's birthday celebration dutifully, that is, simply because a husband is supposed to do something special for his wife on her birthday and because Loretta would be hurt and angry if he didn't. He was relieved that Loretta didn't want a party because that would have required a lot of work.

But then Fred began to get into the spirit of things. He found himself wanting to feel close to Loretta and to make her birthday special. He phoned the hot springs to make an appointment for Loretta with the masseuse she had liked the previous time. He stopped by the restaurant and ordered a special dish—burgundy duck—that required four days' advance notice. And he searched all over town for a gift that would really please her. And he thought he had found it: the nightgown.

Fred imagined how delighted Loretta would be coming home after the special massage and the special burgundy duck and then opening the special gift. Tears would come to her eyes. She would throw her arms around him and want to make love right then and there among the wrapping papers.

But Loretta didn't react the way he hoped. She didn't like the massage. She was impatient during dinner. And she exchanged the nightgown for a bedspread.

When Loretta's fantasy wishes were disappointed, she was clearly upset, although she had difficulty telling Fred what it was about. When Fred's fantasy wishes were disappointed, he just shrugged a little. He didn't seem distressed. He just seemed the same old Fred. His fantasy wishes developed, collapsed, and disappeared almost without a trace. No one would have known that he had them. And he himself had almost no memory of them, although a subtle, almost undetectable sadness crept into his feelings toward Loretta.

How could Fred have been rescued from this situation? If he had been more comfortable with his wish to please her, he might have been able to respond to Loretta's expressing her fantasy by expressing his own.

FRED: It's funny—your hoping for a surprise party—because I had a fantasy too. I was trying to make it the best birthday you ever had.

LORETTA: Yeah, but you wouldn't have wanted to throw me a party. I know you. You wouldn't have wanted to go to all that bother.

FRED: Well, you're right, I was relieved when you said you didn't want a party. It would have been a lot of work. But also, I wanted to have you all to myself—to make things romantic—to have it just the two of us.

LORETTA: Really? Is that true? I didn't know you felt that way. If I knew you cared that much, maybe I wouldn't have even wanted a party.

To a great many people the ability to talk in this way might be even better than a surprise party.

HALF-EXPRESSED FANTASY WISHES

Feeling embarrassed or self-critical about their fantasy wishes, people withhold them. Or, as in the following example, they blurt them out and then get stuck defending them. Arthur and Charlotte are a couple in their thirties. Arthur is struggling to start a consulting business. Charlotte quit her job as a high school music teacher to take care of their three young children.

She supplements their income by giving piano lessons. While driving to the store, Arthur and Charlotte pass a couple on bicycles.

ARTHUR: Why don't we buy bicycles? (This is Arthur's blurted-out fantasy wish.)
CHARLOTTE: Do you think we'd really use them?
ARTHUR: Why do you always put down every idea I have?
CHARLOTTE: Why do you keep having impractical ideas?
ARTHUR: It's not impractical. We'd get a lot of use out of them.
CHARLOTTE: We'd ride them twice a year, *maybe*.
ARTHUR: Why do you always have to be so logical? You take the fun out of everything.
CHARLOTTE: I just don't think it makes sense to get bikes. We can't even pay our rent.

Mr. Skeptic: I can't get very interested in this couple. Arthur is clearly an immature and irresponsible person who has to have everything that strikes his fancy. And Charlotte's not much better. She's a hostile and controlling person who puts down everything that Arthur says. In a way, they deserve one another.

Wile: Of course, in criticizing Charlotte and Arthur for being "immature," "irresponsible," "hostile," and "controlling," Mr. Skeptic, you're using the *character-flaws* way of thinking. If we look more closely, however, we'll see that Arthur and Charlotte got into an argument so quickly that they never had a chance to realize that Arthur really *agrees* with Charlotte. He *isn't* about to engage in "immature" and "irresponsible" behavior. He *too* thinks that it doesn't makes sense to get bicycles.

If he had said everything he was thinking about the matter, it would have come out this way:

ARTHUR: I know we don't have the money and we probably wouldn't even use them that much, but seeing that couple riding bicycles makes me wish we had them. I feel so bogged down by niggling details, money worries, and irritabilities that I wish we could just go off riding together and forget it all.

To which Charlotte might have answered:

CHARLOTTE: Yeah, me too. And I know just the perfect bicycle path we can go riding off together down. In fact, why don't we actually do it? Today even. We can *borrow* some bicycles.

In so saying, Charlotte would be *joining* Arthur's fantasy and turning it into a reality.

The problem with Arthur's original statement ("Why don't we buy bicycles?") is that it doesn't let Charlotte know that he realizes his plan is impractical. She thus feels obliged—she gets stuck—having to point that out. And Arthur then gets stuck having to defend the fantasy. Arthur's spirited idea, a potential contribution to their relationship, has been transformed into a problem.

All Charlotte and Arthur needed is for *one* of them to realize that Arthur is saying what he *wishes* they could do rather than what he expects them to do. If Arthur were suddenly to realize this, he could say:

ARTHUR: Wait a minute. How did I get myself into defending buying bikes? I agree that it doesn't make sense. I just had a fantasy of us riding off together feeling carefree.

If it were Charlotte, she could say:

CHARLOTTE: Wait a minute. Maybe I jumped too quickly. I just assumed that you wanted us to go out right away and get bikes. But maybe you didn't. Maybe you only meant that you *wished* that we could get them.

SKILLFULLY TRACKING DOWN FANTASY WISHES

Couple life is a succession of half-experienced, half-stated, half-fulfilled, easily lost, and quickly forgotten fantasies. I recommend developing skill in tracking them down and in talking about them.

Let's go back to Karen and Joseph, the partners who greeted one another at the door at the end of a difficult day (Chapters 13 and 14).

> On the way home from work, Joseph had the fantasy wish that Karen would somehow magically know that he has had a difficult day. She'd meet him at the door with a spicy Bloody Mary, have the newspaper all set out for him, keep the kids from bothering him, and bring his dinner to him while he watched TV. Later, she'd give him a fantastic back rub and listen with loving concern as he told her the troubles of his day, followed by. . . .
>
> And Karen had her *own* fantasy. She imagined that Joseph would somehow magically know that she has had a difficult day. He'd

bring home a videotape of her favorite movie, listen comfortingly as she explained all that had gone wrong, and insist that she sit down and relax while *he* takes care of the kids and *he* makes the dinner. Later he'd come to her with solutions to all the problems she had that day. And then he'd suggest that they go away for the weekend—just the two of them—and *he'd* arrange the babysitting.

As soon as Joseph walks through the door, however, both partners' fantasy hopes are crushed. Each discovers that the proposed *rescuer* needs to be rescued.

Mr. Skeptic: That doesn't surprise me. Fantasy expectations like that are doomed to disappointment. It's pretty unrealistic to expect your partner to drop everything and immediately start taking care of you.

Wile: But you're forgetting that almost everyone has such fantasy-wishes. And you're forgetting that almost everyone makes do with *fractional fulfillment*. Karen and Joseph had extravagant fantasies of how the other would rescue them, but when it came down to it, neither one needed very much. It might have taken no more than a kind word from the other and a chance to express their frustrations to interrupt the harsh and un-inviting view of the world they had built up that day and to substitute a warmer and more comforting one. They would no longer need their fantasy expectations to be fulfilled, or rather, their expectations would in a sense have been fulfilled.

Mr. Skeptic: I still think it's wrong for people to expect others to take care of them.

Wile: And Karen and Joseph agree with you. As a result, they were unable to talk about their wishes. Rather than telling Karen about his fantasies, Joseph just presented himself at the door with the vague, half-conscious hope that Karen might spontaneously start fulfilling them. And Karen didn't express her wishes either. She simply listed all the things that had gone wrong that day, hoping that Joseph would figure out that she needed to be rescued. And then, when Karen and Joseph saw that their fantasy-wishes *weren't* going to be fulfilled, they immediately forgot them.

Mr. Skeptic: And that's just as well. I can't think of anything useful they *could* do with them. They certainly couldn't talk about them. How can you tell your partner about such ridiculous, self-centered wishes without feeling ridiculous?

Wile: By *admitting* that you feel ridiculous. Joseph could say:

JOSEPH: I know it's unreasonable for me to even think this, but I had the thought that somehow you would magically know that I had a horrible day and you would do all kinds of wonderful comforting things like give me a backrub, bring my dinner to the TV room, do all my chores for me, and just take care of everything.

If Joseph had stated it this way—that is, as a wish that he *knew* was ridiculous, rather than as something that he really expected Karen to do and that he blamed her for not doing—Karen is less likely to have felt attacked. In fact, she might have said something like:

KAREN: That *does* sound nice—I'd like to have done that for you—although, actually, the way my day has gone—first the flat tire and then the dog eating a quarter pound of butter—I would have liked some comforting myself.

Mr. Skeptic: Yeah, but what's your point? Karen and Joseph are making pretty speeches, but nothing really has changed.

Wile: It may look as if nothing has changed. Neither partner's fantasies are getting fulfilled and it appears as if they're not going to be. Each is too in need of comfort himself or herself to comfort the other. But Joseph and Karen are doing something that partners rarely do. They are talking as if:

It's okay to have outrageous, unfulfillable fantasies.
It's possible to talk about your fantasies without having to accuse your partner of not fulfilling them.
It's possible to listen to your partner describe his or her fantasies without having to feel responsible for fulfilling them.

I'm suggesting a whole new way of looking at fantasies. As it is now, fantasies are seen, on the one hand, as something that you shouldn't be having and, on the other hand, as something that your partner should be fulfilling. No one ever has the luxury to be able to just have them without having to do anything about them.

Karen and Joseph wouldn't be having their fantasies fulfilled. Joseph wouldn't be getting his backrub and Karen wouldn't be getting her video. What they would be getting, however, is help from one another in feeling that it's okay to have such fantasy wishes. And with such help, they wouldn't have had to withdraw. What they might be able to do, instead, is commiserate about their bad luck in having difficult days at the same time so that neither was able to help the other. After a day of alienating experiences like the ones that Karen and Joseph just had, a moment of shared commiseration like this can go a long way.

So that's how it's possible to become skillful in tracking down and talking about fantasy wishes. Three things are required:

1. The idea that when something's not quite right between you and your partner, unrecognized fantasies may be hiding down there somewhere. People who are on the lookout for such hidden fantasies will be at an advantage in finding them.
2. The belief that it's okay to have such fantasy wishes.
3. The ability to talk about your fantasies in a way that doesn't make your partner defensive; that is, making clear that you see your fantasy expectations as just that—fantasies—and that you don't really expect your partner to fulfill them.

Mr. Skeptic: I'll tell you *my* fantasy wish.
Wile: Yeah, what?
Mr. Skeptic: That I get to win one of these arguments.
Wile: That truly *is* a fantasy since this is my book. If you want to win an argument, you'll have to write your own book.

20

Using Fantasies as Clues

*O*nce you are able to notice your fantasies, you are then ready for the next step, which is to use them as clues. Let's go back to Katie's fantasy, which I discussed in Chapter 11:

> Katie thinks longingly back on the early days of the relationship, when she and Burt used to party, dance, and stay up all night talking and making love.

Daydreaming about the excitement she felt early in their marriage reveals Katie's concern about its absence now.

> Pearls are clues to the existence of grains of sand in oysters. Fantasies are clues to the existence of wishes and disappointments in people. And the nature of these fantasies reveals the nature of their wishes and disappointments.

But people hardly ever think to use their fantasies as clues. Instead, they lurch into action. That's what Katie does. She says to Burt:

KATIE: Let's go rowing on the lake tonight.

Her hope is to recapture some of the old romantic feeling. Her statement is lurching into action because she doesn't tell Burt that she has been missing the intimacy that they had early in their relationship and that she hopes that rowing under a full moon might bring it back. She simply says "Let's go rowing."

Katie's having a positive fantasy. She hopes rowing under the moon might revive their romance. Burt's having a negative fantasy. He thinks rowing will show how unromantic they've become. So he says:

BURT: Let's talk about it later.

Burt hopes Katie will forget about it. She doesn't forget about it, but she doesn't bring it up again either. She just feels another degree sadder.

Actually, there isn't anything necessarily wrong with lurching into action. I do it all the time and I get a lot out of it. And Katie and Burt could possibly have gotten a lot out of it. If Burt had agreed to go rowing, the two of them *might* have been able to recapture some of the old romantic feeling.

Lurching into action is a problem only when people *limit* themselves to it. I recommend lurching into action *and* talking about the fantasies that are generating the lurch.

Two weeks later, Katie does make an attempt to talk about them. But as often happens with held-back fantasies, when they do eventually emerge, they do so as accusations. Katie tells Burt:

KATIE: Why is it that we never stay up all night talking as we used to do, or going to parties, or dancing, or making love? (She implies that he's the one who doesn't want to do these things).

Burt responds as people generally do when they feel accused. He defends himself. He responds with reasons rather than feelings.

BURT: You know I've got to get up early to go to work. We were in school in those days and we could sleep till noon.

Battle lines have been drawn. Katie answers that they had classes in the morning so that they *couldn't* have slept till noon. Burt says that they *didn't* have classes in the morning and that they *did* sleep till noon. The discussion gets stuck on their schedule twenty-five years ago, and Katie never does get her point across about missing the feeling they used to have about one another. She comes away feeling that Burt won't listen to her. And secretly she worries that she's too demanding.

Katie's mistake is stating her fantasy as a complaint rather than as a wish. Actually, there's nothing wrong with stating a fantasy as a complaint. At least, let's *hope* there's nothing wrong with it because that's what we all do. Certainly that's what I do. It's almost impossible not to slip into accusation when feeling awkward, uncertain, or frustrated. And people often feel awkward, uncertain, or frustrated about their fantasies.

Stating a fantasy as a complaint is a problem only when that's *all* you do. I recommend making the complaint, perhaps having the argument that may result from the complaint, and then coming back later, after the argument is over, and using the fantasy as a clue.

And that's what Katie does. After making her complaint and getting into an argument, she comes back to Burt later, when they have both calmed down, and brings up the same point but in a less accusing way:

KATIE: It was unfair of me to blame you for the fact that we don't have fun the way we used to. We're both to blame. Or maybe neither of us is to blame. Maybe that's just the way things are.

Having approached Burt in this much less accusing way, Katie is now in a position to use her fantasy as a clue:

KATIE: And I don't even know why I got it into my head to go rowing on the lake. . . . Well, maybe I do. I've been kind of sad lately. There doesn't seem to be the same spark between us. I'm missing what we used to have—and I bet you are too—because we seem so distant with each other now.

Even if Katie were to state her fantasy in this seemingly nonaccusing way, Burt might still become defensive. People are so used to being subtly accused that they often assume that comments they don't immediately understand are criticisms. But Burt *doesn't* become defensive. Instead, he says:

BURT: Well, I've been kind of sad too. In fact, I'm glad you're bringing it up because I'm having fantasies of my own. I keep thinking of that summer we went skinny dipping in that lake in the mountains. That's the most special thing we ever did.

Katie's statement of her fantasy has allowed Burt to state his own. Katie is pleased:

KATIE: That's just the kind of thing I'm talking about. I wish we were at that lake now, even though it would be pretty cold since it's the middle of January.

Instead of arguing as they were before, Katie and Burt are now on the same side.

BURT: There was always something exciting happening in those days.

KATIE: And we felt a lot closer to one another then . . . although, I don't know, I'm beginning to feel pretty close to you right *now*.

BURT: Yeah, it helps a lot just to talk about it.

And, of course, "it helps a lot just to talk about it" because that's what Katie and Burt's fantasies are about: they *hadn't* been talking. They had been daydreaming about periods of special intimacy in the past because they hadn't been talking about the feelings they were having *now*.

> As I've been saying, intimacy is the result of talking; it's hearing what's on your partner's mind and telling your partner what's on your mind.

CLUES WE NEVER USE

The ideal is for partners to use their fantasies as clues. But that's hard to do. When have you ever heard anyone say anything like the following?

> "I've been thinking about how we used to stay up all night talking and making love, so it must mean that I'm feeling what I usually feel when I have that fantasy: distant from you."

> "I've been thinking all day about the time we took off all our clothes and went swimming in that lake in the mountains, so it must mean that I'm feeling what I usually feel when I have that fantasy: that things haven't been feeling special enough between us."

> "I've been imagining living alone in a cabin in the woods, so it must mean that I'm feeling what I usually feel when I have that fantasy: that I've agreed to do more things with you—go to parties, go shopping, go skiing—than I really want to do."

> "I've been thinking how wonderful it would be to have another baby, even though I realize that another baby is the last thing we need right now. So it must mean that I'm feeling what I usually feel when I have such thoughts: particularly close to you."

> "I've been thinking again about that affair you had ten years ago, so it must mean that I'm feeling what I usually feel when I begin stewing about that: ignored by you."

"I've been thinking about my former boyfriend, so it must mean that
I'm feeling what I usually feel when I begin thinking about such
things: taken for granted."

"I've been wishing that you would greet me at the door in a particularly
warm, loving, sexy, and charming way (or tell me how much
you care for me, or come over and give me a hug, or suddenly
feel all turned on by me and want to have mad passionate sex),
so it must mean that I'm feeling what I usually feel when I'm
having such wishes: neglected."

People don't talk about their fantasies. And while it's a shame they
don't, it's also understandable that they don't.

If a wife met her husband at the door by saying that she had been
looking forward to being greeted by a charming, masterful, and
rescuing man rather than the depressed, grumpy, and withdrawn
person that she found, he is likely to become upset. And if he
answers that he had been looking forward to being greeted by
a warm, loving, comforting, and rescuing woman rather than the
complaining, frazzled, ill-tempered person that he found, *she* is
likely to become upset.

Even if they were to say these things, however, all is not lost. What
is left for these partners—and it is a very considerable compensation—is
to commiserate with one another. Husband and wife may agree that it is
a shame that neither is able to give the love and caring the other wants
because, among other reasons, at the moment both need to be loved or
cared for themselves.

They'd be comforting each other regarding the human condition—
the fact that many of our most important needs and wishes remain
unfulfilled.

Such sharing of unfulfilled fantasies may go a long way toward fulfilling
them. A husband who has spend half the day at the unemployment
office—standing on long lines, feeling ignored by the civil service em-
ployees working there, being criticized for not accepting dishwashing jobs
—reacts by imagining being affirmed by his wife to the same degree (or
twice as much) that he felt humiliated at the unemployment office. He
thus comes home with a rather extravagant fantasy of how his wife might
express this affirmation. It might take no more than a kind word from her,

however, and a chance to talk with her about the frustrations of the day to interrupt the view of the world he had built up (that is, as hostile and uninviting) and to substitute a more benign and congenial one. He might no longer need his fantasy expectation to be fulfilled; it would in a sense have been fulfilled.

It is not difficult to understand how this might happen. People often respond to frustrations in the sphere of reality by imagining exquisite gratifications in the sphere of fantasy. It might take no more than a fragment of real satisfaction—a kind word from his wife—to make fantasy satisfaction no longer necessary.

USING FANTASIES AS JOINT CLUES

I'm not saying that you should immediately begin telling your partner about all your fantasies.

In fact, a considerable amount of preliminary work may be necessary. If you and your partner are to talk usefully about your fantasies, the two of you may first need to arrive at a shared appreciation that:

1. Everyone has fantasies that he or she finds threatening. So the fact that you and your partner have such fantasies doesn't mean that you have a bad relationship.
2. Since fantasies are often compensations for dissatisfactions in the relationship, or in life in general, they can be used as clues to the existence of these dissatisfactions.

Mr. Skeptic: That sounds good in principle, but let's be real. Let's consider sexual fantasies that you have about people other than your partner. If you told your partner about them, he or she would only feel hurt and insulted.

Wile: Well maybe, but let's take an example and see if there *might* be a way to talk usefully about such fantasies.

Margaret and John are a couple in their late twenties. They have been married a year. Margaret becomes upset when one evening while doing the dishes she has the fantasy of running naked along a secluded beach with the man across the street. They stop. She reaches out to him. She pulls him down upon her. . . . Margaret's appalled. She thinks she shouldn't be having such thoughts and tries to shut them out. A little later, she imagines wearing an incredibly sexy dress and behaving in a daringly intimate manner with an attractive man from work. Suddenly even these clothes disappear, and she reaches for him. . . .

Margaret feels particularly bad about her fantasies because her husband John is spending the evening assembling an automatic garage-door opener that he had brought home as a special surprise for her. "He's always doing thoughtful things like that," she says to herself. "He knows the trouble I have with the garage door. What's wrong with me that I'm thinking about other men?"

> Did I marry John just for security? Was I never really in love with him?
> Am I incapable of love?
> Am I afraid of closeness?
> Am I unfaithful?
> Am I a nymphomaniac?

Certain psychotherapists (those who use the kind of reasoning I most object to) might have some of the same concerns, although expressing them in different language:

> Did Margaret marry a man who is nonthreatening, but unexciting, to deal with what may be her basic fear of men?
> Is she thinking about other men to protect against too much intimacy with her husband?
> Does she have a basic hatred of men that prevents her from fully giving herself over to the relationship?
> Does she need the reassurance of new men finding her sexually attractive to maintain her self-esteem?

Something *is* clearly wrong with Margaret. What's wrong with her, however, is that she *thinks* that's something wrong with her. Margaret's self-criticism about her fantasies makes her forget what she and everyone else know about fantasies—

> Namely, that fantasies are an inevitable accompaniment to life, that everybody has them, that they are compensations for momentary frustrations and deprivations, and that, as such, they provide clues to the existence of these frustrations and deprivations.

If Margaret is having fantasies of passionate adventure, it may be because her life has become humdrum.

And everyone knows—though, like Margaret, everyone continually forgets—that fantasies are *exaggerated* compensations. A man starving out in the wild fantasizes, not about a sandwich and a cup of coffee, but about an orgy of food—a Roman feast. It can be dangerous going marketing when you're hungry because you'll be tempted to buy everything in the store. Fantasy food is not very filling, and one needs an awful lot of it to feel even a little satisfied.

> And a person in a humdrum marriage fantasizes, not about a mild flirtation, but about a torrid affair. Fantasy romance, like fantasy food, is not very fulfilling and one needs a lot of it—a grand passion—to stir the blood even just a little.

Margaret's sexual fantasies are reactions to a creeping humdrumness. She and John no longer have much to say to one another or feel very involved with one another. The prospect of seeing each other at the end of the day just makes them want to yawn. Her fantasies are a kind of humdrum-remover. In them, she does exciting and stimulating things with men who she feels *are* involved with her.

Margaret and John have not discussed and are not even fully aware of the humdrumness that has crept into their marriage. Margaret's sexual fantasies are thus potential valuable clues to this underlying issue. As I said, however, fantasies are clues that hardly anyone ever uses.

Mr. Skeptic: And I don't see how Margaret is going to use *these* fantasies. She can't tell John about them. He'd just get insulted. And so would you. How would you like it if *your* wife came up to you and told you that she was having sexual fantasies about other men?

Wile: Well, if she came up to me out of nowhere and said that, I'd be pretty upset. I'd be wondering what she was trying to tell me. But if we had an understanding that fantasies were clues, and that telling one another about them was a contribution and something we wanted to do, then I wouldn't be so upset. Or, at least, I'd wait to hear more to see whether I *ought* to be upset. And if her fantasy led to an issue that had been bothering me too, I'd be grateful to her for bringing it up.

But you're right, Mr. Skeptic, that Margaret is unlikely to tell John about her fantasies.

MARGARET (to herself): My God! Married only a year and I'm already bored. What does this mean about me? Here I'm this "nice girl" and this "faithful wife," and my mind is a pornographic novel. It's a good thing John doesn't know what I'm thinking. And I wish *I* didn't.

Okay, now let's imagine what Margaret might say to herself if she were able to use these fantasies as clues:

MARGARET (to herself): How interesting. I'm having all these sexual fantasies. I wonder what they mean. If I'm daydreaming about exciting sexual involvements with men, I guess it must mean that I'm feeling unstimulated and uninvolved with John. That explains why I've been feeling so down recently.

Even if Margaret were to have this understanding, and even if she had an agreement with John to talk about fantasies, she might still hesitate to tell him about *these* fantasies, fearing that he'd just get hurt and insulted. But she gives it a try:

MARGARET: I don't know how to say this—I'm feeling really bad about it and I think it'll make you mad—but while you're out there in the garage being a perfect saint and installing the new garage door opener for me, I'm here in the kitchen washing dishes and having sexual fantasies of other men. I feel really embarrassed and upset.

As it turns out, Margaret has good reason to be apprehensive about telling John about her fantasies:

JOHN: *You're* upset? I'm the one who ought to be upset. I'm the one getting greasy installing *your* garage door opener while you're thinking about other men. And who are these men, anyway? And what are these fantasies?

John is more upset than Margaret thought he'd be. She begins to think that telling him about her fantasies might have been a mistake. But there's no backing up now.

MARGARET: You won't believe it—I can hardly believe it—but I was imagining running naked at sunset across Shelter Beach with the guy who moved into the Irvings' old place. I don't even know why him, except I sort of thought he was looking at me the other day. And I *know* you're not going to like the other fantasy. In it I was acting sexy with Patrick from the office. We were standing real close, I was wearing this knockout lowcut gown, Patrick was clearly feeling lucky to be with me, and. . . .

JOHN: Damn right I don't like it. And I particularly can't stand it being Patrick. I wish it were *anyone* but Patrick. He's such a phony.

Margaret is now *certain* that telling John about these fantasies was a mistake.

MARGARET: Yeah, I didn't think you'd like hearing about that.
JOHN: Well yeah, I . . .
MARGARET: I know *I* wouldn't like it if you had such thoughts about that woman in your office who *I* don't like; you know, what's-her-name, Penny.

Margaret is making clear that she feels uncomfortable about her fantasies and that she appreciates how John might feel hurt by them. John begins to soften.

MARGARET: And I feel real bad that those fantasies were about those other guys and not about you.

John is beginning to be won over. In fact, he feels like *reassuring* Margaret.

JOHN: Maybe it couldn't be about me. If I had such fantasies, I might have to leave you out, too. We haven't talked about it, but somehow when we get together these days everything seems to fizzle. Things seem so different than when we were first married.

And suddenly the conversation has become a collaboration with each of them building on what the other says.

MARGARET: Yeah, I don't feel as caught up in you as I used to be. And I sometimes feel that you're not very interested in me.
JOHN: Well maybe that's why you are having these fantasies, then. You're thinking about men who you feel *are* interested in you.
MARGARET: Yeah, even though you came home tonight with the garage-door opener, clearly doing something loving, I still didn't feel loved. I felt a million miles away. And then I had all these fantasies.
JOHN: And I was feeling a million miles away from you. In fact, maybe that's why I bought the gift in the first place. I was feeling a million miles away and I wanted to get closer. I guess buying that gift was my way of getting closer.
MARGARET: The garage door opener didn't do it, but something did, because I'm feeling pretty close right now.
JOHN: Let's go get that gown.
MARGARET: No, let's find that beach.

What made Margaret and John feel closer, of course, was confiding in one another that they didn't feel close. (In fact, their discussion enabled them to *discover* that they didn't feel close.) Margaret and John had used her fantasies as clues to their joint reality.

People view their daydreams as silly things to pay no mind to or as threatening things to get upset about. Partners who realize that their daydreams and fantasies are clues to reality will be able to *profit* from their fantasies. They will be able to use their fantasies to discover what is happening in their relationship.

VII

CONCLUSION: A NEW WAY TO HAVE A RELATIONSHIP

I have always been against the kind of book that I'm now writing—books that promise, for example, "ten ways to a better relationship." How can relationship problems that reflect long-standing personal difficulties possibly be resolved by the simple suggestions generally offered: "be tactful," "learn to compromise," "listen to your partner," "avoid unrealistic expectations," "never go to bed still angry at your partner," and so on?

I now believe that there are, indeed "ten ways to a better relationship." Or, as I would prefer to put it, there are ten (or actually forty-two) things that partners may need to *know* if they are to work out a satisfying relationship. What I think partners need to know, however, differs from what is generally suggested.

> My objection to some of the other self-help books is not that they offer quick solutions, but that the quick solutions they offer may contribute to the problem.

Partners are already reproaching themselves and one another for not being more tactful, more willing to compromise, and so on, and reproach of this kind is much of the problem.

So what I've done in this book is develop my own list of things that I believe partners need to know if they are to work out a satisfying relationship. Many of the items on this list are different from, or even opposite to, what other self-help books suggest.

In Chapter 21, I present this list.

21

It's Not What You Do But What You Know

We are all operating at a terrible disadvantage. There are many things that we need to know if we are to work out a satisfying relationship. Not only are we not told these things, but what we *are* told is often misleading:

> We're told to compromise, but we've already compromised—and that's part of the problem.
>
> We're told that it's important to have a positive attitude (that is, to expect the best) and it is. But it's also important to have a negative attitude (that is, to expect the worst).
>
> We're told we shouldn't take our fantasy-based expectations seriously. In fact, we need to take them much *more* seriously.
>
> We're told that problems come from blaming our partners. But problems also come from trying not to blame our partners.
>
> We're told that dependency is a childish quality we need to outgrow, and that makes it hard to realize that dependency is an adult skill we need to develop.
>
> We're told that intimacy comes from doing things together, and that makes it hard to realize that intimacy comes from talking together about *whatever* we do.

IDEAS THAT PARTNERS NEED TO HAVE

So here, collected from the rest of the book, is my list of ideas that partners may need to have if they are to work out a satisfying relationship.

Mr. Skeptic: Another list? I'm tired of all these lists.

Wile: Well, since it *is* a summary of what you already read, you might prefer to skip it for the time being—perhaps coming back to it at a later date to look at it—and turn to page 269 where I talk about difficulties in *applying* these ideas.

Blocks and Unblocks to Thinking

1. Many of our usual ways of thinking about our problems prevent us from solving them. The character-flaws, you-must-have-wanted-it-that-way, back-to-childhood, bad-habits, and unrealistic-expectations habits of thought *block* our thinking and talking. The ordinary-feelings, point-not-gotten-across, hidden-appropriateness, hidden-clue, solutions-become-problems, universal-issues, and special-sensitivities styles of reasoning *unblock* our thinking and talking. According to them, our seemingly strange, provocative, and off-the-wall behavior:

   Is a distorted expression of an ordinary, understandable, garden-variety feeling.
   Is a result of the failure to get something important across.
   Makes sense once you get to the bottom of it.
   Is a clue to important underlying feelings or hidden issues.
   Is a consequence of solution attempts that have gone awry.
   Is an extreme form of a common or universal feeling or reaction.
   Is an exaggerated reaction caused by a childhood-based special sensitivity to things that are actually happening now.

Makeshift Solutions

2. When people are unable to think or talk effectively about their problems, they engage in makeshift solutions that often lead to worse problems. On the other hand, makeshift solutions sometimes work and are the major way we solve our problems.

Cultural Slogans

3. A great deal of our thinking is self-propaganda; that is, attempts to talk ourselves into or out of our feelings. We employ culturally sanctioned complaints or slogans in an attempt to justify the feelings and

wishes that we are having difficulty justifying or to get across points that we are having difficulty getting across.

Problems

4. A relationship problem is really two problems: (a) it's the problem itself, and (b) it's how you talk (or don't talk) about the problem. How you talk or don't talk about a problem is often the major part of the problem.
5. Certain relationship problems are unsolvable, at least for the moment. The best way to deal with them, accordingly, is to establish an ongoing way of talking about them and to develop skill in recovering from them.
6. We're told that it's important to have a positive attitude, and it is: "If you expect problems," we're told, "you'll find them." But it's also important to have a negative attitude: "If you expect problems," I suggest, "you'll be better prepared to deal with them."
7. No one ever begins a relationship in such a way—it would be too unromantic—but there is value, when choosing a long-term partner, in realizing that you will inevitably be choosing a particular set of unresolvable problems that you'll be grappling with for the next ten, twenty, or fifty years. What people *don't* like about their partners may be the other side of what they *do* like. In fact, a relationship is, in some sense, the attempt to work out the negative side effects of what attracts you to your partner in the first place.
8. Problems can be used as clues to hidden feelings; that is, they can be turned to advantage. A husband criticizes his wife for being a compulsive housekeeper when he feels slighted by her (she fails to greet him when he comes home). He thinks he *shouldn't* feel upset about her not greeting him, but he feels justified in complaining about her fastidiousness. Ideally, this husband could use his sudden preoccupation with his wife's housekeeping as a clue to the fact that he just felt subtly slighted by her.
9. Problems are the result of conversations we fail to have. If this husband had been able to talk about feeling slighted, and if his wife had responded sympathetically, he wouldn't have needed (or wanted) to criticize her housekeeping. People get upset and start doing provocative things or acting crazy when they are unable to get across what they need to get across.

Intimacy

10. Many people think that intimacy comes from spending a lot of time together, enjoying the same things, and having the same interests. But intimacy comes from something quite different. It comes from telling your partner the main things on your mind and hearing from your partner the main things on his or her mind. It's talking about what you're feeling even if what you're feeling is that you aren't intimate. The chance to express feelings and make complaints can have a powerful love-reviving and closeness-reviving effect.

Dependency

11. "Dependent" is a ruined idea. The only way anyone can think, once the term is used, is that the person so labeled just shouldn't be that way. And that's too bad because dependency is a skill that needs to be developed rather than a deficiency that needs to be overcome. Dependency is too important a task to be left to children.

The Curative Power of Relationships

12. One of the major purposes of relationships is to cure. Despite what you might have been told, you *can* expect your relationship to solve your problems, fill gaps in your personality, and help you love yourself.

Conversational Booby Traps

13. Almost all of us repeatedly make the error of giving advice or offering solutions when, instead, our partners want us to appreciate how they feel. The way to deal with this problem is to become good at recognizing when you (or your partner) make this error and to have a matter-of-fact way of talking about it when you do.

14. When you are bored by what your partner says, it's easy to conclude that your partner is "just boring," that you are "just selfish," or that the two of you are "just incompatible." These nightmare ideas keep you from realizing that your partner may be boring as a result of his or her efforts *not* to be boring or because he or she is leaving out the most important parts—his or her feelings. And you may be bored because of your inability to talk about being bored.

Using Communication Errors As Clues

15. We are told to make "I statements" rather than "you statements." But "you statements" are *clues* to hidden "I statements." "You statements" indicate that there is something that needs to be talked about; "I statements" provide the means to do so.

16. We are told not to say "always" or "never." But people say "always" and "never" when they feel that they aren't getting their points across. It's a means of emphasis and an expression of frustration.

17. We are told to listen to our partners and not to interrupt them. But we have a hard time listening (and not interrupting) when, as often happens, we feel unlistened to by them. We are left with a difficult choice: to interrupt, which squelches our partners, or *not* to interrupt, which squelches us.

18. We are told not to "mindread." But "mindreading"—reading our *partners'* minds—might reveals what's on *our* minds and, as such, might be a useful clue to what *we* are feeling. "Mindreading" is often an expression of our feelings—feelings of worry or fear—put in the form of assertions about our *partners'* feelings. The statement, "Why are you so angry at me?" might mean "I'm *worried* that you might be angry at me. Pressures at work have made it so that I've hardly been at home lately, and I'm *worried* that you might be upset about it. *Are* you?"

19. We are told to stick to one topic and not to dig up grievances from the past. But we *don't* stick to one topic—we shift to new ones—when we feel the present topic places us at a disadvantage in the fight we are having with our partner. And we dig up grievances from the past to find clear examples of points we are trying to make about the present.

20. We are told not to name-call and not to get bogged down arguing about irrelevant issues. But we name-call because we are momentarily feeling so frustrated, hurt, stung, put upon, or unlistened to that we are willing to resort to almost anything, even to statements that a moment's reflection would tell us will just make our partners even *less* likely to listen to us. And we argue about irrelevant issues because we are at least momentarily so upset with our partners that we don't want to agree with them about *anything*.

21. We are told not to dump out stored-up complaints. But if we don't dump them out, they might never get out. And it's important that

these complaints get out—that is, that they be brought to the surface—so that they can be talked about.

Fighting

22. Partners may either express anger, which leads to fighting, or suppress it, which leads to boredom, loss of love, *and* fighting. People withdraw in order not to fight, and they fight as a reaction to their withdrawal.

23. What you are saying may be more accusatory than you realize. Accusing turns your partner into someone who can't listen. *Listening* turns your partner into someone who *might* listen.

24. Fights become unresolvable when, as often happens, neither partner is able to get across what he or she needs to get across. In fact, that's what a fight is: two people who are unable to make their points. Partner A has no interest in hearing what partner B has to say until partner B listens to what partner A has to say. But that won't happen because partner B has no interest in hearing what partner A has to say until partner A listens to what partner B has to say.

25. The belief that you are having a discussion when you are really having an argument is what has given talking a bad name. Partners come away from such an interaction all the more convinced that talking just makes things worse.

26. It's difficult to have a fight and a conversation at the same time (although we continually try to do so), and it's necessary to have the fight first. Although a fight isn't a time to expect to work out any issues, it may be only then that we ever bring up these issues. Fights are thus both pathways and obstacles to conversations. It's possible *after* the fight to discuss the important issues revealed by the fight.

27. The initial statements of held-back complaints are exaggerated and inaccurate. The dust may need to settle before you'll be able to find out how angry your partner really is and what he or she is actually angry about.

28. Your partner is more likely to listen to you if you *report* your anger (that is, *say* that you are angry) rather than simply *express* it (say angry things). And your partner is even more likely to listen to you if you report the *hurt* or *disappointment* that underlies your anger.

29. One way to get your partner to listen to you is to discover the ways

in which you agree with what your partner has just said and to go on from there to make your point. Talking about your partner's contribution to the fight is likely to rekindle the fight.

Pursuit and Distance

30. In each couple, one partner typically wants to do a particular thing (talk, spend time together, have sex) at least slightly more than the other does. Soon, the first person (the "pursuer") is seen by both as *always* wanting to do that thing, and the second person (the "distancer") is seen as *never* wanting to do it.

31. Both pursuer and distancer are partly right. The pursuer is right, for example, that it's important to be able to talk about their problems, whereas the distancer is right that they presently don't have a way to do so that doesn't just lead to a fight.

32. The common advice given to partners in a pursuer-distancer interaction is that the pursuer should stop pursuing and the distancer should stop withdrawing. But the pursuer can't stop pursuing and the distancer can't stop withdrawing. Furthermore, the pursuer already spends most of his or her time trying *not* to pursue—and that's part of the problem—and the distancer already makes effortful though hardly noticeable attempts *not* to withdraw. Moreover, the pursuer has good reason to pursue (he or she is the only one noticing how lonely, depriving, and empty the relationship is) and the distancer has good reason to withdraw (he or she is the only one noticing how dangerous the relationship is).

33. Everyone knows that pursuers are deprived. That's why they pursue: to try to get what they're missing. But no one realizes that distancers are *just* as deprived. While the pursuer may be deprived, for example, of having a partner who looks forward to spending time with him or her, the distancer is deprived of having a partner he or she wants to spend time with. In pursuer-distancer relationships, distancers lose part of the wish that they might otherwise have to engage with, talk to, and be affectionate toward their partners, whereas pursuers may lose part of the wish that they might otherwise have to do things on their own.

34. The best way to deal with pursuit and distance or, for that matter, any of the other troublesome couple patterns, is to recognize their inevitability and develop a joint perspective from which to view them.

Bypassing and Nonbypassing

35. In a bypasser-nonbypasser conflict, the bypasser gets caught up in fantasy while the nonbypasser is left behind in reality. Bypassers and nonbypassers have mutually incompatible ways of solving problems. The bypasser's way is to stop talking about it—because that just makes it worse—and to trip off in fantasy. The nonbypasser's way is to *try* to talk about it (even though talking about it *might* makes things worse) because he or she *can't* trip off in fantasy. For the nonbypasser, love requires an ability to complain. For the bypasser, love may require not being complained about.

Compromising

36. People make compromises so quickly and so automatically that they are often unaware of doing so. People may become uncompromising because of the hidden compromises that they are already making. The boredom and devitalization that creep into relationships are unrecognized consequences of the continuous flow of compromises and accommodations.

37. Compromises are calculated risks that people don't even realize they are making. The calculated risk is that they will be able to get away with doing something they really don't want to do without becoming too resentful and without having to withdraw.

Fantasies

38. Fantasies are seen, on the one hand, as something that you shouldn't be having and, on the other hand, as something that your partner should be fulfilling. People rarely have the luxury to be able just to have their fantasies—and to learn from them—without having to do anything about them.

39. Partners can end up on different sides of issues on which they actually agree. While walking through an automobile showroom, a husband says to his wife, "Hey, what do you think about our getting that Ferrari?" The wife, not realizing that he's only *fantasizing* about getting one, says, "Are you crazy? We can't afford that. Where's your brain? We'd be in hock for the rest of our lives." The husband, angered by her tone, stubbornly argues that they *can* afford it. They get into a fight in which the wife gets stuck pointing out reality and

the husband gets stuck defending the fantasy, when, actually, they agree: *both* would like the Ferrari and *both* think they can't afford it.

40. Couple life is a succession of half-experienced, half-stated, half-fulfilled, easily lost, and quickly forgotten fantasies. Everyone knows about the hazard of fantasy-expectations. (People who expect the honeymoon feeling to last throughout the marriage may end up with lots of marriages and lots of honeymoons.) Few people are aware, however, of the hazards of trying *not* to have fantasies. Fantasies provide a direct tap into what you're feeling. Since fantasies are compensations for disappointments in the relationship, they can be used to detect the existence of these disappointments. Fantasies are clues to reality.

IDEAS ARE DANGEROUS

And there is a further idea that people need to have. This further idea, which challenges all the other ideas, is that ideas can themselves be dangerous. They become dangerous when they turn into rules. The important idea that "anger is natural" can quickly be turned into the rule that people *should* express it. Instead of criticizing themselves and one another for expressing anger, these individuals now do so for *failing* to express anger. "You shouldn't hold onto your anger," they say, "You should let it all out."

This tendency to turn ideas into rules seems characteristic of human thinking. Constance Apfelbaum talks about "a reflex-like conversion of insight into moral imperative as a habit of human consciousness," by which she means that ideas that originally have the effect of liberating can themselves become imprisoning.

When "nice" women were allowed to enjoy sex (they were rescued from the Victorian belief that sex for a woman was supposed to be simply an unpleasant duty), they then felt duty-bound to enjoy sex.

When women were allowed to have careers (they were freed from the pre–women's liberation belief that their place was at home), they then felt *responsible* to have careers.

When men were allowed to have feelings (the macho image came into disrepute), they then felt *required* to have feelings.

Closing the door on one rule may result merely in opening it to another. The "Human Potential" or "Growth" movement was founded on an important insight—the realization that certain widely accepted and long-standing social virtues—politeness, propriety, and dutifulness—had serious drawbacks. These virtues produced superficiality in relationships and raised emotional barriers between people. What began, however, as a liberating idea—that people need not always limit themselves to polite conversation—turned into a new pressure. People now felt *required* to express deep feelings and to have meaningful conversations.

So here is idea number 41:

41. Ideas, which potentially can free people (including all the ideas on my list), can turn into rules that further oppress them.

BUT CAN IDEAS REALLY HELP?

Mr. Skeptic: You're saying that ideas are powerful and dangerous. What they *really* are, however, are weak, ineffectual, and beside the point. People would be better off if they stopped thinking so much and just took things as they came. I keep telling my wife—"If only you didn't have to talk so much about *every* little issue that comes up, maybe things would take care of themselves." People talk *ad nauseam* and it just makes things worse."

Wile: I agree, Mr. Skeptic, that a great deal of our talking and thinking *does* make things worse. In fact, my major objective in this book has been to point this out and to provide a way to distinguish the kinds of talking and thinking that are helpful from those that aren't. Take a look at my list. You'll have to admit that the ideas on it *are* useful.

Mr. Skeptic: Well, maybe *some* of them just a little bit. But you're forgetting something, Wile. Ideas are a dime a dozen. They keep drifting in and out of your mind. You think one thing one moment and the opposite the next. So how realistic is it to expect that ideas can really make a difference, particularly when they just come from a book? And how realistic is it to expect that anyone will even remember these ideas a week from now, particularly since they go against what we've always been taught?

Wile: Well, I must admit you're right about that. *I* have difficulty remembering these ideas, and I wrote the book.

But let me tell you about Sybil and Gus, an unmarried couple in their early forties who have been living together for ten years. Sybil is a dietician at a private hospital, and Gus is an architect in a large firm. Sybil and Gus have just read this book. In fact, the book happens to be open and sitting on the kitchen table right in front of them as they have the following conversation.

Gus tells Sybil about the great design that Ben, a colleague in his firm, made of an underground bowling alley to be built in the new Shopping Center across town. As Gus talks about "reinforced arches," "ceiling joists," and "tensile strength," Sybil stifles a yawn.

Gus is about to do what he usually does when Sybil seems bored by what he says: get out of his chair, say, "Well, if you're not interested, forget it," and stomp out of the room. But his chair jams on the table leg and, before he can free it to get up, his gaze falls on this book and he reads:

Idea number 14: *If your partner is bored by what you're saying, maybe you're leaving out the most important part—your feelings.*

So, instead of stomping out of the room, Gus says:

GUS: You don't seem interested in what I'm saying, but maybe it's what this book says: that I'm leaving out the main point. And, you know, I *am*—because the main point is that I'm *envious* of Ben and I'm *angry* about the whole thing. *I'm* the one, after all, who landed the account, and it should be *me* doing the plans. Ben's design isn't bad, but I could have done better, and I should have been given the chance.

Sybil's no longer bored. Instead, she's upset:

SYBIL: Well, it's just not right. You should see your boss the first thing in the morning and tell him that *you* should have been given the bowling design. Better yet—call him right now. Here's the phone.

Gus had wanted a reaction from Sybil, but not this. He feels overwhelmed. Sybil notices that Gus isn't liking what she said, but she doesn't know why. And Gus doesn't know why either; he thinks he should be *appreciating* her advice.

So they grab for the book and begin frantically looking for something that might help them figure out what's happening. And they find it—

Idea number 13: *If your partner isn't appreciating your advice, maybe he or she just wants you to appreciate how he or she feels.*

SYBIL: How embarrassing. Here I am telling you what to do and not giving you a chance to say how you feel. And I've done this before. What's wrong with me that I keep doing this?

GUS: Well, if you believe the rest of what's said here, then there's *nothing* wrong with you. It says that *everyone* repeatedly gives advice when his or her partner really wants to be listened to and that the solution is simply to have a matter-of-fact way of talking about it when you do.

SYBIL: Well that's relieving. But I *still* shouldn't have come on so strong —telling you to call your boss. That's pretty obnoxious.

GUS: Yeah, but look what it says under idea number 9: people get upset and start doing provocative things when they're unable to get across what they need to get across.

SYBIL: Well, if that's so, then there's something that *I* need to get across . . . but I can't think of what it would be.

The conversation's going well. And it could go even *better* if Sybil and Gus *could* figure out what Sybil is needing to get across. Here they are trying to do it—

SYBIL: All I know is that hearing that you were cheated out of the bowling project really got to me.

GUS: Well, it *was* unfair.

SYBIL: It was outright nepotism. Ben's the boss's nephew, for heaven's sake.

GUS: Yeah, that's probably why he got the job all right . . .

SYBIL: It was *rotten*. It was *so* rotten, in fact, that I can't even stand to hear about it. It makes me feel too angry and helpless.

GUS: Well yeah . . .

SYBIL: And *that's* why I told you to phone right away. I needed you to do something because *I* felt so helpless.

And having said this, Sybil feels better:

SYBIL: You know, it's funny, but it helps just to talk about it. If I'd been able to say all this, maybe I wouldn't have needed to tell you to call your boss.

GUS: You wouldn't have had to tell me to call my boss, all right, but that's because I'd *already* be thinking of doing it myself. You'd have helped me realize how upset and helpless *I feel* about it.

Sybil and Gus are now clearly on the same side; they're collaborating. This conversation is very different than the one that they would have had if they *hadn't* read the book. In fact, if they hadn't read the book, they wouldn't be having a conversation at all. Gus would be storming around the block trying to cool down, and Sybil would be sitting in the kitchen fighting off the strongest urge for a cigarette she'd had since giving up smoking two years before.

But how realistic is it to expect Sybil and Gus to have such a conversation even if they *had* just read this book? It's hard to imagine anyone thinking that fast, being so articulate, and having all the ideas they need right when they need to have them. (I made up this conversation, and it took me a lot of time sitting in front of the typewriter to get it to come out right.)

> Fortunately, Sybil and Gus wouldn't have to have the *whole* conversation. Even just a fraction of it could make a big difference.
>
> And they wouldn't have to have the conversation *right away.* Suppose Gus *hadn't* caught his chair on the table leg and, instead, had stormed around the block. While storming, however, he might suddenly realize that Sybil was bored because he hadn't told her how he felt. He might *then* come back into the house and try to talk with her about it.
>
> And they wouldn't have to have the conversation *all at once*; they could have it in spurts. Gus may realize *two days later* that he felt that Sybil hadn't appreciated how he felt. And Sybil may realize *three days after that* that she had come on so strong because she felt helpless. Sybil and Gus could have a conversation bit by bit over the course of days as the information slowly came out.
>
> And, they wouldn't have to have the conversation *at all.* Just *knowing* that he was being boring because he was leaving out his feelings or that Sybil's offensive behavior was the result of her not getting across what she needed to get across, could help a lot. Gus would no longer have to see himself as "just boring." And he'd no longer have to see Sybil as "just selfish" and "just bossy."

We're all used to operating at a severe disadvantage. Just a little edge, now and again, can make a big difference.

My goal in this book is to do for other important ideas what George Bach, in *The Intimate Enemy* and other books, did for the idea of anger. People came away from his books on couple fighting convinced that the anger that they and their partners feel towards one another is ordinary and inevitable rather than, as they feared, a sign that they have a bad relationship. And for some, this newly won insight remained permanently set. My hope is to make the ideas about relationships presented in this book just as familiar, usable, and permanently available to partners.

The ideal in the case of Sybil and Gus would be for them to be able to apply this new knowledge in future situations. But how realistic is this? In a few weeks, they might not even remember very clearly what the book was about.

And even if they did, they're still likely to slip back into their classic (their "real") beliefs that:

> Gus is just boring.
>
> Sybil is too self-involved to care about Gus and his work; she's only interested in *her* work.
>
> Gus refuses to take Sybil's good advice about how to handle his problems at work.
>
> Sybil just comes on too strong.

In other words, Sybil and Gus would have slipped back into their usual *accusing* way of reasoning that blocks useful thinking and talking about the issue.

The problem with the 41 ideas is that they don't stick to your bones. And that brings us to the 42nd and final idea, which is: you're likely to forget the other 41. These ideas are difficult to remember because they go against what we've always been taught.

> But being aware of this danger—that is, knowing that we're likely to forget these ideas—may enable us to keep it from happening or, rather, to *prepare* for it to happen and to feel less upset about it when it does.

And remembering that we won't remember is the most crucial idea of all. That's because:

> The ultimate goal in a couple relationship is the creation by partners of a *joint platform* from which to view their inevitable lapses into

accusatory or self-accusatory thinking in which they forget everything useful that they know.

Mr. Skeptic: What kind of ultimate goal is that? I had hoped for something a little more upbeat. If that's the best you've got to offer, I might as well stick to suppressing complaints, avoiding fights, using self-restraint, maintaining a positive attitude, making compromises, avoiding unrealistic expectations, and trying to get along.

Wile: But Mr. Skeptic, imagine if you'd suppressed complaints, avoided fights, and used self-restraint in *reading this book*. It wouldn't have been as much fun. You wouldn't have gotten as much out of it. And you might have stopped reading it halfway through.

Mr. Skeptic: Possibly.

Wile: And without your comments, this book wouldn't have been as much fun for me, either. I wouldn't have gotten as much out of it. And I might have stopped *writing* it halfway through.

Mr. Skeptic: Well, I'm touched.

Wile: So, in couple relationships, the more of your thoughts, feelings, complaints, wishes, fantasies, disappointments, resentments—everything —you can *include* in your relationship, the more you'll get out of it and the less you'll want to end it halfway through.

Index

ask